SECOND THOUGHTS

Seeing Conventional Wisdom
Through the Sociological Eye

SECOND THOUGHTS

Seeing Conventional Wisdom Through the Sociological Eye

JANET M. RUANE
Montclair State University

■

KAREN A. CERULO
Rutgers University

PINE FORGE PRESS
Thousand Oaks ■ *London* ■ *New Delhi*

For information, address:

 Pine Forge Press
A Sage Publications Company
2455 Teller Road
Thousand Oaks, California 91320
(805) 499-4224
E-mail: sales@pfp.sagepub.com

Sage Publications Ltd.
6 Bonhill Street
London EC2A 4PU
United Kingdom

Sage Publications India Pvt. Ltd.
M-32 Market
Greater Kailash I
New Delhi 110 048 India

Production: Melanie Field, Strawberry Field Publishing
Copy Editor: Carol Dondrea
Interior Designer: Lisa Mirski Devenish
Typesetter: Christi Payne, Book Arts
Cover Designer: Paula Shuhert and Graham Metcalfe
Production Manager: Anne Draus, Scratchgravel Publishing Services
Print Buyer: Anna Chin

Printed in the United States of America
97 98 99 00 01 10 9 8 7 6 5 4 3 2 1

Library of Congress Cataloging-in-Publication Data
Ruane, Janet M.
    Second thoughts : seeing conventional wisdom through the
  sociological eye / Janet M. Ruane, Karen A. Cerulo.
      p.   cm.
    Includes bibliographical references and index.
    ISBN 0-7619-8505-0 (p : alk. paper)
    1. Sociology. 2. Sociology—Quotations, maxims, etc. 3. Maxims.
  I. Cerulo, Karen A.   II. Title.
  HM51.R867   1997
  301—dc21   96-45365
                                                        CIP

 This book is printed on acid-free paper that meets Environmental Protection Agency Standards for recycled paper.

To Mary Agnes, a beloved
source of knowledge

About the Authors

Janet M. Ruane (Ph.D. Rutgers University) is Associate Professor of Sociology at Montclair State University. She has served as coordinator of both the Sociology Graduate Program and Undergraduate Advising since 1992. Professor Ruane's research interests include formal and informal social control mechanisms, domestic violence, media and technology, and applied sociology. She has contributed articles to several journals, including *Sociological Inquiry, Law and Policy, Communication Research, Sociological Focus, The Journal of Applied Sociology, Science As Culture, Simulation and Games,* and *The Virginia Review of Sociology.* She is currently at work on a book addressing family businesses. Over the years Professor Ruane has gained considerable classroom experience, teaching both introductory and advanced level sociology courses as well as graduate courses in applied sociology.

Karen A. Cerulo (Ph.D. Princeton University) is Associate Professor of Sociology at Rutgers University. Her research interests include symbol systems, identity construction, and media and technology. Professor Cerulo's articles appear in a wide variety of journals, including the *American Sociological Review, Social Forces, Sociological Forum, Sociological Inquiry, Sociological Focus, Communication Research, Social Science Research, Science As Culture,* and annuals such as the *Annual Review of Sociology* and *Research in Political Sociology.* She is also the author of *Identity Designs: The Sights and Sounds of a Nation,* a work that won the ASA Culture Section's award for the best book of 1996 (The Rose Book Series of the ASA, Rutgers University Press). Her most recent work, *Deciphering Violence: The Cognitive Order of Right and Wrong* is forthcoming (Routledge). Professor Cerulo's teaching experience includes the Rutgers University Award for Distinguished Contributions to Undergraduate Education.

About the Publisher

Pine Forge Press is a new educational publisher, dedicated to publishing innovative books and software throughout the social sciences. On this and any other of our publications, we welcome your comments.

Please call or write us at:

Pine Forge Press
A Sage Publications Company
2455 Teller Road
Thousand Oaks, CA 91320
Phone: (805) 499-4224
E-mail: sales@pfp.sagepub.com

Visit our new World Wide Web site, your direct link to a multitude of on-line resources:

http://www.sagepub.com/pineforge

CONTENTS

men. We also discuss the powerful role physical attractiveness can play in the construction of self-identity.

CONCEPTS DEFINED AND APPLIED

Cultural inconsistency; self-fulfilling prophecy; cultural capital; social status; identity; socialization; appearance norms; primary socialization; rituals; looking-glass self

STRATIFICATION

CONCEPTS DEFINED AND APPLIED

Intergenerational upward mobility; structural functionalism; functional illiteracy; conflict theory; socialization; tracking; self-fulfilling prophecy.

It is not uncommon for those assigned to teach entry-level sociology courses to experience some trepidation, even dread, about the teaching task ahead. In many ways, intro to sociology is a "tough sell." Some students perceive the discipline as nothing more than a "re-hash" of the obvious; it speaks to every-day life, something many students believe they already know and understand. Other students confuse sociology courses with disciplines such as psychology or social work; they take our courses hoping to "figure out the opposite sex," learn to better "work the system," or overcome their personal problems with regard to deviant behavior or family relations. To muddy the waters even more, many intro students are likely to be in our courses not because of some desire to learn sociology but because the courses satisfy a general education requirement. Taking all of these factors into account, sociology instructors can face substantial resistance. Getting students to "adjust" their vision of the world so as to incorporate the sociological eye is no small feat.

Despite these challenges, it remains essential to achieve success in entry-level sociology courses. From an instrumental point of view, the discipline recruits future sociologists from these courses, thus mandating a sound foundation. Further, departments may gain significant institutional resources by keeping intro course enrollments up. Intellectual concerns also contribute to the importance of entry-level courses. Many sociology instructors believe that intro courses offer a guaranteed "dividend" for the student: the sociological vision represents an essential tool for understanding and surviving our increasingly complex social world. Thus, intro courses provide instructors with a valuable opportunity to plant and nurture the sociological imagination in each new cohort of college students. Thought of in this way, failing the intro student can carry long-term social costs.

Second Thoughts offers a "tried and true" approach to successfully nurturing sociological thinking in the newcomer. The book provides a vehicle with which to initiate dialogue; it allows instructors to meet their students on "common ground." Each chapter in this book begins with a shared idea—a conventional wisdom that both instructor and student have encountered by virtue of being consumers of popular culture. Once this common footing is established, *Second Thoughts* introduces relevant sociological concepts and theories that "mesh" with each conventional wisdom. Sociological ideas and perspective are used to explain, qualify, and sometimes debunk conventional wisdom.

At the conclusion of each chapter, we provide a vehicle by which students can apply their new sociological knowledge beyond the classroom. We have incorporated a set of exercises linked to the subject matter covered in the chapter. The exercises, too, are grounded in the familiar. We encourage students to turn to everyday, common resources for some first-hand learning experiences.

Our own classroom experiences prove the "familiar," a "user-friendly" place to jumpstart discussion, thus laying the foundation for critical thinking and informed analysis. In the classroom, we also have found the "familiar" a useful tool with which to delineate the sociological vision. This book attempts to pass along some of the fruits of our own learning. In pushing beyond the familiar, *Second Thoughts* also exposes students to the sociological advantage. At minimum, readers will accrue the benefits that come from taking time to give conventional ideas some important "second thoughts."

ACKNOWLEDGMENTS

There are, of course, a number of people who have contributed to this book. First and foremost, we would both like to acknowledge the students encountered in the many sociology courses taught at SUNY Stony Brook, Rutgers University, and Montclair State University. These students challenged us to make the sociological imagination a meaningful and desirable option on students' learning agendas. Thanks also go to Maureen Gorman, a patient and skilled reference librarian who always met our information needs with a better than excellent effort. We are grateful to several reviewers for their careful readings and productive suggestions on various drafts of the manuscript: Paul Baker, Illinois State University; Gerald Boucher, Temple University; Lisa Brush, University of Pittsburgh; Diane Carmody, Western Washington University; Tad Krauze, Hofstra University; Judith Lawler-Caron, Albertus Magnus College; Judith Richlin-Klonsky, University of California, Los Angeles; Daniel Schubert, Dickenson College; Marshal Shapiro Rose, Florida Atlantic University; Michelle Stone, Youngstown State University; and Shirley Varmette, Southern Connecticut State University. Their efforts were spearheaded and complemented by Steve Rutter's savvy editorial insight and intellectual acumen. Steve's input improved this work immeasurably. Thanks also go to the solid support staff at Pine Forge, Strawberry Field Publishing, and Scratchgravel Publishing Services. Finally, we would like to thank several friends and family members (Mary Agnes, Anne, Jay, Sam, Joan, and Jane) for consistently asking about "the book" and/or planning a book celebration, thereby indirectly prodding us to stick with the program.

Introduction:
The Sociological Perspective

■

IN THIS INTRODUCTION, WE DISCUSS THE ROOTS

OF CONVENTIONAL WISDOM. WE ALSO CONTRAST

SUCH KNOWLEDGE WITH THAT ACQUIRED VIA

THE SOCIOLOGICAL PERSPECTIVE. IN THIS WAY,

WE INTRODUCE STUDENTS TO A SOCIOLOGICAL

MODE OF THINKING.

■

Conventional wisdom is a part of our everyday lives. We are exposed to its lessons from early childhood, and we encounter its teachings until the day we die. Who among us was not taught, for example, to "be fearful of strangers" or that "beauty is only skin deep"? Similarly, we have all learned that "stress is bad for our well-being" and that "adult life is simply incomplete without children."

Conventional wisdom comes to us in many forms. We encounter it via folk adages, "old wives' tales," traditions, and political or religious rhetoric. We find it in advice columns, cultural truisms, and the tenets of "common sense." **Conventional wisdom** refers to that body of assertions and beliefs that is generally recognized as part of a culture's "common knowledge." These cultural lessons are many and they cannot be taken lightly. They are central to American society, and they are frequently the source of our beliefs, attitudes, and behaviors.

To be sure, conventional wisdom often contains elements of truth. As such, it constitutes a starting point for knowledge (Mathisen 1989). Consider, for example, the well-known truism: "Actions speak louder than words." In laboratory research, results show that those assessing an individual who says one thing but does another are influenced more strongly by the individual's actions (Amabile and Kabat 1982; Bryan and Walbek 1970). Similarly, many studies support the adage that warns, "Marry in haste, repent at leisure." When we define *haste* as "marrying too young or marrying too quickly," we find that those who "marry in haste" report less satisfaction over the course of the marriage than those who make a later or a slower decision (Furstenburg 1979; Glenn and Supancic 1984; Grover et al. 1985; Kitson et al. 1985; Martin and Bumpass 1989; Thornes and Collard 1979).

Complete faith in conventional wisdom, however, can be risky. Social patterns and behaviors frequently contradict the wisdoms we embrace. Many studies show, for instance, that adages encouraging the "fear of strangers" often are misguided; most crimes of personal violence are perpetrated by those we know (see Essay 12). Similarly, research documents that beauty may be merely "skin deep," but its importance cannot be underestimated. Physically attractive individuals fare better than those of more average appearance in almost all areas of social interaction (see Essay 7). Many studies suggest that stress is not always "bad for one's well-being"; it can sometimes be productive for human beings (see Essay 4). And, despite all of the accolades to the presence of children in our lives, research shows that many adults report their highest levels of lifetime happiness take place *before* they have children or *after* their children leave home (see Essay 2).

Second Thoughts: Seeing Conventional Wisdom Through the Sociological Eye addresses the gaps that exist between conventional wisdom and social life.

The book reviews several popular conventional wisdoms, noting the instances in which such adages cannot be taken at face value. Each of the following essays uses social research to expose the gray area that is too often ignored by the bottom-line nature of conventional wisdom. In so doing, *Second Thoughts* demonstrates that social reality is generally much more involved and complex than these cultural truisms imply. The book suggests that reviewing conventional wisdom with a sociological eye can lead to a more complete, detailed understanding of social life.

When Conventional Wisdom Isn't Enough

Although there may well be a kernel of truth to much of conventional wisdom, too often these adages present an incomplete picture. Why is this the case? The answer stems, in part, from the source of most conventional wisdom.

Much of the conventional wisdom we embrace originates from a particular individual's personal experiences, observations, or reflections. Often such adages emerge from a highly specific circumstance; they are designed to address a particular need or event as experienced by a certain social group at a specific place or historical moment. For example, consider this well known adage: "There's a sucker born every minute!" P. T. Barnum coined this now-familiar phrase. But recall Barnum's personal circumstance—he was one of the most famous circus masters in history. When one considers Barnum's unique history, both the source and the limits of his wisdom become clear.

Now consider this maxim: "Don't switch horses in midstream." Abraham Lincoln originated this quote. (His actual words were: "It is not best to swap horses when crossing streams.") But note that Lincoln's frequently cited advice actually represents the political rhetoric of a historical moment. Lincoln coined the phrase as a kind of campaign slogan when seeking reelection to the United States presidency.

Finally, consider the famous quotation: "Good fences make good neighbors." Robert Frost forwarded this thought in his 1914 poem, "Mending Wall." Contrary to popular belief, however, Frost never intended to promote social separatism—quite the opposite. In "Mending Wall," Frost criticized the character who uttered the adage, writing, "He will not go behind his father's saying"—in other words, the character will not break with tradition. In so doing, Frost suggested that the wisdom linking good fences to good neighbors was that of *another* generation in a *former* time; it was not wisdom for *all* time.

Each of these examples shares a common thread. In each case, conventional wisdom was born of a particular experience or a specific social situation. The wisdom took root and grew as it resonated with other people who faced similar events and circumstances. Yet each of these examples also illustrates an inherent weakness of conventional wisdom. The "truth" revealed by such wisdom is tied to the particular circumstances of every maxim's origin. This characteristic can make conventional wisdom a precarious source of generalized knowledge. Because such wisdom is individualistic or situation-specific information, it may not carry the general applications that most people assume of it.

For the sociologist, reliable knowledge mandates that we move beyond individualistic or circumstantial information. Sociologists contend that there is more to the story than any one person's life or the lives of one's associates reveal.

Can one safely conclude that my experiences in raising my four-year-old or my neighbor's experiences with an aging parent will provide others with sufficient knowledge for handling the events of their lives? It is difficult to say. If these experiences are atypical, the wisdom they provide will offer little by way of general conclusions regarding the treatment of four-year-olds or elderly parents. The wisdom will fail to transcend one individual's personal world. Similarly, wisdom born of experience may or may not transcend various social contexts. The maxim "Delay is the best remedy for anger" may prove fruitful in a variety of social sites: romance, work, friendship, parenting. Yet, the adage that instructs you to "keep your cards close to the vest" may lead to success on the job but spell failure for a personal relationship.

Although your life may convince you that "birds of a feather flock together," my experience may reveal that "opposites attract." One situation may convince you that "haste makes waste," although another may convince you to "strike while the iron is hot." To be sure, experientially based or situation-specific information offers us knowledge. But that knowledge presents a fragmented, and thus incomplete, picture of the broader social world.

Relying on individualistic, circumstantial information can prove especially problematic when pursuing information regarding broad social patterns. Consider for a moment the ways in which one's geographic location might influence a person's estimate of general population patterns. The life experiences of Maine residents might lead them to conclude that 99 percent of the U.S. population is white. Such an estimate would greatly exaggerate the racial homogeneity of the nation. In contrast, the experiences of Californians might lead them to estimate that only 69 percent of the U.S. population is white, a vast underestimation of population homogeneity. Based on experience, Californians also might argue that Hispanics are the largest minority in the United States. Yet, the experiences of those in Alabama would rank Blacks, not Hispanics, as the largest minority group. On the basis of experience, residents of Alaska or Wyoming would never guess that the United States averages 70 inhabitants per square mile. In Alaska, the average inhabitant is 1 per square mile, and in Wyoming, the average is fewer than 5. And experience might leave residents of Kentucky or Mississippi baffled by Californians' or New Yorkers' concerns over the number of foreign-born individuals entering the nation and settling in their states. Less than 1 percent of Kentucky's and Mississippi's state populations are foreign-born, while 22 percent of California's population and 16 percent of New York's population hail from another nation.

The point we are trying to make here is really quite simple. Accurate knowledge about society requires that we move beyond the limitations of experientially based conventional wisdom. That leap represents one of the most compelling features of sociology. Sociologists are interested in social patterns. **Social patterns** are general trends—trends that can be seen only when we force ourselves to stand back and look beyond any one, two, or three cases. In essence, sociologists search for the "big picture"—the views that emerge when many individual stories are aggregated into a whole.

The sociologist's emphasis on patterns does not necessarily mean that she or he is never interested in personal stories and experiences. Rather, sociology's strength lies in its ability to place or situate individual stories in a social context. **Social context** refers to the broad social and historical circumstances surrounding an act or an event. Once the sociologist discovers the general trends within a particular group or society, she or he is in a better position to assess the relative meaning of any one individual's personal experiences. General patterns must be documented before we can assess one's personal experiences as typical or as exceptional.

OBSTACLES TO THE SOCIOLOGICAL VISION

Approached in this way, the task of sociology sounds straightforward and even appealing. The discipline encourages us to move beyond the personal and adopt a broader social vision—a vision that promises to improve the accuracy of our knowledge. With such gains at stake, why do so many approach the sociological vision with skepticism or confusion?

Certain obstacles can make it difficult to adopt a sociological view of the world. For example, the sociological vision contrasts with Americans' long-standing cultural value of individualism. A **cultural value** is a general sentiment regarding what is good or bad, right or wrong, desirable or undesirable. In the United States, we like to think of ourselves as special and unique individuals. We view ourselves as "masters of our own fates." This individualistic bias, however, flies in the face of established social patterns and social forces. The notion that our behaviors follow patterns that may act as restraints on our actions is an argument clearly at odds with an individualistic mentality.

In a related vein, adopting the sociological vision also can be hindered by our general preference for "certain" rather than "probable" answers. The study of large-scale patterns commits sociologists to predictions that are based on odds or probabilities. In other words, sociologists can suggest possible outcomes that individuals from particular groups and places, or in particular circumstances, are likely to face. However, they cannot predict *the* definitive outcome for any *one* individual. In a culture that favors individualism, this feature ensures a certain amount of resistance to the sociological approach. Indeed, sociology instructors often note a familiar complaint among newcomers to the field: If sociology can't predict what will happen to *me*, then what good is it?

Developing a sociological vision also can be undermined by the dynamic quality of social existence. Social reality is not static—it changes constantly. So just when we think we know the patterns, new patterns may be emerging. In addition, the very act of examining social phenomena can inevitably influence the entity we are studying. (If you need a concrete example of this, think about how sensitive the stock market is to people's ideas about the economy.) Such dynamics mean that sociologists' work, in a sense, is never done. Further, the conclusions they reach must often remain tentative and open to change. Unlike a physics formula or a mathematical proof, sociological knowledge is rarely final. That dynamic quality often leaves the onlooker questioning its legitimacy.

Another obstacle facing the sociological viewpoint is doubt about the value of *socially* informed knowledge. As conventional wisdom indicates, many people trust only their own personal experiences to teach them about the world, arguing that such knowledge works for them. And, in a certain sense, sociologists must concede the point. Often, it *does appear* as if personal experience is more relevant, or truer, than sociological knowledge. Consider that as thinking human beings we have some capacity to create our own social reality. If we think people are not trustworthy, for example, we won't trust them, and we certainly won't give them the chance to prove us wrong. This course of action, no matter how ill conceived, serves to substantiate our own life experiences and to validate our own personally informed knowledge. For in clinging to such a stance, we create a self-fulfilling prophecy. A **self-fulfilling prophecy** is a phenomenon whereby that which we believe to be true, in some sense, becomes true for us. In this way, self-fulfilling prophecies make personal experience *seem* like the clear victor over social knowledge.

Finally, the sociological viewpoint often is ignored by those who believe they already possess sociological expertise. One of the earliest figures in American sociology, William Graham Sumner, noted the tendency of people to think they know sociology by virtue of living in societies. "Being there" affords the opportunity to make social observations, and, arguably, social observations are the ingredients of which sociology is made. Thus, "being there" mistakenly is deemed by many as sufficient for generating social knowledge and sociological insights. As our previous discussion indicates, however, personal experience is *not* the same as the sociological perspective.

If you consider all of these obstacles, you will better understand why the sociological vision is not more readily pursued or adopted by all. It requires effort to move beyond our personal views or experiences and develop what C. Wright Mills called the sociological imagination. **Sociological imagination** refers to the ability to see and evaluate the personal realm in light of the broader social/cultural and historical arenas.

Why Read This Book?

By introducing this broader picture of reality, *Second Thoughts* encourages readers to step back and sharpen their analytic focus on the familiar. The essays that follow highlight the complex reality of modern-day society—a complexity often missed when we restrict our knowledge to personal experience and the common knowledge or popular assumptions borne of those experiences.

Second Thoughts also introduces readers to many of the concepts central to sociology. In this way, the book can serve as an initiation into the ways in which sociologists frame the world around them. For those who find their sociological eye activated, we provide some of the tools needed for additional research. Each essay concludes with several suggested readings that elaborate on key concepts and ideas introduced in the essay. Further, each essay includes several reliable sources from which facts and figures were derived.

Readers may also find that some of the information presented here moves them beyond curiosity and toward action. To assist such individuals, we have provided an appendix listing the names of organizations involved with certain issues. These listings are not meant as publicity for any body or cause. Rather, we offer them as preliminary leads—starting blocks for those who feel directed toward change.

In moving through the text, it will become clear that we have organized *Second Thoughts* according to topics typically covered in introductory level courses. Those who wish to consider broader applications of this material should consult the "concepts covered" sections in the table of contents. These lists suggest a variety of issues for which one might use a specific conventional wisdom to "jumpstart" critical thinking and discussion.

In Closing

When we open our eyes and carefully examine the world around us, we must concede that the realities of social life often run contrary to our stock of common knowledge. In the pages that follow, we aim to highlight some of these contradictions, and in so doing demonstrate that reviewing conventional wisdom with a sociological eye can provide a valuable "correction" to our vision of the world around us.

LEARNING MORE ABOUT IT

To learn more about developing a sociological vision, see Peter Berger's classic book *Invitation to Sociology* (New York: Anchor, 1963). C. Wright Mills also provides a brilliant theoretical treatise on this subject in *The Sociological Imagination.* (London: Oxford, 1959). A more recent and very readable treatment of these issues is offered by Earl Babbie in *What Is Society?: Reflections on Freedom, Order, and Change* (Thousand Oaks, CA: Pine Forge, 1994).

William Sumner's definition of the field can be found in his essay, "Sociology" [in *Social Darwinism: Selected Essays of William Graham Sumner* (pp. 9–29), Englewood Cliffs, NJ: Prentice-Hall, 1963].

A compelling and humanistic introduction to sociology and its core concepts is offered in Lewis Coser's classic work *Sociology Through Literature: An Introductory Reader* (Englewood Cliffs, NJ: Prentice-Hall, 1963).

All data on state populations were secured from the 1995 *Universal Almanac* (Kansas City: Andrews and McMeel, edited by John W. Wright) and the 1995 *World Almanac* (New York: Pharos Books, edited by Mark S. Hoffman).

EXERCISES

1. Think about the social arrangements of your life—that is, your family relations, your neighborhood, your school and work experiences. If your knowledge of the world were restricted to just these arenas, identify five important facts that you would fail to know.

2. The media give us one view of our social world. Select one week's worth of prime-time TV programs and use them to learn about U.S. society. Put together coding sheets that will allow you to collect basic data on all the program characters you encounter; that is, record each character's age, education, ethnicity, family status, family size, gender, occupational level, race, residence patterns, and so on. Tabulate summary statistics from your data. For example, determine the percentage of characters that are male and female, the average education level, and so on. Obtain a national or world almanac from your local or university library, and compare the data you obtain via TV with comparable real-life demographics for the U.S. population. What can you conclude about the media's picture of American society? How did your particular selections of prime-time programming bias or influence your data?

Culture

■

CONVENTIONAL WISDOM TELLS US . . .

Winning Is Everything

■

CONVENTIONAL WISDOM SUGGESTS THAT COMPETITION AND ACHIEVEMENT GO HAND IN HAND. IN THIS ESSAY, HOWEVER, WE HIGHLIGHT THE MANY STUDIES THAT SHOW THE BENEFITS OF COOPERATION OVER COMPETITION. IN SO DOING, WE REVIEW AMERICAN CULTURAL VALUES, STRATEGIES OF ACTION, AND THE CONNECTION OF THESE ELEMENTS TO BOTH POSITIVE AND NEGATIVE OUTCOMES.

■

Think back to the last Little League baseball game or professional hockey match you attended. Note the number of stores and businesses that celebrate the "salesperson of the week." Consider the mega-dollars spent, or the "hard-ball" tactics used, by most recent contenders for national political office. And who can forget the thrill of victory and the agony of defeat as read on the faces of the most recent World Series, Super Bowl, or Olympic contenders.

These snapshots of American life remind us that competition is central to our culture. As children, we are taught to play hard and fight to win. As adults, we learn to value winning. We equate winning with the most talented or the "best man," and we regularly remind ourselves that "nice guys finish last." In the United States (as well as in most capitalist societies), the emphasis is on beating one's opponent and being the one "on top," the "king of the hill," the one left standing after a "fair fight."

The conventional wisdom on competition represents a cultural value. A **cultural value** is a shared sentiment regarding what is good or bad, right or wrong, desirable or undesirable. In the United States, competition is a positive cultural value (Aronson 1980; Toda et al. 1978). Yet, despite our commitment to healthy competition, research shows that the practice may not always be in our best interest. A growing literature suggests that, in many areas of social life, cooperation leads to more profitable outcomes than competition.

Social psychologists David and Roger Johnson reviewed nearly 200 studies on human performance. The results of their survey indicate that cooperation promotes higher individual achievement, higher group productivity, better problem solving, and more effective learning than do competitive strategies of interaction. These same studies show that the *more* cooperative people are, the better their performance. Thus, when group members periodically take the time to review their efforts while executing a task or attempting to solve a problem—that is, when group members reflect on their actions, ensure the equal distribution of responsibility, and protect open communication channels—the benefits afforded by cooperative strategies often increase (Johnson and Johnson 1989; also see Kohn 1986).

The success of cooperation stems from the strategies of action that it stimulates. **Strategies of action** are the means and methods social actors use to achieve goals and fulfill needs. Research indicates that the cooperative stance allows individuals to engage in more sophisticated and advanced thinking and reasoning than that which typically occurs in competitive environments. Social psychologists refer to these sophisticated thinking strategies as *higher-level reasoning* and *meta-cognitive strategies*.

Why do cooperative environments enable sophisticated thinking? Research suggests that interaction within cooperative settings typically evolves according to a process that sociologists refer to as a dialectic. A **dialectic** is a process by which contradictions and their solutions lead participants to more advanced thought. The dialectic process consists of three steps. In step one—*thesis*—the group experiences conflict. Here, members propose different ideas, opinions, theories, and information regarding the task or problem at hand. This conflict or disequilibrium sparks step two—*antithesis*. In antithesis, members actively search for more information and additional views, thus maximizing their knowledge about the task or problem they face. When the search is complete, the group begins step three—*synthesis*. Synthesis is a period in which group members reorganize and reconceptualize their conclusions in a way that merges the best thinking of all members (Johnson and Johnson 1989; Wichman 1970).

In addition to bettering group and individual performance, cooperation—according to more than 180 studies—enhances the quality of interpersonal relationships. Friends, workers, and intimates who cooperate rather than compete with one another report feeling greater levels of acceptance from their colleagues and partners. As a result, cooperators become more caring and committed to their relationships. Further, those involved in cooperative relationships report higher self-esteem and less psychological illness than those who compete with their friends, colleagues, and partners. Indeed, competitiveness has been repeatedly linked to psychological pathology (Combs 1992; Johnson and Johnson 1989; Kohn 1986).

Some studies also link cooperation to diminished feelings of prejudice. **Prejudice** refers to the prejudgment of individuals on the basis of their group membership. For example, individuals who cooperate with those whom they previously had stigmatized or negatively stereotyped report an increased liking toward such individuals. In contrast, individuals placed in competitive situations with members of a previously stigmatized group report a greater dislike for their competitors. On the basis of such studies, many researchers suggest that interracial, interethnic, and intergender cooperative tasks should become a regular "orientation" strategy in workplaces, schools, civic groups, and neighborhood organizations. Many believe that such cooperation "exercises" could help to reduce prejudice and bigotry in the sites of our daily interactions (Aronson and Cope 1968; Aronson et al. 1978; Aronson and Thibodeau 1992; McConahay 1981; Slavin and Madden 1979; Worchel and Norvell 1980).

If cooperation leads to so many benefits, why do social actors continue to choose the competitive stance? The persistence of competition is a good example of the power of cultural values and the ways in which cultural values can promote a phenomenon sociologists refer to as culture against people. **Culture works against people** when the beliefs, values, or norms of a society lead to destructive or harmful patterns of behavior. When it comes to the value of competition, the culture against people phenomenon couldn't be any stronger. Indeed, several studies suggest that even when individuals are made fully aware that they have more to gain by cooperating with others than by competing with them, they continue to adopt competitive strategies of action (Deustch and Krauss 1960; Kelley and Stahelski 1970; Minas et al. 1960; Schultz and Pruitt 1978).

In one experiment, for example, a college professor told his students that they were participating in an investment research project for the *Wall Street Journal*. The project consisted of several simple exercises. In each exercise, students in the class would be asked to write a number—either 1 or 0—on a slip of paper. Before casting their votes, students were informed that the number of 1 votes cast by class members would determine a financial "payoff" for each student. The professor explained that each exercise was designed such that a unanimous class vote of 1 would maximize *every* class member's payment as well as the total class "pot." The class was also instructed that a single 0 vote could increase *one* voter's payoff, but such split votes would always result in a smaller payment for the remaining class members, as well as a smaller payment for the class overall.

Here is a concrete example of the payoff schedule. If 30 people wrote the number 1, a total of $36.00 would be evenly divided by the class—$1.30 for each class member. But if 29 people chose 1 and one person chose 0, only $35.30 would be paid to the class. The one individual who voted 0 would be paid $1.66; the 29 students who voted 1 would each receive only $1.16. Now consider a situation in which 10 students choose the number 0 and 20 choose the number 1. Here, the class would divide only $29.00. Students choosing 0 would each receive $1.30, but those choosing 1 would receive only $.80. (The professor provided students with a breakdown of all possible payoffs before the class voting began.)

The professor took several votes in his class, allowing class members to debate strategies before each vote. Yet, even when the entire class recognized and agreed that a unanimous 1 vote would be the fairest and most lucrative strategy overall, several class members continued to vote 0 in an effort to maximize their own individual gain (Bishop 1986).

Similar results have emerged from experiments conducted in laboratory settings. The Prisoner's Dilemma, for example, is an experimental game designed to test an individual's preference for cooperative versus competitive strategies. The game is based on a hypothetical problem faced by two suspects and a district attorney, all gathered in a police station. The district attorney believes that both suspects have committed a crime. However, the D.A. has no proof connecting the suspects to the crime. Thus, he separates the two, telling each prisoner that he has two alternatives: confess to committing the crime in question, or not confess. Prisoners are told that if neither confesses, both will be convicted of only a minor offense and receive only a minor punishment (1 year incarceration). If both confess, each will be convicted of a major crime and face fairly severe penalties (10 years in prison). If only one of the prisoners confesses, the confessor will receive full immunity, while the nonconfessor will receive the maximum penalty allowed by law (15 years in prison).

The Prisoner's Dilemma is designed to encourage cooperation. Clearly, silence on the part of both prisoners maximizes the chances of each one. Yet, in experimental trials, prisoners repeatedly favor competition. When faced with both the cooperative and competitive options, players consciously choose confession—the strategy that offers them the potential to maximize their own gain. In other words, players choose to compete even when such a strategy proves riskier than cooperation (Rapoport 1960).

The *Wall Street Journal* experiment (devised by three economists: Charles Plott, Mark Isaac, and James Walker), the Prisoner's Dilemma, and other similar games and experiments all illustrate the way in which our cultural value of competition can work against people. These examples suggest that even when a goal can be realized best via a common effort, significant numbers of individuals will *espouse* cooperation but *act* in a competitive way. Significant numbers of individuals will act to maximize their own gain rather than to act in the best interest of the group as a whole—even if that maximization proves risky and the payoff uncertain.

Can we overcome the allure of competition? Are there any circumstances that motivate individuals to choose the cooperative path? Certain studies suggest that when faced with some type of external threat, individuals will abandon their competitive stance and ban together with others in cooperative strategies of defense or protection (Blake and Moulton 1979; Deustch and Krauss 1960; Dion 1979; Lanzetta 1955; Sherif et al. 1961; Sherif 1966; Wilder and Shapiro 1984). Thus, when the chips are down, there is reason to believe that human beings will extend hands of support—as opposed to gauntlets and challenges—to one another. However, if circumstances fall short of desperation, our culture appears to promote the stance of "every man and woman for himself or herself."

LEARNING MORE ABOUT IT

For an interesting discussion regarding the links between cultural values and strategies of action, see Ann Swidler's "Culture As Action," in the *American Sociological Review* 51: 273–286.

The notion of "culture against people" stems from a line of work that includes Philip Slater's *The Pursuit of Loneliness: American Culture at the Breaking Point* (Boston: Beacon Press, 1970), Richard Sennett's *The Fall of Public Man* (New York: Knopf, 1977), and Robert Bellah and colleagues' *Habits of the Heart: Individualism and Commitment in American Life* (Berkeley: University of California Press, 1985).

Several interesting articles linking cooperation to matters of racial harmony, world peace, and so on can be found in *Cooperation: Beyond the Age of Competition* (Philadelphia: Gordon and Breach, 1992), edited by Allan Combs.

Those interested in a thorough examination of the conditions which foster cooperation and/or in learning how to promote cooperation should consult Robert Axelrod's *The Evolution of Cooperation* (New York: Basic Books, 1984).

EXERCISES

1. To determine the cultural importance of competition, try the following "experiment." Solicit several friends and/or relatives to join you in some traditionally competitive activity, such as basketball, bowling, cards, tennis. Vary the conditions of play with each individual you choose. For example, use normal game rules with some of your "subjects"; tell others that you don't want to play for points or keep score. Note the different reactions, if any, to the different conditions of play. Does playing without keeping score affect the willingness of some to participate? Affect the quality of interaction? Do you note any effects of gender or age in the reactions you observe?

2. Explore the significance of competition for college grading. Prepare a serious proposal that testing be conducted under conditions of cooperation rather than competition. (Cooperative conditions might include group testing, open discussion during the exam, or adjustment in grade calculation methods such that each student's grade is an average of her or his actual performance as well as the performance of the best and worst students in the class.) Conduct a limited survey of your colleagues. Do they support or reject such a proposal? What reasons do they offer for their position? Is their reasoning consistent with American values on competition? On cooperation?

CONVENTIONAL WISDOM TELLS US . . .

Children Are Our Most Precious Commodity

■

WE FREQUENTLY HEAR IT SAID: CHILDREN ARE OUR FUTURE. THEY ARE OUR MOST VALUABLE RESOURCE. HERE, WE PRESENT RESEARCH SUGGESTING OTHERWISE. CHILDREN MAY BE THE MOST OVERLOOKED, THE MOST NEGLECTED SEGMENT OF THE POPULATION DESPITE CURRENT TALK OF FAMILY VALUES AND THE FUTURE OF AMERICAN YOUTH.

■

Children—who doesn't love them? In the United States, we refer to children as our nation's future. Our conventional wisdom celebrates them as society's most precious commodity. National opinion polls repeatedly document that Americans consider children one of life's true rewards. Indeed, couples who *want* children but cannot have them are assured the sympathies and support of their fellow members of society. In contrast, couples who *don't want* children frequently find themselves an object of contempt or suspicion by their peers.

Much of today's political rhetoric is fueled by the cultural value America places on children. Citizens and elected officials are urged to act now in the long-term interest of the nation's youth. Politicians vow to cut today's spending and spare our children and grandchildren a troubled and debt-ladened tomorrow. Many advocate curbing social security and medicare costs so as to protect benefits for future generations. Such prescriptions underscore the importance of children in our youth-oriented society.

Threats to our children can mobilize American sentiments in a way that few other issues can. Consider some landmark moments of the 1990s—moments that joined American citizens in public outrage: responses to the 1994 terrorist attack on New York City's Twin Towers, the 1995 bombing of a federal building in Oklahoma City. In such instances, public outrage was fueled in large measure by the fact that these acts threatened and took the lives of so many children.

Can we take the pro-child rhetoric of conventional wisdom at face value? How do our pro-child sentiments compare with the behavioral realities of America's children?

A review of worldwide infant mortality rates offers one perspective on the matter. **Infant mortality rates** gauge the number of deaths per 1000 live births for children under 1 year of age. Such statistics represent a commonly consulted measure, or social indicator, of a society's behavior toward its children. **Social indicators** are quantitative measures or indices of social phenomena.

Despite the pro-child sentiments of American culture, the United States trails 19 other nations in the fight against infant mortality. To be sure, infant deaths typically are highest within less-developed nations of the world community, such as Afghanistan, Bangladesh, Ethiopia, or Haiti. Yet, the U.S. infant mortality rate is comparable to that found in Cuba, Dominica, or Portugal—nations with far less wealth or international power than the United States (see Figure 2.1). Other major industrial nations, such as Japan, Sweden, Canada, France, and Germany, have been more effective

FIGURE 2.1

Infant Mortality Rates for the United States and All Nations with Comparable or Lower Rates

Infant Mortality Rates (Deaths per 1000 Live Births)

than the United States in fighting infant deaths. Indeed, Japan's infant mortality rate is less than half that of the United States (United Nations Development Programme 1993; U.S. Bureau of the Census 1993b).

Child inoculation rates are another informative measure of a society's behavior toward its children. Using this gauge, the United States again fares rather poorly in comparison to other nations. Among Western Hemisphere countries, the United States outperforms only Bolivia and Haiti in the vaccination of children aged two or younger. All of our other Hemisphere neighbors do a better job of protecting their children against childhood diseases (*Kids Count Data Book* 1991; *The State of America's Children* 1991).

Finally, when it comes to the health and well-being of America's most precious commodity, one statistic may prove most noteworthy of all: In the United States, homicide is now the leading cause of death among children under 1 year of age (Porter 1991).

These facts and figures on the physical well-being of children in America unveil glaring discrepancies between what we say and what we do with regard to children. However, the discrepancies extend well beyond the realm of health and mortality—for, although conventional wisdom celebrates the child, the reality is that American children face a greater and greater risk of poverty with each passing year. More than 20% of American children are currently living in poverty (Children's Defense Fund 1992). For many children, this poverty goes hand in hand with homelessness. Indeed, children account for approximately one-fourth of the current U.S. homeless population. Further, families with young children are the fastest growing segment of the homeless population (Blau 1992; Burt 1992).

Even among children who have a roof over their heads, life is not always easy. National surveys suggest rates of physical and sexual child abuse that are completely inconsistent with America's pro-child rhetoric. One in six Americans reports being physically abused as a child. One in seven Americans reports being sexually abused as a child. (When broken down by gender, statistics show that females are twice as likely as males to be abused.) Such estimates mean that close to 7 million children are assaulted each year. This violence proves fatal for more than a thousand children annually (Gelles and Cornell 1990; Rosewater 1989; Straus and Gelles 1988; 1990).

America's pro-child adages ring hollow as well in homes broken by divorce. Nearly three-fourths of the children in female-headed households (a typical product of divorce) currently live in poverty (Children's Defense Fund 1992; National Center for Health Statistics 1990). Further, in any given year, nearly one-half of eligible American children fail to receive their entitled support payments from "deadbeat" parents. Approximately $4 billion in child support is unpaid each year (Waldman 1992).

American schools—another central institution in children's lives—also show evidence of problems that nullify conventional wisdom's pro-child rhetoric. An American child today may have more reason than ever to dread going to school. U.S. Department of Justice surveys show that one in four urban school children reports fear of physical attack while at school (U.S. Bureau of Justice Statistics 1991). Although this fear is not proportional to the actual incidence of violence in our schools, such anxieties are not unfounded. Several hundred thousand students are the victims of school violence each year. Further, estimates suggest that more than 100,000 guns are carried into our schools every day (Bastian and Taylor 1991).

Our schools appear to fail our children with regard to academic achievement as well. Since the early days of the American space program, many have voiced concern regarding the performance levels of American schoolchildren. These concerns are well grounded. The Educational Testing Service, for example, reports that among the 15 major industrial nations of the world, the United States ranks 14th and 13th, respectively, in standardized math and science test scores (*Washington Post* 1992). The U.S. high school dropout rate far outpaces that of other industrial nations. And in the United States, graduating from high school is itself no guarantee of educational achievement: approximately one in eight American high school graduates leaves school as a functional illiterate—that is, her or his reading and writing skills are inadequate for meeting the demands and needs of everyday life (National Commission on Excellence in Education 1983; U.S. Department of Education 1993).

These everyday patterns suggest that, in America, although we may idealize childhood (especially in our memories), the reality for today's children is often anything but ideal. Indeed, despite our pro-child stance, many children find childhood too difficult to endure. The suicide rate among American youth increased by 240% from the early 1950s to the late 1970s. Today, suicide is the second leading cause of death among adolescents (Ward, Carter, and Perrin 1994).

What meaning can we draw from the discrepancies between conventional wisdom's view of children and the way in which children actually are treated? Are we simply a nation of hypocrites? We gain some perspective on the issue when we consider a distinction sociologists draw between ideal culture and real culture. **Ideal culture** comprises the values, beliefs, and norms each society claims as central to its modus operandi. In other words, ideal culture is about aspirations—the ends or goals of our behaviors. In contrast, **real culture** refers to those values, beliefs, and norms we actually execute or practice. Thus, real culture is about behaviors or the means to a society's ends.

Your own life experiences have surely taught you that humans have a remarkable capacity to be inconsistent: We can say one thing and do another. In fact, Americans have a cultural prescription reflecting this capacity: "Do as I say, not as I do." When sociologists examine the fit between ideal and real culture, they are exploring the "say one thing, do another" phenomenon as it occurs at the social level.

For a society to achieve perfect agreement between its ideal and real cultures, it must achieve *both* consensus on goals and agreement regarding the appropriate methods for achieving those goals. That is, ideal and real cultures are in balance only when a society is free of contradiction between what it says and what it does. If a society cannot synchronize its goals and behaviors, then it experiences a condition sociologists refer to as cultural inconsistency. **Cultural inconsistency** refers to a situation in which actual behaviors contradict cultural goals. Cultural inconsistency depicts an imbalance between ideal and real cultures.

Why do cultural inconsistencies emerge in a society? Conflict theorists offer one possible answer. **Conflict theorists** analyze social organization and social interactions by attending to the differential resources controlled by different sectors of a society. These theorists suggest that the inability to balance ideal and real cultures has much to do with the broader issues of power and social policy. **Power** is the ability of groups and/or individuals to get what they want even in the face of resistance. **Social policies** are officially adopted plans of action.

In American society, social policies often guide social behaviors, or what we are referring to as real culture. Yet, social policies rarely emerge from general population consensus; they are rarely directed toward ideal culture. Rather, such prescriptions inevitably are influenced by the actions and relative power of various sectors of the population—special interest groups, political action committees, lobbyists, and so on.

By definition, special interest groups promote or advance the cause of certain segments of the population, such as the New Christian Right, senior citizens, tobacco manufacturers, trial lawyers. Thus, these groups are unduly responsive to the interests of the few—and necessarily ignore the broader interests of the larger population. Special interest groups vie to prescribe social policy. Ultimately, then, social policy generally reflects the particularized goals of groups sufficiently powerful to influence it.

Lacking control of economic resources or access to the political ballot denies children, as a collective, the typical tools of power. Further, age works against the self-serving collective actions of children. Children are dependents; they must rely on adults to act as their advocates. As a result, the interests and rights of children always will be weighed against those of parents, families, and society at large. The child's voice always will be rendered via an intermediary's perspective.

The drawbacks of the child's indirect political presence is aptly illustrated when we review efforts to combat child abuse in the United States. History reveals a parade of policies consistent with child advocates' views and beliefs regarding the best interest of children. For example, child advocates of the early 1800s believed that abused and neglected children were at risk of delinquency; such advocates saw abused children as threats to society. As a result, social and reform policies of the period demanded the institutionalization of abused children. Protecting society was deemed action in the best interest of the child. In the early 1900s, the newly emerging professions of social work and clinical psychology argued that promoting and protecting intact families would best serve the interests of children. Such policy recommendations remanded abused children to the very sites of their mistreatment (Pfohl 1977).

In the current era, many child advocates continue to cling to the family protection theme. The Family Research Council, for example, is an advisory group that promotes traditional family values. This group rejects any efforts to view children and their rights as an issue separate from the context of the family (Family Research Council 1992). The Family Research Council's position, as well as those of other groups before them, makes the political plight of children clear. Without the ability to organize and lobby solely on their own behalf, children always will be one critical step removed from the social policy process—and the gap between the ideal and real cultures that frame childhood in America will continue to exist.

Given the cultural inconsistency that exists in American society's stance toward children, isn't it hypocritical to continue to espouse the ideals we hold? Shouldn't an honorable society refrain from promoting ends it cannot meet?

Sociologically speaking, there are several important reasons to maintain the concept of an ideal culture—even when society fails to practice what it preaches. First, a gap between goals and behaviors—that is, a gap between ideal and real cultures—does not diminish the value of a society's ideals. We can honestly place a high value on children even though our behaviors may fall short of the ideal. Ideals, goals, and values are aspirations and, as such, they are frequently not achieved.

Second, changing ideal culture to fit a society's actual practices might indeed bring an end to cultural inconsistency. However, such a change would not alter an important fact. Children literally are the future of any group or society. For a society to survive, individuals must be persuaded to reproduce themselves. In preindustrial days, economic necessity was an attractive incentive for reproduction. Children furnished valuable labor power to colonial families. Children were valuable sources of family income in the early days of industrialization as well. In the industrialization era, children regularly took their place alongside older workers in factories and sweatshops (LeVine and White 1992; Zelizer 1985).

Today, the economic incentives attached to childbearing have changed dramatically. Children are no longer regarded as valuable labor power or income sources for families. Further, the cost of having and raising children in our society has risen dramatically over the years. The U.S. Department of Agriculture puts the expense of raising one child at $100,000. If the child attends college, that figure doubles (U.S. Department of Agriculture 1993).

Clearly, the motivation to have children is more problematic today than at earlier points in America's history. (This may explain why many adults report that their highest levels of lifetime happiness occurred *before* they had children or *after* their children left home (White and Edwards 1990). Indeed, the economic and personal costs of child rearing may account for the steady decreases in average family size during the past century. The latest census figures show the median number of children per family is 0.96. Further, surveys indicate that Americans no longer fantasize about "having a house full of children." Rather, most women cite two as the ideal number of children (General Social Survey 1990).

Delayed childbearing also accounts for part of the decline in average family size. Women in the United States are waiting longer to have children, and such delays ultimately translate into fewer total births (McFalls 1990). In addition, increases in education levels, career aspirations, and satisfaction with present life situations appear to be making it easier for some couples to remain childless (Bloom and Bennett 1986; Rix 1989). In the early 1990s, only 37% of all families consisted of married couples *with* children (Ahlburg and DeVita 1992). The majority of families reported no children living in the home (Exter 1992; *The World Almanac* 1995).

A growing trend toward singlehood among the young and middle-aged further complicates overall fertility patterns in the United States. The past two decades have seen a 94% increase in the number of women living alone and a 167% increase in the number of men living alone.

Any society interested in its own survival must keep a watchful eye on such developments. Many European countries experiencing similar drops in family size are treating lower birthrates as a foreshadowing of dangerous population decline. France, for example, has recently undertaken an advertisement campaign to offset its low birthrates. (One campaign ad features a picture of a baby with the caption, "It appears that I am a sociocultural phenomenon.") Viewed in this light, maintaining an ideal culture that values children makes good sense—even when we sometimes fail to practice what we preach. Placing a high premium on children is one important way to ensure that individuals continue to make a financial investment in children. By doing so, they provide the critical raw material for societal survival.

American conventional wisdom on children seems at odds with our behaviors and actions. But this cultural inconsistency is not likely to disappear soon. Indeed, even if the costs of having and raising children continue to increase and the structures of our families continue to change, pro-child rhetoric may grow even stronger in the United States in the days ahead.

LEARNING MORE ABOUT IT

Readers will find a very engaging review of the past two centuries of family life in Stephanie Coontz's *The Way We Never Were: American Families and the Nostalgia Trap* (New York: Basic, 1992).

Viviana Zelizer offers a fascinating historical review on the social value of children in *Pricing the Priceless Child* (New York: Basic Books, 1985).

For an interesting perspective on historical responses to child abuse in the United States, see Stephen J. Pfolh's "The Discovery of Child Abuse" (*Social Problems, 24* (3), 310–323, 1977).

For a discussion on the discrepancy between goals and the paths we choose to achieve them, see Merton's classic 1938 work "Social Structure and Anomie" in *American Sociological Review 3,* 672–682.

Amatai Etzioni provides an interesting discussion on special interest groups and their impact on the American legal system in *Capital Corruption* (New York: Harcourt Brace Jovanovich, 1984).

EXERCISES

1. Take a look at the age graph in Figure 2.2. Pay particular attention to the relative size of the various age groups and the corresponding implications for population trends over the next 10 to 20 years. What does

FIGURE 2.2

Population Breakdown by Age

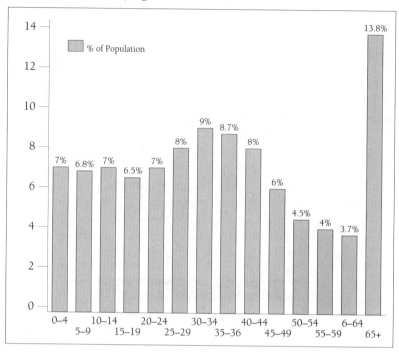

the graph suggest is a likely development with regard to our pro-child culture?

2. Select three family TV programs whose cast of characters includes children. Monitor the content of the programs for a 2–3 week period, noting program incidents and themes. On the basis of your observations, do the programs emphasize ideal or real culture in their portrayal of children in our society? What factors can you offer that might account for your findings?

Social Structure

■

CONVENTIONAL WISDOM TELLS US . . .

Love Knows No Reason

■

IN THIS ESSAY, WE EXPLORE VARIOUS SOCIAL STATUSES—AGE, EDUCATION, GENDER, INCOME, RACE, RELIGION—NOTING THE WAYS IN WHICH THESE FACTORS CAN GUIDE SOMETHING AS SEEMINGLY INDIVIDUALISTIC AS CUPID'S ARROW.

■

Love—that invigorating, addictive sensation, the emotional roller-coaster ride that signals the wonder of being human. Conventional wisdom locates love in the world of passion; adages describe it as an experience that can make us irrational, impetuous, and often oblivious to the real-life events that surround us. There is nothing logical about love. Love bows to emotion, not reason.

The conventional wisdom on love is not easily shaken. For example, in 1974 the National Science Foundation awarded an $84,000 grant for a social *scientific* investigation into the experience of love. But upon hearing of the grant, Senator William Proxmire blasted the investment from the floor of the U.S. Senate, saying:

> I'm against this, not only because no one—not even the National Science Foundation—can argue that falling in love is a science; not only because I'm sure that even if they spend 84 million or 84 billion they wouldn't get an answer that anyone would believe. I'm also against it because I don't want the answer! (quoted in Harris 1978).

Is conventional wisdom accurate when it comes to love? Is the fall into love strictly an emotional journey? Does Cupid's arrow defy reason or direction and truly strike us senseless?

Despite romantic visions, research indicates that the experience of falling in love is much more logical than we might like to admit. Although Cupid's arrow may contain the magic that joins two hearts, Cupid's aim appears to be highly selective, and heavily influenced by the social status of his targets. **Social status** refers to the position or location of an individual with reference to characteristics such as age, education, gender, income, race, religion. Consider the love-and-marriage game. Our choices for the "love of my life" generally occur along highly predictable lines (Buss and Barnes 1986; Epstein and Guttman 1984; Hollingshead 1950; Murstein 1976; Strong and DeVault 1989). Indeed, these choices are guided by "rules" that sociologists refer to as norms of homogamy. **Norms of homogamy** encourage interaction between individuals occupying similar social statuses.

Research shows that the large majority of Americans fall in love and marry mates within 3 years of their own age (Mensch 1986). Further, the look of love seems routinely reserved for those of like races, religions, and classes. For example, only 2% of all U.S. marriages are interracial, and only about a third of American marriages occur between people of different religions (Pagnini and Morgan 1990; U.S. Bureau of the Census 1990a). Better than half of all American marriages unite people of the same social class, and 95% of all U.S. marriages join people who are no more than one socioeconomic class apart (Hout 1982; Simon 1987).

Cupid's arrow also is typically reserved for those with similar educational backgrounds (Mare 1991), similar intelligence levels (Lapidus, Green, and Baruh 1985), and similar physical appearance (White 1980). And, apparently, Cupid's flights are amazingly short. Research documents a 50/50 chance that individuals will marry someone who lives within walking distance of them (Kephart and Jedlicka 1991).

When it comes to love and marriage, research suggests that "birds of a feather seem to flock together," while "opposites rarely attract." Star-crossed lovers may exist in principle, but in practice the stars of love are likely to be carefully charted by social forces—and thus glitter in the eyes of a social peer. Such patterns lead sociologists to characterize both romantic love and marriage as endogamous phenomena. **Endogamy** are practices restricted by shared group membership; they are an "in-group" phenomena. What explains the endogamous nature of love? Endogamy generally results from a societal wish to maintain group and class boundaries. In some cases, these boundaries are formally stated. Certain religious groups, for example, strongly urge their members toward intrafaith marriages. Similarly, traditional caste systems generally prohibit marriage between individuals of different castes. In other settings, however, boundary maintenance occurs via more informal channels, where certain key social players may quietly enforce endogamy in love and marriage.

In U.S. society, parents and peers often play the role of enforcer. It is not uncommon for family and friends to threaten, cajole, wheedle, and even bribe individuals in the direction of a "suitable" mate. Suitability generally translates into a partnership based on similar social profiles. Thus, the "American way" of marriage places the most personal decisions of one's life—falling in love and getting married—under "group control." This subtle control serves as a vehicle by which endogamy can be maintained.

Like romantic love, the development and expression of platonic love or friendship is also heavily influenced by the social location of its participants. Research shows that friendship formation is largely a product of one's daily interaction patterns rather than of chance or "good chemistry."

Friendships tend to develop with the people we see most often—those with whom we work, those enrolled in the same class, or members of our church, health club, and so on. (Insko and Wilson 1977). Similarly, friendships tend to form among those who are in close geographic proximity to us as opposed to those who are further away—i.e. the people in our apartment complex or those who live in our neighborhood (Festinger, Schacter, and Back 1950; Lapidus et al. 1985; Monge and Kirste 1980).

Like romantic love, the platonic love of friendship grows best out of similarity. We tend to build the strongest friendships with those who hold attitudes similar to our own. We also tend to connect with those who share our physical and social characteristics—appearance, income, education level, race, and so on. In the case of friendship, familiarity breeds attraction rather than contempt (White 1980; Zajonc 1970).

Interestingly, our feelings about friendship—the way we define and express it—differ in systematic ways on the basis of our socioeconomic status. **Socioeconomic status** refers to a particular social location—one defined with reference to education, occupation, and financial resources. Studies show, for example, that working-class Americans conceive of friendship as an exchange of goods and services. Gifts and favors come to indicate the strength of a friendship bond. In contrast, material exchange is absent from middle-class definitions of friendship. Middle-class individuals frequently view friendship as an emotional or intellectual exchange; they may also conceive of friendship simply as the sharing of leisure activities.

The "faces" of our friends also differ by social class. Thus, if you are a member of America's working class, your friends are highly likely to be relatives—siblings, cousins, parents, and so on. In contrast, middle-class individuals prefer nonblood relations for friends. Further, among working-class people, friendships are overwhelmingly same sex, whereas middle-class people are more open to cross-gender friendships. Finally, if you are from America's working class, your friendships are likely to be local. Thus, working-class friends interact, on average, once a week or more. In contrast, middle-class individuals have as many long-distance friendships as they do local ones. Because middle-class life in America often involves high levels of geographic mobility, members of the middle class are more likely than their working-class counterparts to maintain a friendship after individuals move out of the immediate geographic area. This distance factor carries a downside, however. Middle-class friends generally report less frequent contact than their working-class counterparts (Allan 1989; Bleiszner and Adams 1992; Elles 1993; Fischer 1982; Gouldner and Strong 1987; Rawlins 1992; Walker 1995).

The patterned nature of love also emerges in matters of self-love, or what social scientists refer to as self-esteem. **Self-esteem** refers to the personal judgments individuals make regarding their own self-worth. Like romantic and platonic love, love of self appears quite systematically tied to an individual's social situation.

On the level of experience, for example, many studies show that one's self-esteem is directly tied to the love expressed toward that individual by her or his significant others. Not surprisingly, when significant others give positive feedback, self-esteem increases. Conversely, consistently negative feedback from significant others lowers self-esteem. Similarly, the character of one's social or work environment clearly influences an individual's self-esteem. Those who are situated among optimistic people in positive, upbeat environments have been shown repeatedly to enjoy better self-esteem than those who find themselves in negative environments with depressed or disgruntled colleagues. Finally, various social attributes can influence levels of self-love or self-esteem, with members of upper classes and racial majority groups routinely faring better than the poor or those in racial minorities (Coopersmith 1967; Felson and Reed 1986, 1987; Gergen 1971).

Romantic love, platonic love, self-love—when findings from these areas are considered together, we must concede that love, in its various forms, is a highly structured phenomenon. There is much rhyme and reason regarding how we find it, define it, experience it, and express it. And that logic is tied to aspects of our social backgrounds and our social locations. Knowing this, we might do better to trade our notions of the irrational heart for knowledge of the social organization of the heart. Indeed, the study of love reminds us that even the most personal of experiences can succumb to the systematic influence of the social.

LEARNING MORE ABOUT IT

Two informative studies on coupling in America can be found in *American Couples: Money, Work, Sex*, written by Philip Blumstein and Pepper Schwartz (New York: Wm. Morrow, 1985), or, more recently, *The Social Organization of Sexuality* by Edward O. Laumann and colleagues (Chicago: University of Chicago Press, 1994).

For an interesting look at the social aspects of friendship, see Rubin's *Just Friends: The Role of Friendship in Our Lives* (New York: Harper and Row, 1985).

Most sociological work on self-esteem is steeped in the writings of Charles Horton Cooley. His classic works include *Human Nature and Social Order* (New York: Scribner, 1902) and *Social Organization* (New York: Charles Scribner, 1909).

EXERCISES

1. Identify the top three traits you desire in a friend. Do these traits correspond to the friendship trends cited here for (a) your social class of origin or (2) the social class to which you aspire? Now, repeat the exercise, this time considering the top three traits that you desire in a spouse. Do your answers suggest the influence of homogamy?

2. Using yourself (if appropriate) and your married friends as case studies, discuss how the rules of homogamy either apply or do not apply in these individuals' selections of marriage partners. Collect similar information about your parents, aunts, and uncles, and compare it with what you found about yourself and your friends. Do you see any important generational changes in the rules for marital homogamy? Are there rule variations that can be linked to class or educational factors?

ESSAY 4

CONVENTIONAL WISDOM TELLS US . . .

Stress Is Bad for Your Well-being

■

OR IS IT? THIS ESSAY REVIEWS THE CONDITIONS

UNDER WHICH STRESS CAN PROVE BENEFICIAL

IN ONE'S EVERYDAY ACTIVITIES. IN SO DOING,

WE HIGHLIGHT THE IMPORTANCE OF

CONSIDERING SOCIAL CONTEXT IN ASSESSING

SOCIAL BEHAVIORS.

■

Stress has become a regular feature of modern-day existence. Finding a parking space at the mall, hooking up a new computer, navigating the university's new automated registration system, getting the supermarket to correct the price on that misscanned item—in today's fast-paced, high-tech environment, stress can weave its way into even the most routine tasks.

Modernization and technological advancement have stress-related costs. To be sure, these phenomena make possible amazing strides, including increased life spans, greater geographic mobility, and heightened industrial and agricultural productivity. Yet, these changes also actively alter a society's social structure. **Social structure** refers to the organization of a society—the ways in which social statuses, resources, power, and mechanisms of control combine to form a framework of operations.

Thus for many, a society's "amazing strides" may translate into commuter marriages, single parenthood, long widowhoods, or "downsized" work environments—conditions often associated with increased stress. In addition, such advances may expand the ranks of the poor, trigger rapid population growth, and increase competition for resources. Such structural changes can increase the day-to-day stress experienced by those in certain social locations. **Social location** is an individual's total collection of social statuses; it pinpoints an individual's social position by simultaneously considering age, education, gender, income, race, and so on.

The pervasiveness of stress makes it important to weigh conventional wisdom's dire warnings on the subject. Will the benefits of modernization ultimately cost us our physical, mental, or emotional health? Just what toll does stress take on our overall well-being?

The links between stress and well-being are complex because the effects of stress vary by social context (Jacobson 1989; Lennon 1989; Pearlin 1989). **Social context** refers to the broad social and historical circumstances surrounding an act or an event. For example, consider the links between stress and health. Many studies link stress to serious physical problems: cancer, heart disease, mental illness, and emotional depression. Research also suggests that stress can trigger increases in smoking, drinking, drug use, and other hazardous behaviors (House, Strecher, Metzner, and Robbins 1986; Pearlin, Menaghan, Lieberman, and Mullan 1981; Ross and Huber 1985; Wheaton 1983). However, these negative effects are largely confined to contexts in which stress is chronic. **Chronic stress** refers to the relatively enduring problems, conflicts, and threats that individuals face on a daily basis. Most researchers agree that chronic stress contexts, such as persistent financial woes, a bad marriage, sites of crime, violence, overcrowding, or even noise, are harmful to our well-being. In contrast, sporadic, short-term stress generally proves less detrimental to well-being

(Aneshensel 1992; House et al. 1986; Kobasa, Maddi, and Kahn 1982; Pearlin 1989).

Now consider the stress generated by certain life events—retirement, children leaving home, the death of a spouse, and so on. Conventional wisdom suggests that such events can be the most stressful experiences of our lives. Again, however, research reveals that the stress associated with these life events varies with the social context in which the event occurs.

For example, retirement actually has been shown to alleviate stress if one is leaving an unpleasant or difficult job. Similarly, when a child leaves home, stress actually decreases for those parents who perceived their family relationships to be troubled or strained (Thoits 1983; Wheaton 1982, 1990). To determine the level of stress associated with any life event, one must explore the circumstances and activities that precede and/or accompany the event; one must assess the life event within its proper social context (Aneshensel 1992; Jacobson 1989; Lennon 1989; Pearlin 1989).

In assessing the conventional wisdom on stress, it also is important to note that the negative effects of stress are not inevitable. Research documents several coping mechanisms that can temper or even cancel the negative impact of stress on one's well-being. For example, individuals who enjoy strong social support networks often are protected from the harmful consequences of stress. A **social support network** consists of family, friends, agencies, and resources—entities that actively assist individuals in coping with adverse or unexpected events.

Studies document, for instance, that widows and widowers who have close friends or confidants report much less stress from the death of a spouse than individuals who lack such support. Similarly, the stress of divorce appears greatly diminished for those with close friends, confidants, or new romantic interests. Certain resources also influence the experience of stress. Research indicates that relaxation techniques can buffer individuals from the negative impact of stress. Similarly, learning strategies that can physically or mentally distance one from the site of stress can help mitigate its harmful effects (Eaton 1978; House et al. 1986; Kessler and McLeod 1985; Kessler, Price, and Wortman 1985; Lin 1982; Menaghan and Merves 1984; Pescosolido and Georgianna 1989; Wheaton 1982, 1990).

Coping mechanisms can offer protection from stress. However, some contend that modern lifestyles may make it difficult for individuals to put these "safeguards" into effect (Dahrendorf 1959; Kornhauser 1959; Pearson 1993). For example, the geographic mobility that characterizes modern society may place friends and family out of one's immediate reach. Similarly, increased access to information may create a mental overload that eats away at one's relaxation time. And technological advancements that allow one to merge work and home sites may make mental distancing strategies difficult to execute.

The successful enactment of coping mechanisms may be largely related to the kinds of social relationships that characterize one's social environment. Ferdinand Tonnies (1855–1936) analyzed such relationships using two distinct categories: Gemeinschaft and Gesellschaft. **Gemeinschaft** refers to an environment in which social relationships are based on ties of friendship and kinship. **Gesellschaft** refers to an environment in which social relationships are formal, impersonal, and often initiated for specialized or instrumental purposes. Modern social environments, with their emphasis on privacy and individuality, reflect the Gesellschaft environment. As such, the social resources from which coping mechanisms develop may not be readily available to modern women and men.

Are there contexts in which stress positively influences our well-being? Social psychologists have demonstrated that task-oriented stress often can lead to visibly productive consequences. **Task-oriented stress** refers to short-term stress that accompanies particular assignments or settings. Individuals who report feeling completely comfortable or relaxed during the execution of certain mental tasks remember and absorb less information than those who experience moderate levels of task-oriented stress. Indeed, task-oriented stress has been linked to enhanced memory of facts and skills and increased learning ability—important attributes in our postindustrial, knowledge-based society (Courts 1939; Ellis 1972). This suggests that the nervous tingles you experience in studying for the law boards, your driving test, or a public speaking engagement may serve you better than a lackadaisical stance.

Studies also show that stress can work *through* other physiological or psychological states to produce quite unexpected, and quite positive, behavioral outcomes. For example, when stress leads to a state of emotional arousal such as anxiety or fear, stressed individuals are more likely to befriend or bond with others. (This may explain why your student colleagues always seem more approachable on the day of a big exam.) Further, when stress leads to anxiety or fear, stressed individuals demonstrate a greater tendency to like and interact with people whom they usually dislike or around whom they typically feel uncomfortable. This "benefit" extends to people who differ from the stressed individual in terms of race, socioeconomic status, and personality. In light of these findings, some researchers contend that under the right circumstances, stress may aid the cause of achieving interracial, intergenerational, or interclass affiliations (Latané and Glass 1968; Schachter 1959; Wrightsman 1960).

It is interesting to note that stress which proves detrimental to the well-being of individuals sometimes may prove productive for societies at large.

Consider one such example in the area of chronic stress. Chronic stress can emerge from a particular type of long-term situation, a condition sociologists refer to as role conflict. **Role conflict** occurs when social members occupy two or more social locations that carry opposing demands. Military chaplains, working parents, or student teachers—all provide examples of potentially conflicting role combinations. Roles that carry opposing demands create a tug-of-war within individuals, a persistent strain characteristic of chronic stress.

Although role conflict can take its toll on an individual's well-being, it sometimes proves the source of positive social change. For example, when role conflict is routinized by changing cultural or economic demands, the resulting stress can actually trigger needed social restructuring. Routinized role conflict can lead societies to institute changes that positively alter the playing field of social interaction. For example, the conflict and stress that emerged from the working-parent role combination served to revolutionize America's work environment. Methods such as flex-time, in-house daycare, and work-at-home options—originally antidotes to the stress of role conflict—are now a productive dimension of work in the United States.

We can take this analysis of the positive consequences of stress one step further. The phenomenon of stress need not be confined to individual-level inquiries; societies as a whole also can experience stress. Sociologists refer to this type of stress as social strain. **Social strain** develops when a social event or trend disrupts the equilibrium of a society's social structure. For example, an economic depression may generate social strain by forcing increases in unemployment and exacerbating poverty. In essence, the depression event disrupts expected patterns of resource distribution. Similarly, a large increase in a society's birth rate may place strain on various social institutions. Schools, hospitals, or prisons may suddenly be presented with more clients than they were designed to serve.

Sociologists such as Talcott Parsons (1951/1964) or Lewis Coser (1956), although coming from different perspectives, both suggest that social strain creates an opportunity for societal change and growth. (Note that Coser refers to the phenomenon of strain as "social conflict.") Social strain disrupts the status quo. Thus, it can force societies to work at reestablishing smooth operations. For example, the strain placed on the U.S. stratification system by the civil rights movement of the 1950s and 1960s resulted in positive strides toward racial and ethnic equality in America. Similarly, consider the growing demands U.S. entitlement programs currently place on the nation's economic system. Many credit such strain with prompting much needed public discourse on major budget reforms.

Is stress harmful to our well-being? Taken as a whole, current research on stress paints a less dismal picture than that promoted by conventional wisdom. To be sure, stress is frequently harmful, and it is rarely a pleasant experience. Yet, its consequences do not necessarily jeopardize personal health and happiness. In fact, when one views stress in context, or at the level of societies at large, it sometimes proves a useful social resource.

LEARNING MORE ABOUT IT

For a good summary of current findings and controversies within the social science literature on stress, see Carol Aneshensel's 1992 review article "Social Stress: Theory and Research" in the *Annual Review of Sociology* (vol. 18, 15–38). One might also consult an interesting symposium on stress, including works by Leonard Pearlin, David Jacobson, and Mary Clare Lennon published in the *Journal of Health and Social Behavior* (vol. 30, 241–269, 1989).

Several interesting experiments document the positive consequences of stress for individuals. Schachter's *The Psychology of Affiliation* (Stanford: Stanford University Press, 1959) represents a classic among such studies.

Stress and conflict within social systems is wonderfully addressed in Lewis Coser's classic theoretical treatise, *The Functions of Social Conflict* (Glencoe, IL: The Free Press, 1956).

EXERCISES

1. Research suggests that stress can increase an individual's likelihood of affiliating with others. Can stress function in a similar way at the societal level? To test the hypothesis that social stress increases social solidarity, see if periods of economic recession or a nation's involvement in a major war are associated with any indicators of increased group cohesion. Using a source like the *Information Please Almanac,* track membership rates in five national organizations for years before and after the economic recession of the 1970s or World War II.

2. Compare two weeks' worth of "Letters to the Editor" prior to a national- or local-level stress event—for example, the declaration of war on Iraq in 1991, the 1995 bombing of the federal office building in Oklahoma, a well-publicized murder or accident in your hometown—with two weeks' worth of "Letters to the Editor" after such an event. Analyze the content of letter writers' remarks concerning their personal feelings and reactions to these events. What does your analysis show regarding the social consequences of stress?

CONVENTIONAL WISDOM TELLS US . . .

The "Golden Years" Are Tarnished Years

■

GROWING OLD—NO ONE LOOKS FORWARD TO IT.
YET, THIS ESSAY ILLUSTRATES THAT OUR
WORST FEARS ABOUT GROWING OLD MAY BE
LARGELY UNFOUNDED, SIMPLY PRODUCTS OF
A "MASTER STATUS" FOR WHICH WE HAVE
BEEN INADEQUATELY PREPARED.

■

Aging is a curious phenomenon. When we are young, we can't wait to be older—or at least old enough to drive, get a good job, and make our own decisions. When we finally reach adulthood, many of us continue to yearn for a later stage in life, a time when we can begin to capitalize on the lessons of youth, a time when we can enjoy the fruits of our labors. Retirement looks like a pretty good deal from the vantage point of youth.

Eventually, however, there comes a time when the benefits of aging seem less clear-cut. We begin to view age as a liability, perhaps even as a thing to be feared. The conventional wisdom on aging seems to support this negative stance. We are warned never to "trust anyone over 30." Those in their forties and fifties frequently are characterized as "over the hill." Advanced age becomes a liability for many practices and occupations: After all, "You can't teach an old dog new tricks." And retiring can earn one the image of "being put out to pasture." Indeed, today, presidential candidates who have earned 65+ years of life experience must convince us that they are not too old for the job!

Despite early desires to "be older," many Americans ultimately develop a rather negative view of growing old. Surveys show that many Americans picture old age as a time of loneliness, vulnerability, and sickness (Harris 1981). Are such images accurate? Is conventional wisdom's negative stance on growing old justified? Research suggests that the "negative press" on aging is not fully supported by the facts. In reviewing several studies on the elderly, one finds many inconsistencies between the public perceptions versus the social realities of old age in America.

Some polls show that roughly two-thirds of the general public believe elderly Americans are plagued by social isolation and loneliness. Yet, these same polls suggest that less than one-eighth of those 65 and older identify loneliness as a serious life problem (Cupito 1986; *Public Opinion* 1986). It is true that the elderly make up a relatively large portion of single households. However, such living arrangements seem to reflect a preference rather than a forced choice. In one study, for example, 85% of elderly respondents indicated they did not *want* to live with their children (Casale and Lerman 1986). And, indeed, fewer than 10% of American elderly ultimately move in with their children (Dentzer 1991).

In addition to living arrangements, several other behavioral patterns contradict the loneliness stereotype. For example, America's senior citizens regularly report active companionship in a variety of settings, not the least of which is the family. Studies show that the majority of America's elderly report having children they can count on if necessary (American Association of Retired Persons [AARP] 1989). In addition, better than three-fourths of those over 65 live within 1 hour of at least one of their children. Among such families, frequent family visitation is the norm rather than the exception. Indeed, more than three-fourths of the American elderly report seeing their children at least once a week, and approximately half of those over 65 say that they see their children at least once a day (Bengston, Rosenthal, and Burton 1990; Casale and Lerman 1986; Gibbs 1988).

Loneliness is only one of the misconceptions about old age. Public perceptions also paint the elderly as frequent victims of violent crime. Yet, violent crime against the elderly has declined drastically over the past 20 years. Further, age and victimization are inversely related—as age goes up, crime victimization goes down (Livingston 1996). Thus, those between the ages of 50 and 64, for example, are twice as likely to be victims of crime than those over the age of 65; individuals between the ages of 25 and 49 are more than five times as likely to become crime victims. In fact, the "over-65 crowd" displays the lowest crime victimization rate of all American age groups (Vito and Holmes 1994).

The "crime myth" that surrounds old age is not without its consequences; the myth generates a great deal of anxiety among the elderly. Indeed, those 65 and older exhibit a higher level of fear toward crime than any other age group in the population (Brillon 1987).

Public perceptions also suggest that old age is a time of poverty. Until the 1970s, the elderly were more likely than any other age group to live in poverty: Twenty-five percent of those over the age of 65 were classified as poor. In contrast, the poverty rate for the population at large was only 13%. But changes in the social security system—in particular, changes linking benefits to cost-of-living increases—have helped reduce the percentage of elderly living in poverty. Today the poverty rate for those over 65 years of age is just under 13%. Thus current poverty rates for the elderly are slightly below the national average (U.S. Bureau of the Census 1994a).

Images of physical and mental deterioration also invade public perceptions of old age. To be sure, age does result in some changes on this front: Ten percent of those 65 years of age and older experience some vision impairment; 30% of this age group experience some hearing loss (U.S. National Center for Health Statistics 1989). Yet, it is important to note that *health*, not disease, is the norm for the elderly—even for those over 85! Only about 5% of the American elderly report serious physical incapacitation; less than 1% are bedridden. Indeed, a full 65% of senior citizens report no restrictions in physical mobility, with an additional 30% reporting only minimal difficulties in mobility (Atchley 1994; Kart 1990; Mutchler and Burr 1991; U.S. National Center for Health Statistics 1989) Less than 10% of those between 65 and 84 and only about a fourth of those 85 or older are relegated to nursing home care (Atchley 1994).

In terms of mental health, the elderly fare quite well. Indeed, the highest rates of mental illness are found among those who are much younger—those 25 to 34 years of age (Kessler et al. 1994). Although senility is frequently associated with old age, it afflicts but 20% of those over 80. Further, the vast majority of these cases result from nonneurological problems that are susceptible to treatment (Shanas and Maddox 1976). Overall, aging appears to bring an elusive mental benefit to the elderly: They are more at peace with themselves than any other age group (Casale and Lerman 1986).

The facts about old age in America seem to contradict "common knowledge." Why do such misconceptions exist? The concept of a master status may provide one insight in the matter. A **master status** refers to a single social status that overpowers all other social positions occupied by an individual. A master status directs the way in which others see, define, and relate to an individual.

Master statuses are powerful identity tools because they carry with them a set of qualities or characteristics that they impose on those who occupy the status. For example, those who occupy the master status of doctor are assumed to be knowledgeable, wealthy, rational, and usually white and male. Similarly, those that occupy the master status of mother are presumed to be caring, nurturing, stable, and female.

In short, a master status and the traits and characteristics that accompany it have a tremendous capacity to influence what others "see" or assume to be true in their social interactions. Thus, although I can look at a doctor and see that *she* is not a male, the story doesn't end here. Expectations that stem from the master status "doctor" might nonetheless continue to influence my interaction with my doctor—I may question whether or not *she* possesses other key traits of the master status such as knowledge or rationality. I may doubt her ability to diagnose.

During two periods in our lives, childhood and our senior years, age serves as a master status. In childhood, the master status of age is equated with qualities such as dependency, unbounded energy, innocence, inquisitiveness, irresponsibility, and the ability to be uninhibited. As senior citizens, the master status of age is associated with characteristics such as dependency, frailty, loneliness, and the potential for poor health.

In essence, age becomes a master status early and late in life due to a lack of competition. We begin to accumulate statuses more powerful than age only as we move out of childhood and through adolescence, young adulthood, and our middle-age years. It is during life's middle stages that we embark on careers, take spouses, raise children, join clubs and associations, become homeowners, and pursue leisure-time or self-fulfilling interests. During life's middle stages, occupational and family statuses typically assume the master status position.

In our later years, we exit many of our occupational and family statuses. Children leave home, people retire, spouses die, and homes are sold. When such status losses occur, age and the characteristics associated with it once again return to the forefront of our identities.

Misconceptions about our golden years may also result from a lack of anticipatory socialization. **Anticipatory socialization** refers to socialization that prepares a person to assume a role in the future. Consider that, as children, we "play" at being mommies and daddies, teachers and fire fighters. As we move through the early stages of our lives, anticipatory socialization provides a road map to the statuses of young adulthood and the middle years. High school and college put us through the paces via internships, apprenticeships, and occupational training. We receive on-the-job instruction when initiated to the work force. Such preparation is simply not given to the tasks involved in senior citizenship. At no time in our lives are we schooled in the physiological changes and social realities that surround retirement, widowhood, or other events of old age.

This lack of anticipatory socialization should not surprise us. Preparing for old age would be inconsistent with typical American values and practices. We are an action and production-oriented society—we generally don't prepare for doing less. As a society, we don't encourage role playing for *any* statuses that carry negative traits and characteristics, such as being old, criminal, terminally ill, widowed, and so on.

Switching our focus to a macro-level analysis provides additional insight regarding the misconceptions on aging. A **macro-level analysis** focuses on broad, large-scale social patterns as they exist across contexts or through time. Consider aging as a historical phenomenon. Old age in America is a relatively new event. In the first census, in 1790, less than 2% of the U.S. population was 65 or older; the median age was 16. (Historians suggest that these statistics most likely characterized the population from the early 1600s to the early 1800s; see Fischer 1977.) Thus, old age was an uncommon event in preindustrial America. Those of the period could not reasonably expect to live into old age. Indeed, individuals who did reach old age were regarded as exceptional and often were afforded great respect. Life-earned experience and knowledge were valuable commodities in a preindustrial society (Fischer 1977).

The youthful age structure of early America meant the absence of retirement. Preindustrial societies consisted of home-based, labor-intensive enterprises. Thus, the ability to produce, not age itself, was the relevant factor for working. Prior to the 20th century, most Americans worked until they died.

With the rise of modern society and industrialization, this pattern changed. The skills, experience, and knowledge of older workers did not resonate with the demands and innovations of factory work. Younger and inexperienced (that is, cheaper) workers were the better economic buy for employers. Such changes in the knowledge and economic base of American society profoundly impacted social and culture views on aging (Watson and Maxwell 1977). With this shift, old age ceased to be exalted, and a youth-oriented society and culture began to develop.

The youth mentality of the industrial age is clearly articulated in one of the 20th century's most influential pieces of legislation: the Social Security Act of 1935. This act can be credited with setting the "old-age" cutoff at 65. (Note that older workers lobbied for a higher age cutoff and younger workers lobbied for a lower age cutoff at the time of the act's passage.) Further, the act legally mandated that older workers must make way for younger ones. The directive has been successful: Only about 12% of those 65 and over are still in the work force (U.S. Bureau of the Census 1994a).

The forced retirement instituted by the Social Security Act contributed to the negative image of old age. Retirement signifies both a social (occupational) and an economic "loss." (Despite the reality of social security benefits, the elderly as a whole have less income than most other age groups. See U.S. Bureau of the Census 1994a.) When one couples these losses with the natural physiological and social changes that accompany aging (increasing risk of chronic diseases, some vision and hearing impairment, relinquishment of parental and spousal roles, and so on), it becomes easier to understand the development of old age's negative image.

Before leaving this discussion, it is important to note that the analysis of old age in America must be qualified with reference to social context. **Social context** refers to the broad social and historical circumstances surrounding an act or an event. Those in certain social circumstances can find the aging experience to be a greater hardship than do others. For example, although poverty among the elderly *as a whole* has diminished over the past 30 years, some segments of that population still experience high poverty rates. (See Figure 5.1.) Elderly women, elderly minority members, and, in particular, elderly black women continue to suffer rates of poverty that exceed the national average (Soldo and Agree 1988). Similarly, *overall* the elderly experience high rates of emotional calm or peace of mind. However, such rates can vary widely among subgroups of the elderly population. For instance, coping with the trauma presented by the loss of a spouse appears particularly difficult for older males.

FIGURE 5.1

Poverty Among Segments of the Elderly Population—U.S.

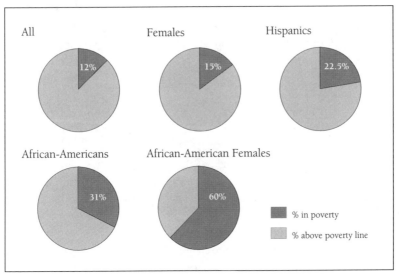

Thus, elderly widowers are seven times more likely to commit suicide than married men in the same age bracket (Seligmann 1994).

Despite the multiple sources for our misconceptions on aging, all of our views on the matter may soon undergo significant revision. The changing age structure of the U.S. population helps to explain such a shift. **Age structure** refers to the distribution that results from dividing a population according to socially defined, age-based categories: childhood, adolescence, young adulthood, middle age, and old age.

Since the early 1900s, the median age in America has risen steadily; so too has the proportion of our population that is 65 or older. Today, approximately 13% of the population is over 65. With the aging of "baby boomers," these numbers will increase significantly. It is estimated that, by the year 2050, the median age of our population will be 45; approximately one-fifth of the population will be over 65 (Spencer 1989). Such fundamental changes to the age structure of our society will produce major consequences for both the image and the reality of old age.

The 65+ age group has the highest voting rates of any age group. On age-related issues, they constitute a powerful voting block (Soldo and Agree 1988). The elderly also benefit from the lobbying efforts of the largest interest group in politics today: the American Association of Retired Persons

(Cockerham 1991). The members of this interest group represent 25% of all registered voters in the United States (Ornstein and Schmitt 1990)

The political clout of the elderly already has resulted in a significant reduction in the percentage of elderly living in poverty. Such clout also has figured in positive changes with regard to medical care (via medicare) and lifestyles of the elderly (tax breaks for people over 65). Indeed, the voting power of the old and "near old" has helped make social security and some of its related assistance programs the "third rail" of American politics. As the size and political power of the elderly continues to grow through the aging of the baby boomers, we should expect to see significant "corrections" in our social views of old age in America.

Are the golden years tarnished? Research suggests not. We have used several sociological tools—master status, anticipatory socialization, macro-historical analysis, and contextual analysis—to understand the discrepancy between the myths and realities of aging.

However, the story on aging in America is hardly complete. Perhaps more than any other social phenomenon, aging is an extremely dynamic process. Consider that current population estimates for the year 2050 place life expectancy near 100 (Siegel and Taeuber 1986). Such a shift means that many of us will be facing futures in which one-third of our lives will be spent in old age! Think of the changes this will bring to family, economic, and social relations. At present, the average adult woman in the United States can expect to spend as much time caring for her aged parents as she spent raising her children (Beck 1990). The future may see such time commitments double. Similarly, when the Social Security Act was first passed, approximately 50 workers "supported" each social security recipient. Today, the burden of support falls on just three workers for every retiree. What will happen to this ratio in the not too distant future when the aging baby boomers hit retirement?

To be sure, the "aging" story is one that will continue to evolve; it is a story that will continue to demand our attention. Thus, old age in America is an area to which all of us must apply careful "second thoughts."

LEARNING MORE ABOUT IT

To learn more about the concept of master status, consult Everett C. Hughes' "Dilemmas and Contradictions of Status" (*American Journal of Sociology* 50 (5), 353–359, 1945), Howard Becker's *The Outsiders* (Glencoe, IL: Free Press, 1963), or J. L. Simmons' "Public Stereotypes of Deviants" (*Social Problems 13*, 223–232, 1966).

To probe more deeply into the process of anticipatory socialization, check Robert K. Merton's *Social Theory and Social Structure* (Glencoe, IL: Free Press, 1957) or "Adult Socialization," an article by Jeylan T. Mortimer and Roberta G. Simmons appearing in the 1978 *Annual Review of Sociology* (vol. 4, 421–454).

David Hackett Fischer offers an interesting history of aging in America in *Growing Old in America* (New York: Oxford University Press, 1977).

EXERCISES

1. Try a little fact finding yourself. Ask some friends and family members what they believe to be true about the financial and social situations of those 65 and over. For instance, what social characteristics do your subjects associate with the elderly? What percentage of the elderly do your "subjects" believe are still employed? Are the elderly financially secure? Are the elderly happy after retirement? After you've solicited several opinions, compare your results with your library's holdings on the latest census figures or with the results of a recent survey executed by the American Association of Retired Persons. How do the social locations of your respondents influence their knowledge of the elderly?

2. It is not always possible to know in advance which status will emerge as one's master status. Consider the following individuals and try to identify the master status for each: Bill Clinton, Anita Hill, Jesse Jackson, Ronald Reagan, Pete Rose, Barbra Streisand, Mother Theresa, and yourself. Be prepared to discuss your selections.

3. We've offered the concepts of master status and anticipatory socialization as useful devices for understanding conventional wisdoms regarding old age. Consider some of the other sociological ideas introduced in previous chapters. Select and discuss two of them that you feel also offer insight into the misconceptions of old age. (*Hint:* Do the dynamics of a "self-fulfilling prophecy" feed a negative view of old age?)

Socialization and Identity

■

CONVENTIONAL WISDOM TELLS US . . .

What's in a Name? That Which We Call a Rose by Any Other Name Would Smell As Sweet

■

THIS ESSAY EXPLORES THE POWER IN A NAME,

HIGHLIGHTING THE CENTRAL ROLE OF SYMBOLS

AND LABELS IN THE CONSTRUCTION OF

IDENTITY.

■

Shakespeare's verse argues for substance over labels. It is a sentiment common to much of the conventional wisdom on names. Adages such as "Sticks and stones may break my bones, but names will never hurt me" or "The names may change, but the story remains the same" and quips like "Call me anything, but don't call me late for dinner"—all such truisms consistently downplay the importance of names. Are the labels we give to people and things as inconsequential as conventional wisdom suggests? Do names really lack the power to influence or the force to injure? Would a rose really command such deep respect and awe if it were known as a petunia or a pansy?

A large body of social science literature suggests that conventional wisdom has vastly underestimated the significance of names. Indeed, names in our society function as powerful symbols. **Symbols** are arbitrary signs that come to be endowed with special meaning and, ultimately, gain the ability to influence behaviors, attitudes, and emotions.

The symbolic nature of names makes them much more than a string of alphabetics. Rather, names function as calling cards or personal logos. They signify important aspects of one's history and heritage; they pinpoint an individual's social location and group affiliations. Based on our names, others make important decisions regarding our nature and temperament. In this way, names serve as important symbols of identity. **Identity** refers to those essential characteristics that both link us and distinguish us from other social players and, thus, establish who we are.

The link between names and identity helps to explain why forgetting someone's name often is viewed as a social faux pas. Similarly, we view situations that preclude the linking of name to identity with great pathos. Consider the sadness that surrounds every tomb of an unknown or unnamed soldier. In settings where one's name remains unknown, it is not unusual for an individual to feel alienated or disconnected. Think of those large lecture courses in which neither the professor nor other students know your name.

Names contribute to the construction of identity in a variety of ways. Family surnames, for example, provide instant knowledge of an individual's history. These surnames serve as a roadmap to the past; they guide us through an individual's lineage and archive one's traditional group affiliations and cultural ties. Thus, historically, children who were denied their father's surname were denied a legitimate social location. Without this signifier to chronicle their paternal past, such children were considered faceless and anonymous, with no rightful place in their social environment.

A name's ability to pinpoint personal histories leads some individuals to abandon their family surnames and adopt new ones in their place. A well-chosen replacement name can bring one closer to groups or social histories that seem more in vogue, more powerful, or more in tune with one's future aspirations and endeavors. The entertainment industry is ripe with examples of the practice. Many performers readily acknowledge the necessity of name changes in building a successful career. In particular, personalities with ethnic surnames often feel the need for more mainstream, English-sounding names. Consequently, Larry Ziegler's fans now know him as broadcaster Larry King. Movie fans know Winona Horowitz as Winona Ryder. Young George Kyriakou Panayiotou was reborn as pop idol George Michael. Thomas Mapother earned his fame as actor Tom Cruise. And credit singer Madonna for understanding that names such as Louise Ciccone are not the stuff of which pop idols are made.

In each of these cases, and countless others like them, a name change became a tool for impression management. **Impression management** is a process by which individuals manipulate or maneuver their public images so as to elicit certain desired reactions. In the process of impression management, new surnames become the foundation upon which broadly targeted identities are constructed.

First or common names function as powerful symbols as well. Consider the care and consideration frequently given by parents as they set about naming a newborn. Many parents start the process months before the child is born. Such care may represent a worthy investment, for research suggests that the selection of a personal name can have long-term consequences for a child. Several studies show that individuals assess others' potential for success, morality, good health, and warmth on the basis of names. Thus, when asked to rate other people on the basis of first names alone, subjects perceived "James" as highly moral, healthy, warm, and likely to succeed. In contrast, "Melvin" was viewed as a potential failure, lacking good character, good health, or human caring. Similarly, individuals with names that correspond to current norms of popularity—in the 1990s, these include Brian, Eric, Michael, Brenda, Karen, and Lisa—are judged to be more intelligent and better liked than individuals with old-fashioned names such as Albert, George, Sam, Betty, Judy, and Phyllis (Anderson 1985; Evans 1992; Young, Kennedy, Newhouse, Browne, and Thiessen 1993).

Personal names can influence more than just the perception of performance and ability. Some studies show a significant association between uncommon, peculiar, undesirable, or unique names and *actual* outcomes such as low academic performance, low professional achievement, and psychological maladjustment (Busse and Seraydarian 1978; Ellis and Beechley 1954; Lansky and Sinrod 1990; Willis, Willis, and Grier 1982). Indeed, so strong is the influence of personal names that some nations actually regulate the process of naming. French law, for example, allows officials to reject any name deemed at odds with a child's well-being (Besnard and Desplanques 1993).

In charting the role of personal names, it is interesting to note that child name selection follows some predictable patterns. For example, naming patterns initiate and reinforce certain gender scripts. Parents quite frequently select trendy or decorative names for their daughters—for example, Autumn, Heather, Jennifer, Krystal, Tiffany. In contrast, parents prefer traditional or biblical names for their sons—Adam, David, John, Michael, Thomas. (Think about it. Have you ever met a man named after a flower or a season?) Further, although little boys frequently are given the name of their father or grandfather, little girls rarely share a name with any family member (Alford 1988; Lansky and Sinrod 1990; Lieberson and Bell 1992; Lieberson and Mikelson 1995).

In addition to establishing identity, names often demarcate shifts in identity or changes in social status. In this way, names facilitate a process sociologists refer to as boundary construction. **Boundary construction** is the social partitioning of life experience or centers of interaction. When we cross the boundary from childhood to adulthood, for example, we often drop childlike nicknames—Mikey, Junior, or Princess—in favor of our full birth names. Similarly, when acquaintances become close friends, the shift is often signaled by a name change. Mr. or Ms. so-and-so becomes Bob or Susan; Henry becomes Hank, or Alison becomes Ali.

A shift from singlehood to marriage, a religious conversion, or an occupation change often are marked by the changing of names. Thus, Siddhartha's religious conversion was signaled by his new name, Buddha. With a similar experience, Saul became Paul. In the modern day, a change in religion transformed Cassius Clay into Mohammed Ali. In the occupational arena, "Ike," "The Gipper," and "Bill Clinton" all became "Mr. President" when they moved into their new status.

Name changes accompany the shifting identities of places as well. With the reemergence of Russia's nationhood, for example, Leningrad reverted to St. Petersburg. Similarly, with political reorganization, the plot of land once known as Czechoslovakia was renamed as the Czech Republic and Slovenia. And the place once known as Yugoslavia is now called Bosnia, Croatia, and Serbia. Although the physical terrain of these areas remains the same, new names serve to reconfigure each location's identity.

Beyond person and place, names can illustrate changing collective identities. In this regard, consider the experience of African Americans in the United States. Note that when the name "Negro" appeared in the United States, the term was synonymous with the status of slave. In order to distance themselves from slavery, free African Americans of that period elected to call themselves "African" rather than "Negro." However, when a movement developed in the 1830s encouraging slaves and their descendents to return to Africa, free African Americans renamed themselves "Colored" or "People of Color." The color term was adopted to underscore disapproval of the "return to Africa" movement. Interestingly, the name "Black" was repeatedly rejected as a name for this collective. The term *Black* appeared on the scene only with the social and legal changes of the 1960s and 1970s (Isaacs 1975).

Postmodern theorists suggest that collective identities generated by a shared group name can sometimes prove more harmful than helpful. **Postmodern theory** represents an approach that destabilizes or deconstructs fixed social assumptions and meanings. Collective names imply a unity of identity—a sameness—among all members of a group. In this way, collective names can mask the diversity that exists within groups. Collective names can lead us to conclude that all "Hispanics," "Women," or "Senior Citizens" think or act in identical ways by virtue of their shared classification. Postmodernists also warn that collective names can give a false sense of distinctiveness to groups. Labeling collectives in unique ways suggests that "Whites" *are* profoundly different from "Blacks," "Men" irreconcilably different from "Women," and "nations" unique unto themselves (Collins 1990; Foucault 1971; Riley 1988; Smith 1991).

Just as name changes symbolize shifts and movement, they can also function to immortalize certain identities. The name often becomes the tool of choice in poignant and permanent commemorations of extraordinary human efforts. Special individuals are honored by attaching their name to a building or a street. War memorials elicit heightened emotions by listing the names of those they honor. (Witness the deeply moving response consistently elicited from the now famous Vietnam War Memorial in Washington, DC)

Extraordinary athletes find their numerical names, or numbers, retired, indicating that there will never be another Yankee number 7 (Mickey Mantle) or another Jets number 12 (Joe Namath). The recent retirement/rebirth of the Chicago Bull's Michael Jordan underscored the significance of names in this regard. Recall that upon Jordan's exodus, his numerical name—23—was ceremoniously retired by his team. When he returned to the Bulls, his new beginning was signaled by the assignment of a new number—45. These numerical names served to distinguish the old, proven Jordan from the new, mysterious Jordan. Indeed, the NBA viewed the boundary protected by these symbols to be so sacred that they fined Jordan heavily the first few times he tried to wear his old number during one of his "second life" games.

Names can be used to indicate possession or control. It is not unusual for valuable belongings such as homesteads, boats, aircraft, cars, or pets to be named by their owners. In the same way, conquerors reserved the right to name the continents they discovered or acquired, as well as the indigenous people living there. Columbus, for example, named the indigenous people he met "Indians," a term that came to be used generically for all native peoples. Similarly, colonial populations frequently were renamed by those controlling them so as to reflect the cultural standards of the ruling power. In one case, a mid-19th-century Spanish governor replaced the Philippine surnames of his charges with Spanish surnames taken from a Madrid directory as a method of simplifying the job of Spanish tax collectors (Isaacs 1975).

Family names function as a sign of ownership as well. In bestowing their surnames on children, parents identify the children as "theirs." And, historically, wives were expected to take the names of their husbands to indicate to whom the women "belonged." All of these examples highlight a normative expectation: That which we name belongs to us. This expectation may help us to explain why adopted children are more likely to be named after a parent or relative than are biological children. In the absence of shared genes, names become a mode of establishing familial connection. And, indeed, research shows that namesaking generally strengthens the bond between father and child (Furstenburg and Talvitie 1980; Johnson, McAndrew, and Harris 1991).

Perhaps the importance of the power of naming is best revealed in research on labeling. **Labeling theory** is built around a basic premise known to sociologists as Thomas's theorem: If we define situations as real, they are real in their consequences. In other words, the names or labels we apply to people, places, or circumstances influence and direct our interactions and, thus, the emerging reality of the situation.

Thomas's theorem was well documented in a now famous study of labeling practices in the classroom. After administering intelligence tests to students at the beginning of the academic year, researchers identified to teachers a group of academic "spurters"—that is, children who would show great progress over the course of the approaching school year. In fact, no such group of academic spurters really existed. Rather, researchers randomly assigned students to the spurter category. Yet, curiously enough, when intelligence tests were readministered at the end of the academic year, the spurters showed increases in their IQ scores over and above the "nonspurters." Furthermore, the subjective assessment of the teachers indicated that the spurters surpassed nonspurters on a number of socioeducational fronts. The researchers credited these changes to the power of labels. When teachers came to define students as spurters, they began to interact with them in ways that guaranteed their success (Rosenthal and Jacobson 1968).

A famous study in the area of mental health also demonstrates the enormous power of labels. David Rosenhan engaged colleagues to admit themselves to several psychiatric hospitals and to report symptoms of schizophrenia to the admitting psychologists. (Specifically, Rosenhan's colleagues were told to report hearing voices.) Once admitted to the hospital, however, these pseudopatients displayed no signs of mental disorder. Rather, they engaged in completely normal behavioral routines. Despite the fact that the pseudopatients' psychosis was contrived, Rosenhan notes, the label schizophrenia proved more influential in the construction of reality than did the pseudopatients' actual behaviors. Hospital personnel "saw" symptomatic behaviors in their falsely labeled charges. The power of the label schizophrenia caused some normal individuals to remain hospitalized for as long as 52 days (Rosenhan 1973).

The labeling phenomenon is not confined to what others "see" in us. Labels also hold the power to influence what we see in ourselves. Recent emphases on politically correct (PC) speech is founded on this premise. The PC movement suggests that by selecting our labels wisely, we may lead people to more positive self-perceptions. There is, after all, a difference between calling someone "handicapped" and calling that person "physically challenged." The former term implies a fundamental flaw, whereas the latter suggests a surmountable condition. Many believe that applying such simple considerations to the use of positive versus negative labels can indeed make a critical difference in the self-esteem levels of those we label.

Similar logic can be found within the literature on social deviants. Some contend that repeated application of a deviant label—class clown, druggie, slut, troublemaker, and so on—may lead to a self-transformation of the label's "target." Sociologists refer to this phenomenon as secondary deviance. **Secondary deviance** occurs when a labeled individual comes to view herself or himself according to that which she or he is called. In other words, the labeled individual incorporates the impressions of others into his or her own self-identity. Thus, just as positive labels such as "spurter" can benefit an individual, negative or deviant labels can help to ensure that an individual "lives down" to our expectations (Lemert 1951).

The power of names and labels may be best demonstrated by considering the terror typically associated with the unnamed. Things that are unnamed, in a very real sense, remain beyond our control. The most feared diseases, for example, are those that are so new and different they have not yet been named. The lack of a name implies unknown origins, and thus little hope for a cure. In contrast, the mere presence of a diagnosis, even one that connotes a serious condition, often is viewed as a blessing by patients. Think of the number of times you've heard a relieved patient or family member say, "At least I know what the problem is."

Alzheimer's disease also illustrates the terror that accompanies name-lessness. For many people, the most frightening aspect of Alzheimer's disease is its ability to steal from us the names of formerly familiar people and objects. Generally, our life experiences are rendered understandable via insightful naming and labeling.

In another realm, note that anonymous callers and figures can strike dread in their targets. The namelessness of these intruders renders them beyond our control. Wanted "John Does" frequently are perceived as greater threats than known criminals because of their no-name status. Recall the intensive search efforts for John Doe II following the Oklahoma City bombing. Similarly, note the frantic aura that surrounded the hunt for the unknown "Unabomber."

When we experience disruptive behaviors that appear new or unusual, our first step toward control involves naming. We coined the label "rumble," for example, to characterize the violent and frightening gang fights that began to erupt on urban streets in the 1950s. We applied the label "wilding" to the new and shocking acts of violence from packs of children that emerged as a phenomenon of the 1980s.

What's in a name? Obviously more than conventional wisdom implies. Names and labels can effectively reshape an individual's past, present circumstance, or future path. Indeed, research seems to leave little doubt: A rose by any other name . . . would somehow be different.

LEARN MORE ABOUT IT

For more on the power of personal names, see A. Mehrabian's *The Name Game: The Decision That Lasts a Lifetime* (Bethesda, MD.: National Press Books, 1990). The link between names and identity is poignantly illustrated by C. Allen in "First They Changed My Name" (*Ms 4* (4), 25–27, 1994).

For the classic work on impression management, see Erving Goffman's *The Presentation of Self in Everyday Life* (New York: Anchor, 1959).

Harold Isaacs offers some interesting reflections on collective naming in his well-known treatise, *Idols of the Tribe* (Cambridge: Harvard University Press, 1975). For postmodern perspectives on collective naming and identity, see Michael Foucault's *The Order of Things: An Archeology of Human*

Sciences (New York: Pantheon, 1971), Denise Riley's *Am I That Name?* (Minneapolis: University of Minnesota Press, 1988), or Anthony Smith's *National Identity* (Reno: University of Nevada Press, 1991).

For more on the links between symbols and identity, see Karen A. Cerulo's *Identity Designs: The Sights and Sounds of a Nation* (New Brunswick: Rutgers University Press, ASA Rose Book Series, 1995).

Howard Becker provides a highly readable discussion of labeling in *The Outsiders* (Glencoe, IL: Free Press, 1963). An informative discussion of labeling as it pertains to women comes from Edwin Schur in *Labeling Women Deviant* (Philadelphia: Temple University Press, 1984).

EXERCISES

1. Choose one or two good friends and intentionally call them by the wrong name several times over the course of a day. Record your friends' reactions. What do these data tell you about the power of personal symbols?

2. Research the names of various buildings on your campus, especially those named for an individual. Taken as a whole, what identity do these names confer on your institution? What lessons of naming can you deduce from the list? Are the norms of naming time-bound? Class-bound? Gender bound?

CONVENTIONAL WISDOM TELLS US . . .

Beauty Is Only Skin Deep

■

THIS ESSAY DOCUMENTS THE SOCIAL ADVANTAGES ENJOYED BY PHYSICALLY ATTRACTIVE INDIVIDUALS—TALL, SLIM, AND BEAUTIFUL OR HANDSOME WOMEN AND MEN. WE ALSO DISCUSS THE POWERFUL ROLE PHYSICAL ATTRACTIVENESS CAN PLAY IN THE CONSTRUCTION OF SELF-IDENTITY.

■

"Beauty is only skin deep" goes the old adage. It's a lesson we learn early in life. From youth to old age, we are promised that, ultimately, we will be judged on the basis of our inner qualities and not simply by our appearance.

The conventional wisdom on beauty is echoed on many fronts. Religious doctrines teach us to avoid the vanity of physical beauty and search for the beauty within. Popular Broadway shows such as *Phantom of the Opera* or *Beauty and the Beast*, fairy tales like *The Ugly Duckling* or songs such as *I Love You Just the Way You Are* promote the notion that appearances are too super-ficial to seriously influence our fate. All in all, our culture warns us not to "judge a book by its cover" for "all that glitters is not gold."

The conventional wisdom on beauty is reassuring, but is it accurate? Do social actors really look beyond one another's facades when interacting with and evaluating one another?

One finds considerable cultural inconsistency surrounding the topic of beauty. **Cultural inconsistency** refers to a situation in which actual behav-iors contradict cultural goals. Cultural inconsistency depicts an imbalance between ideal and real cultures. Although we say that appearances don't matter, our actions indicate something quite to the contrary. Indeed, a large body of research suggests that an individual's level of attractiveness dra-matically influences others' assessments, evaluations, and reactions.

Several studies show that attractive individuals—tall, slim, and beauti-ful or handsome women and men—are better liked and more valued by others than individuals considered to be unattractive. These preferences are amazingly widespread. In seeking friends, individuals prefer the compan-ionship of attractive versus unattractive people (Marks, Miller, and Maruyama 1981; Reis, Nezlek, and Wheeler 1980). In the workplace, attractive people are more likely to be hired than their unattractive com-petitors, even when an experienced personnel officer is responsible for the hiring (Cash and Janda 1984; Marvelle and Green 1980). When being judged or evaluated, individuals are most influenced by the opinion of attractive "judges" (Sigall and Aronson 1969). And within the political arena, attractive candidates regularly garner more votes than unattractive candidates (Effran and Patterson 1974). Only in the search for a lifetime mate does the influence of physical attractiveness wane. Studies show that people tend to choose long-term partners whom they judge to be of com-parable attractiveness (Murstein 1976; Walster, Aronson, Abrahams, and Rottman 1966).

The link between physical attractiveness and being liked and rewarded exists at all stages of the life cycle, including infancy and childhood. Stud-ies show, for example, that attractive babies are held, cuddled, kissed, and talked to more frequently than unattractive babies. This pattern holds true even when one restricts the focus to mother–child interactions (Berscheid 1982). When attractive children make their way to the schools, they tend to be more frequently praised and rewarded by teachers than their less attractive counterparts (Clifford and Walster 1973). Further, studies show that children themselves come to equate attractiveness with high moral character (Dion 1979; Dion and Berscheid 1974; Langlois and Stephan 1981). The typical children's fairy tale is one source of this lesson. Remember Cinderella and her evil stepsisters? Or Snow White and her wicked stepmother who is disguised as an ugly witch? And how about Oz's beautiful, "good" witch of the North versus the ugly and "wicked" witch of the West? The stories of our youth regularly couple beauty with goodness, while ugliness is usually indicative of wickedness.

In addition to issues of liking, reward, and moral character, physically attractive individuals are perceived as having a host of other positive and highly desirable characteristics. Research shows that "beautiful people" are assumed to possess pleasing personalities, personal happiness, great intelligence, high status, and high success in marriage. Further, these perceptions persist, even when the facts contradict our assumptions (Chesler and Goodman 1976; Dion, Berscheid, and Walster 1972; Feldman 1971; Hatfield and Sprechter 1986; Jones, Hansson, and Phillips 1978).

Some researchers feel that our perceptions of attractive people and their lifestyle may create a self-fulfilling prophecy. A **self-fulfilling prophecy** is a phenomenon whereby that which we believe to be true, in some sense, becomes true for us. Thus, when we expect that handsome men or beautiful women are happy, intelligent, or well-placed, we pave the way for expectation to become reality. This may explain why attractive individuals tend to have higher self-esteem and are less prone to psychological disturbances than unattractive individuals (Hatfield and Sprechter 1986; Jackson 1992).

By contributing to a self-fulfilling prophecy, social reactions to physical appearance may endow handsome men and beautiful women with valuable cultural capital. **Cultural capital** refers to attributes, knowledge, or ways of thinking that can be converted or used for economic advantage. Cultural capital is a concept originally introduced by contemporary theorist Pierre Bourdieu. According to Bourdieu, one accumulates cultural capital in conjunction with one's social status. **Social status** refers to the position or location of an individual with reference to characteristics such as age, education, gender, income, race, religion, and so on. The more privileged one's status, the better one's endowment of cultural capital.

Bourdieu argues that an individual's cultural capital works like a good investment. The capital itself—typically defined as family background, education, communication skills, and so on—has inherent value and gains for the individual entry into "the market." "Working" one's cultural capital enables its "owner" to "buy," or accumulate, additional social advantages.

The many studies reviewed in this essay suggest that physical attractiveness also forms another type of cultural capital, one that operates according to the same dynamic as described by Bourdieu. Physical attractiveness provides individuals with an extra resource in meeting life's demands. Beauty places individuals in a preferred, or more powerful, position (Finkelstein 1991; Haug 1986). As such, appearances are frequently converted to economic gain.

Thinking of beauty as cultural capital helps to explain Americans' propensity for physical alterations. In the United States, over 393,000 cosmetic surgery operations occur each year, almost all of them performed for aesthetic reasons rather than reasons of necessity. Teenagers constitute 25% of this business, indicating that our concerns with beauty start young (The American Society for Aesthetic Plastic Surgery, Inc. 1995). National figures also indicate that over $62 billion is spent in the United States each year on cosmetics, perfumes, hair care, and health clubs. This figure was twice as high in 1995 as it was only 10 years ago. Interestingly, the figure surpasses the dollar amounts Americans devote each year to legal services ($51.4 billion), higher education expenses ($48.1 billion), or books ($13.3 billion) (World Almanac 1995).

"Buying" beauty is not strictly an American phenomenon. In Korean culture, for example, a growing value on American facial features has resulted in a dramatic upsurge in eyelid, nose, and facial reconstruction surgery among Korean women (Kaw 1994). Similarly, the Wall Street Journal reports massive increases in cosmetic sales throughout rural China, and Advertising Age describes long lines in Moscow as Muscovites fight to purchase Estée Lauder and Christian Dior cosmetics (Iams 1990). All in all, human behavior may confirm Aristotle's ancient claim: Beauty may be better than all the letters of recommendation in the world.

The effects of physical attractiveness go beyond our interactions with others. An individual's "attractiveness quotient" also proves one of the most powerful elements in the construction of one's self-identity. **Identity** refers to those essential characteristics that both link us and distinguish us from other social players and, thus, establish who we are.

Research suggests that physical attractiveness is critical to positive self-assessments. Physical attractiveness greatly boosts one's level of self-esteem and strengthens one's confidence. Unattractiveness, in contrast, appears to sow self-doubt and impede social interaction skills (Cash and Pruzinsky

1990; Locher, Unger, Sociedade, and Wahl 1993; Mishkind, Rodin, Silber-stein, and Striegel-Moore 1986).

When considering attractiveness and its impact on identity, body weight proves a particularly crucial factor. Each year, Americans spend over $33 billion on weight-loss programs, diet aids, and low-calorie foods in an effort to shed those extra pounds (McLean 1994). We trim down, pump up, tan, tattoo, and even surgically reshape our bodies, all in the hopes that a "new" and more beautiful body will boost our sense of self.

In theory, connections between body weight and identity should be quite straightforward. Throughout the socialization experience, we are exposed to what sociologists call appearance norms. **Socialization** refers to the process by which we learn the norms, values, and beliefs of a social group, as well as our place within that social group. **Appearance norms** refer to a society's generally accepted standards of appropriate body height, body weight, distribution or shape, bone structure, skin color, and so on.

When individuals conform to appearance norms, they enjoy positive feedback from intimates, peers, and social members at large. These reactions enable one to develop a "normal" body image and a heightened sense of self. In contrast, individuals who deviate from appearance norms are likely to be negatively sanctioned. As such, those who stray from average body weight may develop deviant or negative self-identities (Goffman 1963; Millman 1980; Schur 1984).

The process sounds straightforward. Yet in the everyday world of expe-rience, body weight and its connection to identity can be quite complex. For example, several studies document that when certain individuals move from thin to fat (in American society, a shift from a normal to a deviant body), such individuals nevertheless maintain a slim and, hence, normal, body image. This sense of normalcy often persists even in the face of objec-tive evidence to the contrary—evidence such as scale readings or clothing size (Berscheid 1981; Degher and Hughes 1992; Gettleman and Thompson 1993; Millman 1980). Similarly, some individuals who achieve "normal" bodies via diet or surgery continue to identify themselves as overweight (Altheimer 1994; Rubin, Shmilovitz, and Weiss 1993).

What explains the failure to incorporate a "new" body into one's iden-tity? Some believe the phenomenon may be a function of one's childhood years—in particular, the "first impressions" such individuals formed of their bodies during their primary socialization. Sociologists define **primary socialization** as the earliest phase of social "training," a period in which we learn basic social skills and form the core of our identities.

Children who develop "slim and trim" images of their bodies often suc-ceed at maintaining that image as they build their adult identities. In essence, that skinny kid of an individual's past can cover her or his adult eyes so as to obscure the portly grown-up in the mirror (Laslett and Warren 1975; Millman 1980). In contrast, individuals who are labeled as "fat" during the early years of life seem never to fully embrace the notion of a normal or thin body, even when they achieve body weight within or below national weight guidelines (Altheimer 1994; Rubin et al. 1993).

Can those affected by first impressions of their body ever synchronize their identities with their current physical condition? Research shows that certain rituals prove helpful in this regard. Sociologists define **rituals** as a set of actions that take on symbolic significance. When body transitions are marked by some sort of "rite of passage," individuals are more likely to adjust their identity to reflect their new weight. So, for instance, patients opting for surgical weight loss may request a "last meal," write a will, or burn old clothing and photographs. Such rituals prove quite powerful in signaling the death of one's "old" body. Similarly, dieters often engage in rituals such as clothing shopping sprees or body-boasting beach vacations to mark the achievement of a target weight. Dieter's report the power of these rituals in signifying a physical "rebirth" (Rubin et al. 1993).

Intense social feedback also appears critical to synchronizing identity with body weight. Repeated reaction to one's actual weight can eventually alter faulty self-perceptions. Thus, although the overweight individual may be able to neutralize the numbers that appear during his or her morning weigh-in, that same individual proves unable to ignore repeated stares or blatant comments on weight gain by family, friends, or strangers. Similarly, the newly thin often report the wide-eyed gasps, exclamations, and smiles of those viewing their new bodies for the first time as the factors most significant to their adoption of a true sense of body size (Altheimer 1994; Rubin et al. 1993).

Note, however, that some sources of social feedback can hinder the synchronization process. For example, when individuals use TV images as a measuring rod for their own appearance, they tend to overestimate their body weight. Such overestimations, in turn, negatively impact self-identity. Women appear particularly susceptible to such media influence. Although the media present the "acceptable" male in a variety of shapes and sizes, "acceptable" females rarely deviate from the thin standard (Levine 1987).

Work by communication researchers Philip Myers and Frank Biocca (1992) demonstrates that daily exposure to as little as 30 minutes of TV programming may contribute to the self-overestimation of body size typical among women. Further, these same short periods of TV viewing may indirectly increase the incidence of anorexia nervosa and bulimia among women.

Social feedback on weight and the use of such feedback in identity construction illustrates the utility of Charles Horton Cooley's concept, the looking-glass self. The **looking-glass self** refers to a process by which individuals use the reactions of other social members as mirrors by which to view themselves and develop an image of who they are. From Cooley's perspective, individuals who seem unable to "see" their current bodies may be using reactions of the past as their mirrors on the present. Similarly, the use of TV "mirrors" in the definition of self may lead to "fun house" type distortions. The key to accepting one's current body type is collecting appropriate contemporary mirrors and elevating them over those of the past.

Thus far, we have discussed the various effects exerted by an individual's physical appearances. But it is interesting to note that the influence of physical appearance goes beyond the realm of the person. Appearances influence our evaluation of objects as well. Often, we judge the value or goodness of things in accordance with the way they look.

Some researchers have discovered, for example, that the architectural style of a home can affect the way in which others describe the atmosphere within the structure. Farmhouses, for instance, are generally identified with trustworthy atmospheres. Colonial-style homes are perceived to be the domains of "go-getters." And Tudor-style homes are associated with leadership (Freudenheim 1988).

Such links between an object's appearance and notions of quality or identity are, of course, at the heart of the marketing industry. Indeed, in the world of advertising and public relations, "packaging" a product so as to convey the right image is truly the name of the game.

Beauty is only skin deep? After reviewing research findings on physical attractiveness, we cannot help but view this conventional wisdom with some skepticism. When it comes to evaluating and reacting to others, ourselves, and even inanimate objects, beauty matters. The more attractive the proverbial "cover of the book," the more likely we are to value its story.

LEARNING MORE ABOUT IT

For more information on the cognitive process by which we attribute characteristics to people, places, and things, see Fritz Heider's classic work, *The Psychology of Interpersonal Relations* (New York: Wiley, 1980) or Lee Ross's 1977 article "The Intuitive Psychologist and His Shortcomings: Distortions in the Attribution Process," in L. Berkowitz (ed.) *Advances in Experimental Social Psychology*, vol. 10 (New York: Academic Press).

Charles Horton Cooley's *Human Nature and Social Order* (New York: Scribner, 1902) and George Herbert Mead's *Mind, Self and Society* (Chicago:

University of Chicago Press, 1934) are two classic sociological works on self and identity.

A particularly good discussion of obesity and its social consequences is offered by Marcia Millman in *Such A Pretty Face: Being Fat in America* (New York: W.W. Norton, 1980). A very readable study of general female appearance norms can be found in Edwin Schur's *Labeling Women Deviant* (Philadelphia: Temple University Press, 1984).

EXERCISES

1. Choose approximately 10 bridal pictures from your local paper. Using conventional cultural standards, choose brides of varying attractiveness. Remove any identifying names and show the pictures you've selected to five "judges." Supply the judges with a 5-point scale, where 5 equals just right and 1 equals inadequate, and have the judges rate the brides on the following standards:

attractive	*sensual*
good-humored	*sophisticated*
happy	*successful*
intelligent	*trustworthy*
pretty	*wealthy*

   Check the judges' ratings: Is there any relationship between the answers addressing physical attractiveness and those pertaining to personality characteristics?

   Now, repeat exercise 1 using pictures of men from your local newspaper. In choosing your pictures, be sure to select men who are similarly dressed and of similar ages.

2. For this exercise, you will need to gather 20–30 ads that feature *both* products and people. In making your selections, choose ads for "glamorous" products (perfume, clothing, vacations, and the like), as well as ads for nonglamorous products (antacids, cleansers, insecticides). Analyze the patterns you find (if any) between the type of product being marketed and the attractiveness of the people used in the product's ad.

3. Review the personal ads in three newspapers: the *Village Voice,* your local town newspaper, and your college newspaper. Content-analyze 3-days' worth of ads that feature people. Record all information about their physical appearance—weight, height, facial characteristics, and so on. What do your data tell you about current appearance norms? Using your data, discuss the similarities and differences in the appearance norms that govern each of these three contexts.

Stratification

■

CONVENTIONAL WISDOM TELLS US . . .

The More We Pay, the More It's Worth

■

IF SO, OUR GARBAGE COLLECTORS ARE WORTH
MORE THAN OUR TEACHERS, AND BASEBALL
PLAYERS ARE WORTH MORE THAN THOSE
SEARCHING FOR A CURE TO AIDS. THIS ESSAY
ADDRESSES THE INCONSISTENCIES OFTEN
FOUND BETWEEN WHAT WE PAY FOR WORK
AND THE VALUE WE PLACE ON IT.

■

Price tags mean a lot to consumers. With time and experience, most consumers come to embrace the notion that "you get what you pay for." To be sure, many shoppers frequently are driven to find a good bargain. But on the whole, "bigger is better" proves the more popular market pattern.

Americans' willingness to equate high price with quality has led to some ingenious marketing strategies. The founders of Haagen Dazs ice cream, for example, readily admit to conscious price inflation in introducing their product on the market. Given consumer tendencies to gauge product value and attractiveness by price, the owners of Haagen Dazs correctly perceived a high price tag as the best path to high sales (Cowe 1990).

The link between price and worth is not restricted to matters of the taste buds. Worldwide standards in art substantiate such thinking as well. Indeed, the willingness of retired Japanese industrialist Ryoei Saito to pay $82.5 million for Van Gogh's *Portrait of Dr. Gachet* drastically changed the value not only of that single painting, but of Van Gogh's entire body of work (*Los Angeles Times* 1990).

The more we pay, the more it's worth. Conventional wisdom seems "on the money" with regard to patterns of product consumption. However, it is important to note that the adage falls short when we apply it to other economic arenas. For example, in the area of human efforts or work, what we pay is not always a signal of the worth of one's work. Determining the social worth of work requires that we look far beyond an individual's paycheck.

We might begin our inquiry by asking: What do we pay for work? What occupations draw the biggest paychecks in the United States?

Chief executive officers of large corporations earn the highest yearly wages in America. The median wage of CEOs in New York, for example, a state considered the hub for the country's largest, most influential corporations, is $1.6 million per year. On a national level, the CEOs of America's five largest corporations all earn a yearly wage of $2.5 million or more. Currently, the average paycheck for CEOs at the helm of Fortune 500 companies is 157 times higher than the average American factory worker, and 113 times higher than the average U.S. schoolteacher (*Business Week* 1993).

Close on the heels of the CEOs are major league baseball players. Along with long winter vacations and high adulation, the "boys of summer" enjoy an average yearly wage of $1.04 million.

Not surprisingly, physicians also fall near the top of the nation's pay scale. But note that within the profession, the distribution of salaries is somewhat varied. A heart specialist (average yearly salary range: $83,766 to $258,000), for example, earns only two-thirds the salary of an anesthesiologist (average yearly salary range: $144,200 to $367,659)! And a general practitioner (average yearly salary range: $65,000 to $159,990) may not be making much more money than a local dentist (average yearly salary range: $46,228 to $154,650).

In the United States, certain banking occupations can earn one a healthy paycheck. However, the cultural stereotype that pairs bankers with great wealth needs some qualification. Although mortgage bankers are among the highest paid people in the United States, averaging $380,000 per year, your local bank branch manager takes home, on average, a modest $28,355 per year.

What occupations generate the smallest paychecks in the United States? The average yearly salaries of bank tellers, childcare workers, hospital orderlies, and secretaries all fall below $15,000, making them among the lowest paid full-time workers in the United States.

Are members of highly paid occupations worth the paychecks they collect? Is income the true measure of worth in the United States? **Income** refers to the amount of money earned via an occupation or investments during a specific period of time. One theoretical position in sociology—the Davis-Moore thesis—supports the connection between income and worth. The **Davis-Moore thesis** asserts that social inequality is beneficial to the overall functioning of society. According to Davis and Moore, the high salaries and social rewards attached to certain occupations reflect the importance of these occupations to society. Further, high salaries and social rewards ensure that talented and qualified individuals are well motivated to pursue a society's vital jobs. Inequality, then, is an important source of occupational motivation; income variation ultimately works to the benefit of society as a whole (Davis and Moore 1945; Jeffries and Ransford 1980).

The Davis-Moore thesis represents a functional analysis of society. A **functional analysis** focuses on the interrelationship between the various parts of a society. The approach is ultimately concerned with the ways in which such interrelationships contribute to social order. But not all sociologists share this functionalist view.

Proponents of conflict theory question the social benefits of salary discrepancies. **Conflict theorists** analyze social organization and social interactions by attending to the differential resources controlled by different sectors of a society. Conflict theorists note that certain occupational salaries far outweigh the occupation's contribution to society. Furthermore, negative attitudes and bias can prevent some people from occupying jobs for which they nonetheless are qualified. Thus, conflict theorists suggest that salary variations reflect discrepancies in wealth and power, discrepancies that allow a select group of individuals to determine the financial rewards of various occupations (Tumin 1967). **Wealth** refers to the totality of money and resources controlled by an individual (or a family). **Power** is the ability of groups and/or individuals to get what they want even in the face of resistance. Consider, for example, that in 1990 the CEOs of the biggest U.S. companies managed to award themselves sizable pay increases—on average, 10% increases. Such raises occurred despite the fact that the stock prices of the companies run by these CEOs fell an average of 10% (Crystal 1991). The conflict perspective suggests that these salary increases are not reflective of the CEOs' social contribution. Rather, the increases occurred because the CEOs had the capacity, or the power, to command them.

Similar reasoning is used to explain the $1 million plus salaries of some baseball stars. From the conflict perspective, these megasalaries do not reflect the contributions of these athletes. Rather, wealthy team *owners* pay the salaries because they are convinced that they will reap the financial benefits of such investments. Baseball stars can generate huge baseball revenues for club owners by attracting paying customers to the stadium gates and to home TV screens.

Note that income, wealth, and power do not tell the whole story when it comes to defining the social worth of one's work. Worth is also a function of occupational prestige. **Occupational prestige** refers to the respect or recognition one's occupational position commands. Occupational prestige is determined by a variety of job-related factors: the nature of the job, the educational requirements for the job, honors or titles associated with the job, the job's use of "brainpower" versus "brute strength," and the stature of the organizations and groups affiliated with the job.

Periodically, Americans give insight into the prestige factor by rating hundreds of U.S. occupations. Researchers then use such ratings to form an occupational prestige scale. The **occupational prestige scale** provides relative ratings of select occupations as collected from a representative national sample of Americans. In reviewing these ratings, we can quickly see that prestige complicates the road to worth. High income, power, and prestige do not always travel together (Gilbert and Kahl 1993).

CEOs, for example, enjoy great wealth and can wield immense power. Yet the prestige associated with this occupation is comparatively weak. CEOs score only 72 when rated on the 100-point prestige scale. Now note that doctors and dentists earn similar average salaries. Yet doctors enjoy significantly more prestige for their work, earning a rating of 86 versus a 72 rating for dentists.

Bank tellers and secretaries find themselves near the bottom of the income scale. Yet their prestige ratings are more moderate in magnitude;

these occupations receive rankings of 43 and 46, respectively. And a rating of 65 suggests that if prestige were currency or power, U.S. teachers would take home much larger paychecks.

Occupational prestige ratings also can take us beyond the workplace and into the realm of general American values. Often, such insight presents a disturbing commentary. Consider that the lifesaving acts of a firefighter (rated 53) are given no more social recognition than the cosmetic acts of a dental hygienist (rated 52). Similarly, police officers, our legally sanctioned agents of power (rated 60) appear only slightly more valued than the actors who entertain us (rated 58). The information highway seemingly has bull-dozed the heartland, for the farmers who grow our food appear equal in prestige to the telephone operator who answers our information questions (both rated 40). Trades that played a central role in building the nation—carpenters, masons, and miners—no longer command our favor when it comes to prestige (their ratings are 39, 36, and 26, respectively). And, inter-estingly, the midwife who delivers a baby (rated 23) fares slightly worse than the waitress who delivers food (rated 28), the bellhop who delivers bags (rated 27), and the bartender who deliver drinks (rated 25) (*General Social Survey* 1993).

When we note that income, power, and prestige are not always a "pack-age deal," we come to realize the complexity of the U.S. stratification system. The **stratification system** ranks individuals hierarchically with regard to their control of a society's resources, privileges, and rewards.

Those on the highest rungs of the stratification ladder enjoy a critical combination of wealth, power, and prestige. Knowing this helps to explain why electricians or plumbers are rarely considered members of the "upper crust." Their incomes may be high, but their prestige levels are mitigated by a lack of higher education, title, and the use of manual labor in their jobs. Similarly, major league baseball players rarely are classified among the elite. Although their incomes are high, their level of prestige is moderate (rated 65). Further, the historic baseball strike of 1995 suggests that the high income associated with this occupation does not always translate into power.

Individuals who enjoy high income and prestige but are barred from the inner circles of power will never gain full entry to the American upper class. Indeed, many argue that it is this very condition that impedes the progress of political minorities—African Americans, Hispanics, women, youth, and so on—in our nation. Our public rhetoric suggests open access to advanced education, good jobs, and thus high incomes, but our behaviors often block members of minorities from entering the professional and social networks through which power is "brokered."

The more we pay, the more it's worth? Conventional wisdom needs some qualification here. When it comes to the value of certain objects, conventional wisdom may be accurate. But with regard to other aspects of the economy, such as human effort or work, research suggests that the more we pay simply means the more we pay.

LEARNING MORE ABOUT IT

For a good review of occupations in the United States, see Barbara Reskin and Irene Padavic's *Women, Men and Work.* (Newbury Park, CA: Pine Forge Press, 1994).

The definitive work on the three dimensions of stratification—wealth, prestige, and power—can be found in Max Weber's classic work *Economy and Society* (New York: Bedminster 1968; original work published 1922).

For a classic review of the functionalist versus conflict perspectives on stratification, see Arthur Stinchcombe's article, "Some Empirical Consequences of the Davis-Moore Theory of Stratification" (*American Sociological Review 28,* 5, 1963).

All salary information in this essay was drawn from Maze and Mayall's *The Enhanced Guide for Occupational Exploration* (Indianapolis: JIST Works, Inc., 1991) and Reddy's *American Salaries and Wages Survey,* 2d ed. (Detroit: Gale Research, Inc., 1993). The information on prestige rankings comes from the *General Social Science Surveys 1972–1993: Cumulative Codebook* (Chicago: NORC, 1993).

EXERCISES

1. Make a list of all the occupations mentioned in this chapter. Classify each occupation with regard to the gender, race, and ethnicity of those typically associated with the occupation. What patterns can you determine with reference to income and prestige as the occupations vary by gender, race, and ethnicity?

2. Ask 10 of your relatives and/or friends to list their occupations. Then ask them to rate the prestige of the occupation on a 100-point scale. Compare the occupation ratings given by your "subjects" with the national ratings found in your library's copy of the General Social Science Survey. Did your subjects underestimate, overestimate, or pinpoint their prestige levels? If errors were made, were there any patterns to these errors, patterns that might be related to the age, ethnicity, gender, or race of your subjects?

CONVENTIONAL WISDOM TELLS US . . .

Money Is the Root of All Evil

■

THIS ESSAY DOCUMENTS THE IMPACT

OF INCOME ON ISSUES OF MORTALITY AND

LIFE CHANCES. MONEY, WITH ALL ITS ALLEGED

DOWNFALLS, CAN STILL MEAN THE DIFFERENCE

BETWEEN LIFE AND DEATH.

■

When it comes to issues of wealth and poverty, conventional wisdom spins a compelling tale. On the one hand, we are warned of money's ills. Money is touted as the "root of all evil," an intoxicating drug with the power to enslave us. (Charles Dickens's *Scrooge* could tell us something about that!) Biblical scripture contains similar cautions, noting that one "cannot serve God and money." And adages of popular culture warn that "money can't buy happiness or love."

In conjunction with admonitions regarding the perils of wealth, conventional wisdom often paints a rather comforting picture of poverty. From Shakespeare one hears that "poor and content is rich, and rich enough." In the modern era, Gershwin promoted a similar sentiment, writing that "plenty o' nuttin" is plenty enough. These messages reflect a more general belief that poverty brings serenity and simplicity to one's life. The poor are lauded as free of the possessions that can cloud the mind and tempt the spirit. Indeed, the conventional wisdom on poverty suggests that it can breed great character. Such beliefs may explain why politicians—Abraham Lincoln, Richard Nixon, and Bill Clinton among them—love to remind us of their humble beginnings.

Is money the root of all evil and poverty a blessing in disguise? The everyday world of wealth and poverty contradicts such conventional wisdom. Indeed, when we review the connections between one's wallet and one's well-being, it becomes quite clear that the difference between wealth and poverty can literally have life and death consequences.

Consider, for example, the issue of mortality. Mortality rates suggest that the length of one's life is greatly influenced by one's socioeconomic status. **Mortality rates** document the number of deaths per each 1000 members of the population. **Socioeconomic status** refers to a particular social location—one defined with reference to education, occupation, and financial resources.

Those in America who have the highest socioeconomic status live significantly longer than those who have the lowest status (Cockerham 1995; Colburn 1992; Gilbert and Kahl 1993). In fact, some sources suggest that a privileged person's life span can exceed that of a disadvantaged person by as much as 6.5 years (U.S. Bureau of the Census 1993a). Patterns of infant mortality paint a similar picture. **Infant mortality** rates gauge the number of deaths per 1000 live births for children under 1 year of age. Rates of infant mortality are twice as high among the disadvantaged as they are among the privileged (Children's Defense Fund 1991; Crowley 1991).

The link between poverty and mortality stems, in part, from issues of health care. The economically disadvantaged have less access to health care than do members of any other socioeconomic status. Further, the quality of care received by the disadvantaged is significantly worse than that enjoyed by those with higher incomes. Thus, people at the bottom of the U.S. economic hierarchy face the greatest risk of contracting illness and disease. When the disadvantaged get sick, they are more likely to die from their ailments than those who are more economically privileged (Braveman, Egerter, Bennett, and Showstack 1990; Rivo, Kofie, Schwartz, Levy, and Tuckson 1989; Vernacci 1992).

Poor individuals, for example, are much more likely to suffer fatal heart attacks or fatal strokes or to die from cancer than members of any other socioeconomic status (Dutton 1989; Mosley and Cowley 1991). Interestingly, these economic patterns of health hold true even for diseases nearly eradicated by modern medicine. Disadvantaged patients are several times more likely to die of tuberculosis, for example, than their more privileged counterparts. Similarly, the poor are more likely than are members of any other socioeconomic strata to die from generally nonfatal illnesses, such as influenza, stomach ulcers, and syphilis (Gilbert and Kahl 1993; Syme and Berkman 1987). These trends led former U.S. Surgeon General C. Everett Koop to remark, "When I look back on my years in office, the things I banged my head against were all poverty."

Poverty's relationship to life and death, to health and well-being is a worldwide phenomenon. According to the World Health Organization, 1 billion people around the world—approximately 20% of the world population—suffer from serious illnesses attributable to poverty. Poor sanitation, nonvaried diet, and malnutrition all set the stage for this condition. The lack of medical care also greatly contributes to the high rates of death and disease among the poor. Note that in the world's most disadvantaged nations—places such as Cambodia, The Ivory Coast, or Malawi—there are fewer than 5 doctors for every 100,000 of the country's inhabitants! Nations with slightly more resources do not fare much better. Throughout Indonesia and approximately 75% of African nations, there are fewer than 20 doctors for every 100,000 people (*Peters Atlas of the World* 1990).

The effects of world poverty seem especially harsh when one considers the plight of children. Despite the technological advancements of the 20th century, children in poor societies of the 1990s die at the same rate as children did in the Europe of the 1750s (George 1977; Harrison 1984). Indeed, 10% of children in poor societies die during their first year of life. In many nations, half of the child population never sees adulthood (George 1977; Harrison 1984).

Poverty also helps to explain the short life expectancies of those living in the poor nations of the world. **Life expectancy** refers to the average number of years that a specified population can expect to live. For example, although a U.S. citizen might expect to live 70 years or more, individuals in most African nations can expect a life span of only 50 years. In the most deprived of the world's nations, such as Afghanistan, Ethiopia, or Laos, life expectancies average as few as 40 years. Clearly, for many parts of our world community, poverty might be viewed as the leading cause of death (*World Bank* 1994).

Poverty's link to mortality goes beyond issues of health and hygiene. Simple membership in a society's lower economic status, regardless of one's health, increases the risk of premature death. The sinking of the *Titanic* in 1912 offers a stark illustration of this phenomenon. Among passengers on that ill-fated cruise ship, socioeconomic status was a major determinant of survival or death. When disaster strikes on the high seas, norms dictate that women and children should be the first evacuated. On the *Titanic*, however, that norm apparently applied only to wealthier passengers. Forty-five percent of the women in third class met their deaths in contrast to the 16% death rate of women in second class and the 3% death rate of women in first class. What explains the discrepancy? Historians tell us that first-class passengers (both male and female) were given the first opportunity to abandon ship, while those in third class were ordered—sometimes forced at gunpoint—to stay in their rooms. It was only when the wealthy had been safely evacuated from the ship that third-class passengers were permitted to leave. Thus, for many aboard the *Titanic*, mere membership in the ranks of the poor proved to be a fatal affiliation (Hall 1986; Lord 1981; Zeitlin, Lutterman, and Russell 1977).

The link between poverty and mortality, so dramatically witnessed on the decks of the *Titanic*, haunts every corner of American life. In the United States, poverty doubles one's chances of being murdered, raped, or assaulted. Similarly, members of the lower economic strata are more likely than others to die as a result of occupational hazards—that is, from diseases such as black lung, from machinery injuries, and the like (Cockerham 1995; Mirowsky and Ross 1989; U.S. Bureau of the Census 1993a & b). Among children, those of the lower class are more likely to drown, to die in fires, to be murdered, or to be killed in auto accidents than their more affluent counterparts (Cockerham 1995). And during wars, it is sons of the poor that are most likely to serve in the military, and most likely to be casualties (Dunne 1986).

Physical health, life, and death—poverty influences all of these. But the negative effects of low socioeconomic status extend beyond physical well-being. Many studies document that poverty can also negatively influence mental and emotional states. For example, over one-third of the poor report worrying all or most of the time that their household income will be insufficient to meet their basic family expenses. Similarly, the poor are less likely to report feelings of happiness, hope, or satisfaction than their more wealthy counterparts. As a result, the poor are more likely to greet the day with trepidation, despair, and depression rather than with enthusiasm, drive, and stamina (Ladd 1987).

Negative life events also befall the disadvantaged more frequently than those of any other socioeconomic status. **Negative life events** refer to major and undesirable changes in one's day-to-day existence, such as the loss of a spouse, divorce, unemployment. For example, divorce occurs most frequently among the poor, with rates steadily decreasing as one moves up the socioeconomic hierarchy. Similarly, job loss and unemployment are most common among those of the lower socioeconomic strata (Lee 1990; Price and McKenry 1988). The frequency with which the poor experience such events affects their mental and emotional well-being as well. Negative life events have been linked to increases in depression, low self-esteem, and increased use of drugs and alcohol (Hamilton, Broman, and Hoffman 1990).

One's socioeconomic status can also influence an individual's ability to effectively cope with life's struggles; the poor again appear at a disadvantage in this regard. Consider that family members typically constitute the support networks of the poor. This stands in contrast to the networks of the privileged, which typically consist of friends, neighbors, and colleagues. The restricted outlets of the poor are not without cost. Research indicates that the poor experience less security in social exchanges with nonfamily members and greater distrust and fear of the "outside world" than those in more privileged segments of the population (Gilbert and Kahl 1993).

Poverty's links to premature death, physical disease, and poor mental and emotional health suggest that membership in the lowest socioeconomic strata can severely limit an individual's life chances. **Life chances** are the odds of one's obtaining desirable resources, positive experiences, and opportunities for a long and successful life.

Poverty damages the general quality of life. The condition also limits one's ability to improve or change one's circumstances. In the face of disease, depression, unrest, or danger, it becomes hard to summon the motivation necessary for upward mobility.

Given the debilitating consequences of poverty, why have societies been so ineffective at combating it? Sociologist Herbert Gans (1971) suggests that poverty may serve some positive social functions for society. In this regard he offers a functional analysis of poverty. A **functional analysis** focuses on the interrelationship between the various parts of a society. The approach is ultimately concerned with the ways in which such interrelationships contribute to social order.

Consider the economic benefits afforded by the existence of poverty. The poor constitute an accessible pool of cheap labor; they fill jobs that are highly undesirable, yet completely necessary to a functioning society: garbage collector, janitor, poultry processor, and so on. The existence of poverty also generates jobs for those in other socioeconomic strata. Social workers, welfare agents, and public defenders, for example, occupy positions created either to service the poor or to isolate them from the rest of society. A society's poor also provide a ready market for imperfect or damaged goods. By consuming products that others would not consider, the poor help many manufacturers avoid financial loss.

At a social level, the poor provide a measuring rod against which those of other socioeconomic statuses gauge their performance. In this way, the continued existence of a poor class reassures the more privileged of their status and worth. Finally, the poor often function as social scapegoats, symbols by which the larger society reaffirms its laws and values. The poor are more likely to be arrested and convicted of crimes than are members of any other socioeconomic strata. By focusing the social audience on the "sins" of the poor, societies can effectively convey the message that crime doesn't pay.

Reviewing the realities of money and poverty and their place in a society casts serious doubt on conventional wisdom. Money may not guarantee happiness; it may not buy love. Money may trigger greed and, ultimately, personal pain. Yet the disadvantages of money wane in comparison to the absence of money and its effects. Poverty has clear, negative consequences for social actors. In fact, it can be argued that poverty has been a more destructive force in this nation than any medical disease or any international threat. Yet poverty also has clear, positive social functions for society as a whole. Perhaps this point best explains a harsh fact of our times: Despite society's "war on poverty," poverty has proven a tenacious opponent. The battle wages on, with casualties growing in number. Yet, victory over poverty may come at a cost too high for the nonpoor to embrace.

LEARNING MORE ABOUT IT

A poignant account of the lives and conflicts faced by men near the bottom of the economic scale is offered in Richard Sennett's and Jonathan Cobb's *The Hidden Injuries of Class* (New York: Vintage, 1972).

Jeffrey Reiman offers a highly readable look at the ways in which poverty influences justice in *The Rich Get Richer and the Poor Get Jail* (New York: Macmillan, 1990).

For an interesting excursion into the symbolic value of money, see Viviana Zelizer's *The Social Meaning of Money* (New York: Basic Books, 1994).

EXERCISES

1. Essay 5, on aging, introduced the concept of master status. Consider the ways in which an individual's financial position can function as a master status in our society. What auxiliary traits or characteristics are presumed to accompany the status of rich? Of poor? Under what conditions does one's financial status fail to operate as a master status?

2. Consider the ways in which money affects the life chances of a college student. Being as systematic as possible, identify academic and nonacademic activities that increase one's chances of successfully negotiating a college career. How does the ready availability of cash facilitate or impede these various activities? What are the implications of your findings?

CONVENTIONAL WISDOM TELLS US . . .

You've Come a Long Way, Baby

■

IN THE PAST 30 YEARS, WOMEN HAVE MADE

GREAT STRIDES TOWARD EQUALITY WITH MEN.

BUT HAVE THEY JOURNEYED FAR ENOUGH?

HERE, WE FOCUS ON GENDER RELATIONS IN THE

HOME, THE SCHOOLS, AND IN THE WORKPLACE,

ILLUSTRATING THE GAINS AND LOSSES FACED BY

WOMEN AND MEN IN THE CURRENT ERA.

■

"You've come a long way, baby." This is a common phrase that acknowledges the dramatic change in women's social roles and achievements. Drop in on any historical period, and chances are great that you will find evidence of a past filled with gender inequality.

- *Dateline, preindustrial Europe*: Artisan guilds limit apprenticeships to men, thereby ensuring the exclusion of women from their ranks and consequently from the master crafts (Howell 1986).

- *The shores of colonial America:* The Doctrine of Coverture, which subsumes a woman's legal identity and rights to those of her husband, is adopted from British common law (Blackstone 1765–1769/1979).

- *United States, circa 1870*: The "conservation of energy" theme is used to support the argument that education is dangerous for women. The development of the mind is thought to occur at the expense of the reproductive organs (Clarke 1873).

- *The State of Virginia, 1894*: The U.S. Supreme Court rules that the word *person* in a Virginia regulation was properly equated with "male" not "female" and thereby upholds the state's decision to deny a law license to a "nonperson" female (Renzetti and Curran 1989).

- *Turn-of-the-century America*: Twenty-six U.S. states embrace the doctrine of "separate spheres" and pass laws prohibiting the employment of married women. The doctrine asserts that a woman's place is in the home, while a man's is in the public work sphere (Reskin and Padavic 1994; Skolnick 1991).

Today, much has improved for women. Thousands of women have moved into traditionally male jobs. Marital status is no longer a legal barrier to the employment of women. Court rulings have struck down gender-based job restrictions. Women participate in higher education at rates equal to or higher than men. And the law has made concerted efforts to advance and protect the legal rights of women. Yet, despite the long way that "baby" has traveled, a careful assessment of gender relations in the United States indicates that "baby" has a long haul ahead.

Obstacles to gender equality begin with gender socialization. **Gender socialization** refers to the process by which individuals learn the culturally approved expectations and behaviors for males and females. Even in a child's earliest moments of life, gender typing, with all its implications, proves a routine practice. **Gender typing** refers to gender-based expectations and behaviors. For example, one study asked 30 first-time parents to describe their newborn infants. The exercise revealed that parents' responses were heavily influenced by prominent gender stereotypes.

Stereotypes are generalizations applied to all members of a group. Thus, daughters were most often described using adjectives such as "tiny," "soft," and "delicate." In contrast, boys were most frequently described with adjectives such as "strong," "alert," and "coordinated" (Lake 1975; also see Rubin, Provenzano, and Luria 1974). Another study explored the gender typing of a single infant. When the infant was dressed in blue overalls and identified as "Adam," mothers participating in the study described the infant in masculine terms and tried to play with "him" using "male" toys such as trains and cars. When the *very same* infant was dressed in pink and identified as "Beth," mothers participating in the study described the infant in feminine terms and offered "her" a doll (Will, Self, and Dalton 1976).

Gender typing continues during the toddler years. Observation studies of toddlers reveal that parents are rougher and more active with infant sons than they are with infant daughters. Studies also show that parents teach their toddlers different lessons on independence. For example, fathers teach boys to "fend for themselves," while encouraging daughters to "ask for help." These distinctions occur even among parents who claim identical child-rearing techniques with reference to their male versus female children (Basow 1992; Richardson 1988; Ross and Taylor 1989; Witkin-Lanoil 1984).

The gender typing of infants and toddlers is not confined to parents. In one study, for example, college students watched a video in which a baby began to cry after being exposed to a jack-in-the-box toy. When students were told that the infant was male, they attributed the baby's crying to anger. In contrast, when told that the baby was female, the students attributed the crying to fear (Condry and Condry 1976).

Gender typing continues in the schools and can result in a strikingly different educational experience for boys and for girls. For example, research documents that elementary and junior high school teachers give more attention and praise to male students. Further, boys tend to dominate classroom communication and receive more support than girls when working through intellectual problems (Chira 1992; Sadker and Sadker 1985; Thorne 1995).

Social scientists contend that such differential treatment can have long-term consequences. Teacher response patterns send an implicit message that male efforts are more valuable than female efforts. Teachers' gender-driven responses also appear to perpetuate stereotypes of learning. For example, gender stereotypes suggest that boys are more skilled at math than girls. Yet, over 100 studies document that during the elementary and middle school years, girls actually perform better than boys in math. Some suggest that the decline in girls' math skills during the high school years occurs because teachers begin tracking boys and girls in drastically different directions.

Teachers urge boys to value math and science skills, while girls are taught to devalue them (Feingold 1988; Hyde, Fennema, and Lamon 1990).

Perhaps the most telling "lesson" regarding the relationship between gender and education, however, is that schooling leads to greater financial benefits for males than it does for females. In the 1990s, a female high school graduate's earnings are *still* less than those of a male high school dropout. Similarly, national statistics show a $10,000 gap between the earnings of male versus female college graduates. Indeed, it takes a college degree for a female worker to exceed the average earnings of a male with a high school diploma. The gender gap in earnings grows still larger for those with graduate training. American males with some graduate school earn approximately $47,000 per year, while females with the same amount of graduate training average less than $32,000 per year (U.S. Bureau of the Census 1993a).

In addition to parents and the schools, the mass media contribute to gender inequality by prioritizing the male experience in both explicit and subtle ways. For example, studies show that nearly two-thirds of prime-time TV characters are male, a figure clearly nonreflective of the population at large (Signorielli and Morgan 1988). Further, in comparing the presentation of male versus female characters, one finds that males are more likely to be aggressive, powerful, and accomplished, whereas females are more frequently depicted as either attractive sexual objects obsessed with appearance and dating or troublesome, bothersome shrews (Kalisch and Kalisch 1984; Sidel 1991).

The prioritization of males occurs on more subtle levels as well. One study challenged viewers to turn on their TV sets, close their eyes, flip through the channels, and note the gender of the first voice they heard on each station. With few exceptions the voice turned out to be male, a trend suggesting that men are the appropriate gatekeepers of the airways (Atkin 1982).

Gender bias seeps beyond prime-time programming. Children's programming also retains a clear male bias. Indeed, network officials defend this imbalance as a valid, indeed sensible, marketing call—nothing more. Marketing research shows that although girls will watch male-dominated shows, boys will not "cross over" to female-dominated programs. And because boys watch more TV than girls, networks bow to the preference of their male audience members (Carter 1991).

When boys and girls become men and women, they carry learned gender differences into the domestic sphere. Thus, despite current rhetoric to the contrary, the division of labor on the domestic front is anything but equal. Studies show that stay-at-home moms devote an average of 50 hours per week to household duties and chores. Their working husbands, in contrast, average only 11 hours per week. Such a difference may seem just if we view the domestic arena as the stay-at-home mom's workplace. Yet, when such women enter the formal workforce on a full-time basis, research shows that they continue to carry the brunt of domestic chores. Although the full-time working mom spends approximately 30 hours per week on household chores, her working husband's 11-hour contribution remains unchanged (Cowan 1991; Hochschild 1989; Pleck 1985).

Most sociologists agree that the greatest strides toward gender equality have been made within the workplace. Despite such strides, however, the old industrial practice of separating work along gender lines continues. Gender segregation is common practice in many workplaces and within many occupations. **Gender segregation** in the work sphere refers to the separation of male and female workers by job tasks or occupational categories.

Approximately half of all working women are concentrated in "female" occupations (occupations where the overwhelming majority of workers are female). Ninety-four percent of registered nurses, 97% of receptionists, 97% of child-care workers, and 99% of secretaries are female (U.S. Census Bureau 1994a). The histories of these occupations point to an economic motive for such segregation. Within these areas, employers used female workers to reduce their wage costs. Employers were able to pay female workers a lower wage than males. Further, by confining their hiring to young, single women, employers ensured a high worker turnover in their businesses (young, single women left their jobs to marry), as well as a continuous supply of inexperienced, low-wage workers (Reskin and Padavic 1994).

We may be tempted to think that gender segregation can lead to certain positive outcomes. For example, an abundance of women within certain occupations suggests arenas of power born from numbers. However, it is important to note that there is a negative relationship between the percentage of female workers within an occupation and that occupation's earnings. Occupations dominated by women enjoy less pay, less prestige, and less power than occupations dominated by males. Furthermore, once an occupation becomes female dominated, it is effectively abandoned by men. The opposite trend—the male displacement of female workers—is unusual (Reskin and Padavic 1994). Indeed, it is a trend typically limited to instances where immigrant men replaced native-born women, as they did in American textile mills or in the cigarmaking industry (Hartman 1976; Kessler-Harris 1982).

In general, male workers dominate managerial and craft occupations. In addition, the most prestigious professions are primarily the domain of men. Indeed, only 11% of working women are found in male-dominated occupations (Kraut and Luna 1992): Only 8% of engineers, 10% of dentists, 17%

of architects, 19% of lawyers, and 20% of physicians are female. Less than 5% of top management positions are held by women (Sharpe 1994).

Women who do enter nontraditional occupations are likely to face gender segregation *within* the occupation. For example, females in medicine are most likely to specialize in pediatrics and gynecology, while neuro-surgery and radiology remain the preserve of male physicians (Epstein 1988). Similarly, women have greatly increased their numbers in public relations work, but they are more likely to be assigned to technical than to managerial positions (Donato 1990). In the realm of real estate, women sell homes while men sell commercial properties (Thomas and Reskin 1990). (Guess which is the more lucrative branch of the field.) Even in the world of waiting tables, gender segregation persists. Expensive restaurants tend to hire waiters; inexpensive eateries and diners hire waitresses.

The gender segregation of jobs and occupations takes a financial toll on women. Such costs are reflected in a statistic referred to as the pay gap. The **pay gap** refers to a ratio calculated when women's earnings are divided by men's earnings. Historically, a pay gap favoring men over women is a well-established tradition. Currently, the pay gap is approximately 70%—that is, for every $10,000 paid the average male worker, the average female worker is paid just under $7000.

The pay gap can vary according to the age and race of workers. For example, the gap increases when we compare the salaries of older female and male workers as opposed to those just entering the work force. Simi-larly, the gap increases when we compare the salaries of African-American or Hispanic female workers with those of their male counterparts (Reskin and Padavic 1994).

Ironically, one area in which women do appear to be achieving equity is in the realms of disease and mortality. Traditionally, women have enjoyed a health advantage over men. Females display lower rates of infant mortality than males. Females enjoy longer life spans than males. Male death rates generally are higher than female death rates within all age categories. But as women embrace more of the behaviors traditionally associated with the male role (such as alcohol consumption, smoking, and so on), and as they make inroads into male occupations, their health advantage may be waning.

For instance, the increased incidence of smoking among women appears associated with increased rates of lung cancer. Women are now nearly equal to men when it comes to deaths linked to lung cancer. Indeed, more women die of lung cancer each year than do women from breast cancer (National Center for Health Statistics 1992). Similarly, women's increased representation in the work force has been linked to increases in female heart disease. Heart disease is now the leading cause of female deaths. Women who face the greatest risk are those who enter the work force *and* report guilt-related stress over the need to leave the home (Cockerham 1995; Haug and Folmar 1986; Silberner 1990; Verbrugge 1985).

Despite women's greater representation in cancer and heart disease rates, however, several studies show that the female experience receives only secondary consideration by medical researchers. As a result, heart disease in women tends to be less effectively detected and treated than it is in men. Similarly, fewer research dollars are devoted to traditionally female cancers such as breast and ovarian compared to traditionally male forms such as prostate or colon cancer (Silberner 1990).

The longest journey begins with the first step. Women have taken that step, but their journey is far from complete. Perhaps the greatest evidence of the distance yet to be covered is found in the area of politics. Governorships, senate seats, and house seats are noteworthy for their near absence of women. Social psychologist Sandra Lipsitz Bem (1993) contends that the male dominance of political power has created a male-centered culture and social structure. Such an environment works to the clear advantage of men. A male-centered perspective on the world dictates a set of social arrangements that systematically meets the needs of men while leaving women's needs unmet or handled as "special cases."

Witness, for instance, the influence of the male perspective within the legal arena, specifically no-fault divorce laws. Such laws treat parties to a divorce as equal players despite their unequal work and occupational histories. Present social arrangements are such that a husband's earning power is enhanced over the course of a marriage. Consequently, in the wake of no-fault divorce laws, ex-wives typically experience a decrease in their standard of living while ex-husbands typically enjoy an increase (Hoffman and Duncan 1988).

Male-centered social arrangements also permeate current disability policies. Such policies recognize nearly all "male" illnesses and medical procedures (circumcision, prostate surgery, and so on) as potentially eligible for compensation. In contrast, the female condition of pregnancy is defined as a "special condition" unique to women and, therefore, ineligible for coverage. In essence, models or standards of normalcy and behavior are male-oriented, a situation that automatically puts women at a disadvantage (Bem 1993; Crocker 1985).

By increasing their numbers and voice in the political arena, women may achieve an effective "check" on social inequality. Without such a development, it will remain far too easy to sustain policies and practices that work to the disadvantage of women. Gender inequality will continue to be business as usual.

LEARNING MORE ABOUT IT

An interesting and provocative discussion of gender inequality is offered by social psychologist Sandra Lipsitz Bem in *The Lenses of Gender: Transforming the Debate on Sexual Inequality* (New Haven: Yale University Press, 1993).

Several studies document the grave inaccuracies of the stereotypes of boys and girls and their learning skills. Interested readers can consult the work of Janet Shibley Hyde and colleagues in "Gender Differences in Math Performance" (*Psychological Bulletin 107,* 139–155, 1990) or "Gender Differences in Verbal Ability" (*Psychological Bulletin 104,* 53–69, 1988). Also see A. Feingold's article "Cognitive Gender Differences Are Disappearing" (*American Psychologist 43,* 95–103, 1988).

A very readable and interesting discussion of the working woman's disproportional domestic duties is offered by Arlie Russell Hochschild in *The Second Shift: Working Parents and the Revolution at Home* (New York: Viking, 1989).

Barbara Reskin and Irene Padavic have constructed a very readable review of gender and its relationship to work. Readers can consult *Women and Men at Work.* (Thousand Oaks, CA: Pine Forge Press, 1994).

EXERCISES

1. Using your own experiences and the experiences of friends and classmates, construct a list of paying jobs typically performed by adolescent boys and girls. Be sure to note the activities, duration, and rate of pay that normally characterize these jobs. Discuss the anticipatory socialization (see Essay 5) implications of your findings.

2. Using your college catalog, examine the gender distribution across the various academic departments and administrative levels. Note the total number and percentage of female faculty and administrators. Are women equally likely to appear in all fields and levels of work? Within specific fields and departments, is there any evidence of job-level segregation? (i.e., Are women more likely to occupy adjunct or assistant professor positions?) Review some recent course registration materials and see if there is any pattern to the courses assigned to female faculty. Are your findings consistent with the image projected by your institution in its promotional materials?

CONVENTIONAL WISDOM TELLS US . . .

America Is the Land of Equal Opportunity

■

IS THE UNITED STATES AN EVEN PLAYING FIELD FOR ALL AMERICANS DESPITE RACE? IN THIS ESSAY, WE REVIEW THE MANY ARENAS OF CONTINUED SEGREGATION AND RACISM IN THE UNITED STATES. FURTHER, WE EXPLORE THE BASIS FOR DETERMINING ONE'S RACE, NOTING THAT WITH ALL OF THE IMPLICATIONS THE CLASSIFICATION HOLDS, CATEGORTIZING RACE IS, AT BEST, A TENUOUS PROCESS.

■

Several years ago, an editorial in the *Wall Street Journal* (1993) urged civil rights leaders to tone down the rhetoric on racism. The authors argued that, although pockets of racism may still exist, equality is winning the day in the United States. The editorial is consistent with a rather popular sentiment held by many Americans today: If African Americans, Hispanic Americans, or Native Americans fail to succeed, the fault must lie with members of these groups, and not with the system at large.

For example, respondents in one national survey were asked why African Americans have worse jobs, income, and housing than White Americans. Forty-nine percent of the respondents agreed with a statement that offered "a lack of motivation and will power among Blacks" as an explanation for the phenomenon (*General Social Science Surveys* 1993, 293–294). Similarly, a study conducted by the National Opinion Research Center found that 62% of non-Black respondents believed that African Americans simply are lazy; among the same group, 78% believed that African Americans prefer to live on welfare rather than work (Smith 1990). In still another national study, 50% of young White respondents reported that they believe White Americans are hurt more by reverse discrimination than African Americans or Hispanic Americans are by racism (People for the American Way and Peter D. Hart Research Associates 1992).

Clearly, current conventional wisdom suggests that racial inequality is a thing of the past. Progress has been made, and the nation is now an "even playing field." Are such claims accurate? Has racial equality been achieved in the United States? Further, when inequalities do arise, are they rightfully attributable to race or racism? A **race** is a group of individuals who share a common genetic heritage or obvious physical characteristics that members of a society deem socially significant. **Racism** refers to prejudice and discrimination based on the belief that one race is superior to another. **Prejudice** refers to an unfavorable prejudgment of an individual based on the individual's group membership. **Discrimination** refers to unfavorable treatment of individuals on the basis of their group membership.

Racial divisions in America remain bold and visible. Consider housing patterns in the United States. Despite the civil rights movement, affirmative action programs, and other equality initiatives, housing segregation is still a fact of American life. In a recent poll, 73% of White respondents said they would be unwilling to live in a neighborhood that was more than one-third African American. More than one-fourth of the White respondents said they would be unwilling to live in a neighborhood with more than 8% African Americans (Massey and Denton 1993).

Attitudes on neighborhood living arrangements reflect actual residential patterns in the United States. In a phenomenon referred to as "tipping," figures show that White residents begin to relocate from neighborhoods when the African-American population exceeds the 8% threshold. With African Americans constituting approximately 12% of the U.S. population, the tipping phenomenon makes full integration virtually impossible (Chideya 1995). Further, segregated living imposes a financial burden on African Americans. Studies show that home loan applications for Blacks are rejected at a higher rate than those for Whites, regardless of the applicant's income levels (Brenner and Spayd 1993; Conner and Smith 1991; Dedman 1989). When one considers the centrality of home ownership in determining an individual's overall wealth, it becomes clear that the implications of discriminatory practices in the home loan business are profound and long-lasting.

Race bears direct links to inequality in American schools as well. In 1954, the U.S. Supreme Court's *Brown v. Board of Education* decision ordered American schools to desegregate with all deliberate speed. Yet, after 40 years, full integration still eludes schools. In many cases, White communities effectively circumvented the desegregation ruling by relocating their children to private schools. Thus, in areas such as Atlanta or Washington, DC, Whites constitute less than 10% of the public school population (Jordan 1993; Kozol 1991).

Some sociologists contend that race segregation in the schools ultimately translates into knowledge segregation. The financial stability of predominantly White private schools results in better materials, resources, and teachers than those found in non-White urban counterparts. Similar contrasts exist between public schools located in predominantly White versus predominantly non-White neighborhoods. Because most public school budgets are tied to local economic resources, schools in wealthy White neighborhoods fare better than those in poor non-White neighborhoods.

Sociologist Jonathan Kozol (1991) dramatically documented the vast resource differences that characterize White versus non-White schools. For example, Kozol found that the poor resources of one predominantly African-American Chicago Southside school forced chemistry teachers to use popcorn poppers as Bunsen burners. In contrast, students in a nearby predominantly White suburban school were enjoying a facility that housed seven gyms, an Olympic-size pool, and separate studios for fencing, dance instruction, and wrestling. Similarly, Kozol found that PS 261 in the South Bronx housed 400 more students than permitted by local fire codes. Just a few bus stops away in the wealthy Riverdale section of the Bronx, PS 24 touted class sizes well below the city average.

In addition to the unequal distribution of resources, researchers note that the lessons taught in predominantly White versus predominantly non-White schools can differ dramatically. Students in predominantly White schools learn to be self-directed, inquisitive, and ambitious. In contrast, students in predominantly non-White schools are taught to obey rules and maintain the status quo (Bowles and Gintis 1976; Kozol 1991; Polakow 1993).

Race lines are maintained within the workplace as well. Despite laws to the contrary, studies show that discrimination in hiring affects approximately 20% of African-American job applicants (Equal Employment Opportunity Commission 1993). In one study, researchers assembled ten White and ten African-American males matched for age, height, weight, speech patterns, and so on. The men were given fictitious résumés, thus equalizing their job and educational backgrounds as well. Matched pairs of applicants—White and Black—then applied for 476 randomly selected entry-level positions that were advertised by private corporations in the *Washington Post* and the *Chicago Tribune*. In 20% of the cases, White applicants were given an unfair advantage over Black applicants. For example, White applicants were invited to apply for jobs that were unavailable to Black applicants. In some cases, Black applicants were directed to less desirable positions than their White counterparts. White applicants also were hired more frequently than their Black counterparts. These discriminatory practices were most pronounced in jobs offering the highest wages and income potential (Turner, Fix, and Struyk 1991).

Once on the job, discrimination continues. Blacks earn less than Whites within various sectors of the employment market. For example, Black men with college degrees earn only 80% of what their White counterparts earn. When comparisons are made between Black and White incomes across *all* jobs (white and blue collar), statistics show that Black men earn only 61 cents to the White male dollar. Further, although this income gap closed significantly between 1930 and 1970, little movement has occurred since 1970 (Hacker 1992).

Clearly, many inequalities still exist in the various sectors of U.S. society. Yet many contend that such inequalities are not the product of racism. Many continue to believe that race, as a biological attribute, indicates some inherent differences in individuals' ability to achieve.

At first glance, this argument may appear valid. Biology would appear to be the unequivocal determinant of racial group distinctions. Thus, different biologies could conceivably lead to different levels of ability. Yet a biological definition of race does not produce a simple or clear racial classification scheme. In fact, identifying groups who share obvious physical characteristics proves a less than obvious task.

Using a biological definition of race, biologists and physical anthropologists can "find" as few as 3 or as many as 200+ different races. These classifications are muddied further when we note that generations of inter-group marriage and breeding ensures that no "pure" races exist. Indeed, a remarkable similarity exists across the genes of all humans: Of the DNA molecules that account for racial categories, 95–99% are common across all humans (Shipman 1994). Thus, if the human essence is "all in the genes," then racial similarities, not distinctions, are most noteworthy.

From a biological perspective, racial differences are best understood as beneficial, adaptive changes for our human species (Molnar 1991). For instance, the dark skin of peoples living near the equator serves as vital protection against dangerous sun rays. Similarly, the longer, narrow noses found among those living in colder northern climates help to warm the air before it reaches the temperature-sensitive lungs. If the earth were to shift on its axis so that the northern hemisphere moved into direct line with the sun, we would expect an adaptive change in the skin color and nose configuration of the northern population (Rensberger 1981).

A biological approach to the race issue is really insufficient for understanding the dynamics of racial categories. Indeed, the task of identifying discrete racial categories has largely been abandoned by many physical anthropologists. Sociologists suggest that race is more properly understood as a *social* rather than a biological phenomenon: race is socially constructed. The **social construction** of reality occurs when individuals create images, ideas, and beliefs about society based on their social interactions.

The social constructionist approach suggests that racial categories emerge from social interaction, social perception, and social opinion. Social encounters repeatedly expose individuals to specific definitions of race. If these definitions suggest clear and natural boundaries and rankings between various groups of people, the definitions can institutionalize racism as part of a society's stock of knowledge. Such definitions come to reify, or substantiate, racial distinctions that may not be supported in fact. **Reification** refers to the process by which the subjective or abstract erroneously comes to be treated as objective fact or reality. From such a perspective, we must view race as a characteristic that resides in the "eye of the beholder." Change the group doing the perceiving and defining—that is, change the eye of the beholder—and you will change the racial distinctions being made.

For example, it is estimated that over 70% of Black Americans have some White ancestors (Kilker 1993; Roberts 1975). Yet, this biological lineage does not alter public perception. Despite evidence of White ancestry, such individuals are still classified as Black. U.S. classification patterns resulted from a long-standing legal practice that mandated "percentage of blood" standards for determining racial classifications. Until 1983, for instance, the law of Louisiana dictated that individuals with one-thirty-second of "Negro blood" were properly classified as belonging to the Black race. Were we to change the setting of this classification, however, a very different designation of race would emerge. In Brazil, for example, any individual who has "some" White ancestry is classified as belonging to the White race. Consequently, by Brazilian standards, most Black Americans would be classified as White (Denton and Massey 1989).

At first glance, perceptual differences of race may not seem very significant. Such differences merely underscore a major premise of the sociological perspective: Social context is an important factor in understanding, explaining, or predicting human attitudes and behaviors (see the introduction). **Social context** refers to the broad social and historical circumstances surrounding an act or an event. But the intriguing nature of race as a social creation becomes clearer when we view it as a significant social status. **Social status** refers to the position or location of an individual with reference to characteristics such as age, education, gender, income, race, religion, and so on.

All of us have many different relationships; social actors all possess a status set. A **status set** refers to the collection of statuses that a social actor occupies. Some of the statuses we occupy are the result of our own personal efforts; these are achieved statuses. An **achieved status** is one earned or gained through personal effort. One's statuses as Red Cross volunteer, parent, or worker are all achieved statuses. In contrast, some of our statuses are "assigned" to us, independent of our personal efforts, desires, or preferences; these are ascribed statuses. An **ascribed status** is one assigned or given without regard to a person's efforts or desires. Age, gender, and racial statuses are all ascribed statuses.

The average reader of this book will occupy many of the following statuses (try classifying each as achieved or ascribed): son or daughter, student, friend, spouse, sibling, male or female, citizen, voter, consumer, employee. Often, however, one of our many statuses will dominate the rest. This dominant status forms a master status (see Essay 5). A **master status** is a single social status that overpowers all other social positions occupied by an individual. A master status directs the way in which others see, define, and relate to an individual.

If we consider race in light of these status distinctions, we begin to more fully appreciate the implications of race as a social creation. For although race is a social creation, it is also an ascribed status. As such, race is imposed on the individual; one's race is beyond one's control. Race also frequently serves as a master status. As a master status, race has the ability to influence the social identity and life chances of an individual. **Identity** refers to those essential characteristics that both link us and distinguish us from other social players and, thus, establish who we are. **Life chances** refer to one's odds of obtaining desirable resources, positive experiences, and opportunities for a long and successful life. For races classified as social minorities, this influence is often negative. A **social minority** is a group regarded as subordinate or inferior to a majority or dominant group. Social minorities are excluded from full participation in society; they experience inferior positions of prestige, wealth, and power.

Note the irony here. Ascribed master statuses are beyond the individual's control. They are assigned, yet they have a remarkable capacity to control the individual. Indeed, certain ascribed master statuses can prove more important to one's identity than personal efforts. The irony intensifies when we acknowledge that race, an assigned status, is nonetheless a social creation. Racial designations can change as audience perceptions change.

The significance of these last few points becomes more apparent when we reconsider the real-life consequences of racial designations (U.S. Bureau of the Census 1992; 1993b):

- Recent census data indicate that the median family income for Whites stands near $38,000. The median family income for African Americans and Hispanic Americans hovers around $21,000 and $23,000 respectively.

- Approximately 22% of the White population earns a college degree compared to only 11% of the African-American population and approximately 9% of Native Americans and Hispanic Americans.

- As of the early 1990s, the average life expectancy for Whites is approximately 76 years. Life expectancy for African Americans is 7 years shorter, at 69 years.

- The infant mortality rate for White babies is 8 deaths per 1000 live births. The rate for African-American babies is 19.

Indeed, take any set of statistics regarding life chances—poverty rates, divorce rates, mental health rates, and so on—and you will undoubtedly come to the conclusion that race matters.

This essay suggests that racial distinctions cannot be equated with biological or genetic differences. Race is not a simple matter of physiology. Rather, racial distinctions are more properly understood as social creations. Skin color proves the primary marker of racial distinctions in U.S. society; other cultures have focused on such characteristics as height or hair and eye color. No matter what a society's marker, once certain characteristics are deemed worthier than others—that is, once racial categories are created—

powerful social processes such as prejudice and discrimination are set into motion.

Still, race has proven itself a highly dynamic process; the human species has shown a remarkable capacity to adapt to environmental demands. The pressing question for today and the near future is whether our social definition of race will prove equally adaptive to changes in our social and cultural environments. It is presently projected that by the year 2050, the United States will be a land where Whites will be a numerical minority. Given these projected demographic changes, rethinking the race issue may well be a social and cultural necessity. Perhaps by stressing the *social* nature and origins of racial distinctions, we will find that such distinctions are more amenable to change than conventional wisdom currently allows.

LEARNING MORE ABOUT IT

To learn more about the continued presence of racial inequality in the United States, see Andrew Hacker's *Two Nations: Black and White, Separate, Hostile, Unequal* (New York: Scribner, 1992). Statistical analyses are included.

W. E. B. DuBois offers a classic treatise on the dynamics of U.S. race relations in *The Souls of Black Folks* (New York: Penguin, 1982; original work published 1903). Cornel West thoughtfully grapples with issues of race in a more contemporary book entitled *Race Matters* (Boston: Beacon Press, 1993). Similarly engaging is F. James Davis's very readable book *Who Is Black: One Nation's Definition,* a history of the "one drop rule."

In *The Declining Significance of Race: Blacks and Changing American Institutions,* 2d ed. (Chicago: University of Chicago Press, 1980), William Julius Wilson posits the controversial thesis that social class is more significant than race in defining opportunities for African Americans. In a later work, Wilson gives special attention to the plight of Blacks caught in the grip of the inner city underclass. See *The Truly Disadvantaged: The Inner City, The Underclass, and Public Policy* (Chicago: University of Chicago Press, 1987).

EXERCISES

1. Imagine that height is a critical marker for social ranking in the United States: shortness valued, tallness devalued. Speculate on the ways in which the social structure of your hometown might change were residential, educational, and occupational patterns influenced by prejudice and discrimination based on human height.

2. Racial categories are social creations that emerge from social interaction. Gather a sample of ads from two magazines that target different classes of readers. For example, one magazine might be targeting an elite readership (for example, *Martha Stewart's Living* or *Gourmet*), whereas the second targets a more general, less affluent readership (for example, *Family Circle* or *Good Housekeeping*). Are racial lessons delivered through these ads? Do the ads indicate any differences in life aspirations by race or ethnic group? Consider the data on life chances as presented in this essay. How does reality compare to the lifestyles projected in your sample of ads?

Deviance, Crime, and Social Control

■

CONVENTIONAL WISDOM TELLS US . . .

Murder Is Becoming All Too Commonplace on the Streets of Our Nation

■

FOR DECADES, AMERICANS HAVE IDENTIFIED MURDER AS THE CRIME THEY FEAR MOST. IS THAT FEAR JUSTIFIED? HERE, WE EXPLORE THE WAYS IN WHICH PUBLIC PERCEPTIONS AND FEARS OF MURDER OFTEN RUN COUNTER TO THE CRIME'S ACTUAL OCCURRENCE. AS SUCH, THE ESSAY EXPLORES THE MANY PROBLEMS SURROUNDING THE DETECTION AND PERCEPTION OF CRIME.

■

When Americans are asked to name the country's most troubling problems, they rank crime high on the list. In fact, Richard Berke of the *New York Times* writes that "crime is becoming the nation's top fear" (1994: 1). Drive-by shootings, gang warfare, metal detectors at the doors of our schools: In the 1990s, these images have become all too common, and they are images that can provoke a sense of terror.

The crimes that Americans fear most are violent crimes, especially murder. And increasingly, Americans are acting on these fears. Recent Gallup polls show that Americans are doubling and tripling the number of protective measures they take against murderers and other violent criminals. In the 1990s, Americans were two to three times more likely to install special locks or alarms in their homes, buy dogs or guns for protection, or change their nighttime walking patterns than in the prior decade (Flanagan and McLeod 1983; Maguire and Pastore 1994).

Is the rising fear of murder justified? Is conventional wisdom correct in suggesting that our streets have become more dangerous than ever before? Just how likely is it that any one of us will become the victim of a murderer?

Americans do indeed face a greater risk of being murdered than the inhabitants of *any* other nation in the world. Murder, as well as violent crimes such as assault and rape, occur four to nine times more frequently in the United States than in the developed nations of Europe. The United States also displays higher murder rates than nations suffering from intense poverty or political turmoil—places such as Costa Rica, Greece, India, etc. (Archer and Gartner 1987; Fingerhut and Kleinman 1990; Heiland, Shelley, and Katoh 1991).

The ranking of the United States as number one on the worldwide murder scale is compelling. Indeed, it seems to support the conventional wisdom on murder. However, the information must be carefully interpreted. To gain an accurate picture regarding the likelihood of one's falling victim to murder, we must view data on the crime in light of some important facts regarding the actual number of murders that occur.

The public's persistent fear of murder suggests that the crime has a high rate of occurrence. Yet, national statistics reveal that murder is quite rare within the world of crime. In the United States, rape occurs 4 times more frequently and robbery occurs 27 times more frequently than murder. Americans are 46 times more likely to be assaulted than they are to be murdered, and nearly 64 times more likely to have their cars stolen than to be victimized by a murderer (U.S. Federal Bureau of Investigation 1994). (See Figure 12.1.) Indeed when it comes to fatal victimization, statistics show that Americans are more likely to take their own lives than to be killed by a violent criminal (*World Almanac* 1995).

FIGURE 12.1

Victimization Rates by Select Crimes—U.S.

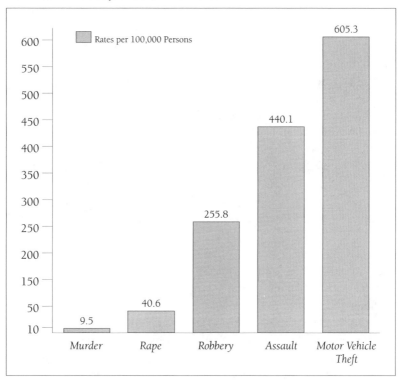

The public's persistent fear of murder also reflects a perception of the crime's random nature; Americans tend to view murder as an event that can strike anyone at any time. However, crime statistics do not substantiate this image. In fact, murder exhibits several striking social patterns. For example, murder is largely a "friendly" crime. The large majority of murders— 80%—are committed by relatives, friends, or acquaintances of the victim. Murder also is a crime of the young. An individual's risk of being murdered peaks at age 25, regardless of race or gender. (Recall from Essay 5 that senior citizens are *most* fearful of violent crime. Yet, crime statistics show that seniors are *least* likely to become murder victims.) And murder is a "male" crime; better than 85% of all perpetrators and 75% of all victims are male. (Maguire and Pastore 1994; U.S. Federal Bureau of Investigation 1993).

In addition, murder systematically varies by race and socioeconomic status. Murder is an overwhelmingly intraracial crime; Whites tend to murder other Whites, Blacks tend to murder other Blacks, and so on. (U.S.

Federal Bureau of Investigation 1994). The crime also occurs dispropor-tionately among the poor. Further, socioeconomic status appears related to when and how a murder occurs. Members of lower socioeconomic strata, for instance, are most likely to be murdered on a Saturday night, and the grizzly event is likely to involve alcohol and emotions. In contrast, mem-bers of the upper strata are murdered with equal frequency during all days and times of the week. In addition, murders among the "privileged" typi-cally result from premeditation rather than passion (Parker 1989; U.S. Fed-eral Bureau of Investigation 1994; Williams 1984.)

Our worst visions of murder seem not to match the realities of the crime. Contrary to perceptions of frequency and randomness, murder is rare and highly patterned. Given these facts, what explains Americans' persistent fears and misperceptions?

One might be tempted to explain them by referring to the high cost of the crime—namely, death. However, if the risk of death alone stimulated such fears, we would find similar trepidation surrounding other high mor-tality settings and events. Consider the area of occupation-hazards. Although fewer than 25,000 Americans are murdered each year, almost 61,000 U.S. workers die annually due to occupational diseases or unsafe working conditions. However, one can document little stated fear of occupation-related deaths (Reiman 1990). Similarly, certain diseases should instill greater fear in Americans than that provoked by murder. Cancer, heart disease, and stroke still account for approximately 70% of all deaths in the United States. Yet, the public's fear of murder often outweighs its fear of dis-ease (*World Almanac* 1995). Finally, Americans are nearly twice as likely to die in automobile accidents than they are to be murdered. However, few would cite a level of fear that precludes one's "taking to the roads" (*World Almanac* 1995).

In contrast to human costs, one might suggest that the economic costs of murder explain Americans' disproportionate fear of the crime. Yet, the economic costs of murder are minimal when compared to other, less feared crimes. The economic costs of corporate crime, for example, can range from $100 billion to $200 billion annually (Livingston 1996; Meier 1989; Simon and Eitzen 1990). **Corporate crime** refers to planned and deliber-ate illegal acts committed by corporate officials or employees for the ben-efit of a corporation. Based on these figures, corporate crime costs Americans several times more than the eight FBI Index crimes combined. The **FBI Index crimes** are crimes counted under the Uniform Crime Reports Index for Serious Crime. The index crimes are murder, rape, assault, burglary, robbery, larceny, motor vehicle theft, and arson. Yet, corporate crimes elicit little fear or concern from the general public (Meier 1989; Simon and Eitzen 1990).

Considerations regarding human and economic costs contribute little to our understanding of Americans' fear of murder. As a result, some sociologists contend that the fear of murder may be socially constructed. The **social construction** of reality occurs when individuals create images, ideas, and beliefs about society based on their social interactions. The social constructionist approach suggests that certain social encounters expose individuals repeatedly to information on murder—information that suggests the crime occurs frequently, randomly, or at the hands of strangers. As a result, these data—even though they represent misinformation—come to form the public's "reality" of the crime.

The mass media, especially television, are the greatest source of misinformation on murder. Research conducted by scholars at the Annenberg School of Communication illustrates the point. Since 1967, Annenberg scholars have been meticulously analyzing the content found in sample weeks of prime-time and daytime television. Their findings show that the rates of murder and other types of violence in "TV land" are disproportionately high compared to real-world figures.

The Annenberg data reveal that during any week night, viewers see an average of 5 to 10 violent acts per hour. On Saturday mornings, a time period dominated by child viewers, the rate of violence increases to 20 to 25 acts per hour. Based on these data, some estimate that by the time most children leave high school, they have viewed approximately 13,000 murders on TV!

The figures on TV violence are significant, for they suggest a world quite different from everyday reality. In the real world, fewer than $1/2$% of all Americans become involved in violence. In TV land, 64% of all characters are involved in violence. Therefore, those who rely on television as their window on reality may come to view the world as a perilously dangerous place.

To substantiate this claim, the Annenberg research group regularly compares both heavy and light television viewers with regard to their perceptions of violence. Respondents participating in these studies are asked a series of questions requiring them to estimate rates of murder, rape, and assault. Respondents are generally presented with two choices in making these estimates. One choice typically reflects real rates of violence in the United States, whereas the other choice better reflects rates of violence in TV land.

In each of the Annenberg studies, results consistently show that heavy television viewers are much more likely to overestimate rates of violence than those who watch little or no television. Heavy television viewers routinely favor TV-land estimates of violence over real-world estimates. Further, heavy television viewers perceive the world to be a more dangerous place than those who watch little or no TV. Thus, heavy viewers are more likely than light viewers to take the protective measures mentioned earlier: installing special locks or alarms in their homes, buying dogs or guns for protection, or changing their nighttime walking patterns (Gerbner and Gross 1972; Gerbner, Gross, Jackson-Beek, Jeffries-Fox, and Signorielli 1978; Signorelli and Morgan 1988).

Complementing the social constructionist view is the view suggested by others that Americans' disproportionate fear of murder emerges from a long-standing cultural value that supports a fear of strangers. A **cultural value** is a general sentiment that people share regarding what is good or bad, right or wrong, desirable or undesirable. A **fear of strangers** refers to a dread or suspicion of those who look, behave, or speak differently than oneself. Such fears can ultimately make the world seem unfamiliar and dangerous.

In the United States, cultural values instill a sense of mistrust and foreboding toward those we do not know. Couple this phenomenon with the fact that most Americans view murder as a stranger crime, and the misinformation that links murder to an already feared social category—strangers—serves to exacerbate and perpetuate public fears of the crime (The President's Commission on Law Enforcement and Administration of Justice 1968).

The public's misplaced fears and misperceptions of murder are not without serious consequences. Such misconceptions sometimes result in the ineffective control of the crime. For example, high-profile murder cases such as the Charles Stuart case in Boston, Massachusetts (1989) or the Susan Smith case in Union, South Carolina (1994) illustrate the dangers of equating murder with strangers. In both cases, the murder victims were killed by an immediate family member: Stuart murdered his wife; Smith murdered her children. Yet in both cases, resistance to the notion of "friendly" murder initially led to the detention of innocent people. (The false leads in both cases also involved black males; indeed, 35 black males were questioned in the Smith case.) Such "mistakes" substantiate the power of socially constructed scripts—scripts that depict the "typical" nature of murder and the "likely" perpetrator of the crime (Brown 1994).

These misplaced fears and misperceptions of murder also can detract attention from the critical sites of murder in the United States. To be sure, Americans display greater concern for violent crimes on our nation's streets than they do for violence in the home. Yet, sociologist Richard Gelles notes that aside from the police and the military, the family is the single most violent institution in our society.

The dangers in our homes extend beyond the crime of murder. Assault and battery, for example, is the single major cause of injury to women. More women are battered in their homes each year than those injured in auto accidents or street crimes. Further, studies of hospital services indicate that assaults by an intimate account for approximately one-third of all injuries to women seen in urban hospital emergency rooms.

Similarly, the United States witnesses approximately 2 million instances of parent to child violence annually. Further, experts estimate that anywhere from 1 to 13 children are killed each day as a result of parental violence (Bean 1992; Ferraro 1989; Gelles and Straus 1988; Gil 1986; Lystad 1986; Newberger and Bourne 1985; Ruane 1993; Straus and Gelles 1986; Straus, Gelles, and Steinmetz 1980; Van Hasselt, Morrison, Bellack, and Straus 1987).

Any instance of murder represents one death too many. In this sense murder may indeed be all too common in the United States. Can the tide of such crimes be turned? It is difficult to say. But any solutions to murder require us to adopt a more accurate picture of the scope and patterns that characterize violent deaths in America.

LEARNING MORE ABOUT IT

A comprehensive study regarding the facts and fictions of murder can be found in Martin Daly and Margo Wilson's *Homicide* (New York: Aldine de Gruyter, 1988).

Philip Schlesinger and colleagues offer an interesting perspective on the role of media in female perceptions of murder and violence. Consult *Women Viewing Violence* (London: BFI, 1992).

For the classic theoretical treatise on the social construction of reality, see Peter Berger and Thoman Luckmann's *The Social Construction of Reality* (New York: Anchor, 1967).

A classic essay by Georg Simmel, "The Stranger," offers an insightful exploration into our cultural beliefs about those we do not know. See *The Sociology of Georg Simmel*, edited by K. Wolff (New York: Free Press, 1950, pp. 402–408).

Some recent and very readable essays on the topic of family violence can be found in *Current Controversies on Family Violence*, edited by Richard J. Gelles and Donileen R. Loseke (Newbury Park, CA: Sage, 1993).

EXERCISES

1. Interview 10–15 people about their working "models" of crime. Be sure to obtain information on such things as the appearance of the typical criminal, the location of the typical crime, the typical criminal offense, and so on. Determine if a general model emerges, and discuss how this model allows certain acts to escape the label "criminal."

2. This chapter provides a profile of the social patterns of murder: age, gender, site, social class. Go to your local or university library and collect similar statistics for the crimes of assault, robbery, and burglary. Based on your data, speculate on the ways in which the "face" of murder differs from other personal crimes . . . from property crimes.

CONVENTIONAL WISDOM TELLS US . . .

Honesty Is the Best Policy

■

. . . EXCEPT, OF COURSE, WHEN REPORTING YOUR
INCOME, REVEALING YOUR AGE, SPARING THE
FEELINGS OF ANOTHER—THE LIST CAN GO ON
AND ON. IN THIS ESSAY, WE EXPLORE THE
CONDITIONS UNDER WHICH LYING IS VIEWED AS
NORMAL. IN SO DOING, WE USE LYING AS A CASE
STUDY THAT APTLY DEMONSTRATES BOTH THE
PERVASIVENESS AND THE RELATIVE NATURE
OF DEVIANCE.

■

"Honesty is the best policy," wrote Ben Franklin. From an early age, parents and teachers urge us to embrace this sentiment. We learn cultural fables and tales that verify the value of truthfulness—remember Pinocchio or George Washington and the cherry tree? Similarly, religious doctrine turns honesty into law with lessons such as "Thou shalt not lie." In civics class, individuals learn that perjury—lying while under oath—is an illegal offense.

Prohibitions against lying are among the earliest norms to which individuals are socialized. **Norms** are social rules or guidelines that direct behavior. They are the "shoulds" and "should nots" of social action, feelings, and thought. These lessons continue throughout life. As we grow older, we witness firsthand the ways in which dishonesty can lead to the downfall of individuals, families, careers, communities—even presidencies. Indeed, many social commentators identify the Watergate incident, and the high-level lying that accompanied it, as the basis for today's widespread public distrust toward the U.S. government (Ekman 1992; Leone 1994).

The conventional wisdom on honesty is strong. Yet, it is interesting to note that almost as early as we learn prohibitions against lying, we also learn how to rationalize the telling of lies. We learn that "little white lies" are not as serious as "real lies." We learn that context matters: lying to strangers is not as serious as lying to friends; lying to peers is more excusable than lying to parents or authorities. We learn that lies don't count if we cross our fingers or wink while telling them. And we learn that lies told under duress are not as awful as premeditated or "bald-faced lies" (Ekman 1992).

Thus, despite conventional wisdom to the contrary, lying stands as a ubiquitous social practice. Children lie to parents, and parents lie to grandparents. Employees lie to employers, and employers lie to regulators. Presidents lie to Congress and governments lie to their people. Indeed, there may be no social sphere to which lying is a stranger.

What explains the prevalence of lies when conventional wisdom so strongly supports honesty? What accounts for the discrepancies between what we say about lies and what we do? Is lying wrong? Is it deviant or not?

Society's contradictory stance toward lies illustrates a critical point about the overriding issue of deviance. **Deviance** is typically defined as any act that violates a social norm. Definitions of deviance are rarely "black and white." Rather, determining what is deviant is a relative process because norms can vary with time, setting, or public consciousness. Thus, today's deviant behaviors may be tomorrow's convention. (Think of some of the recent "deviant behaviors" that subsequently entered the realm of conformity: long hair on men, jeans on students, smoking among women.)

Because lying, like all deviant acts, is variable, sociologists distinguish between two types of lies: deviant lies and normal lies. **Deviant lies** are falsehoods always judged to be wrong by a society; they represent a socially unacceptable practice, one that can devastate the trust that enables interaction within a complex society of strangers. **Normal lies** are a socially acceptable practice linked to productive social outcomes. Individuals rationalize and legitimate normal lies as the means to a noble end: the good of one's family, colleagues, or country. A lie's relative deviancy or normalcy depends on who tells it; when, where, and why it is told; to whom it is told; and the outcome of its telling (Manning 1974, 1984; Ruane, Cerulo, and Gerson 1994).

For example, withholding your AIDS diagnosis from your elderly mother may be viewed as an act of mercy. In contrast, withholding the diagnosis from a sex partner likely would be viewed as immoral or potentially criminal. Similarly, lying about one's age to engage a new romantic interest is likely to be defined as significantly less offensive than lying about one's age to secure social security benefits. As with all forms of deviance, lie classification is based on context. We cannot classify a lie as deviant or normal on the basis of objectively stated criteria.

Although deviant lies can destroy social relations, normal lies can function as a strategic tool in the maintenance of social order. Normal lies become a "lubricant" of social life; they allow both the user and receiver of lies to edit social reality. Normal lies can facilitate ongoing interaction (Goffman 1974; Goleman 1985; Sacks 1975).

If our boss misses a lunch date with us, we tell her or him it was "no big deal," even if the missed appointment led to considerable inconvenience in our day. Similarly, we tell a soldier's parents that their son or daughter died a painless death even if circumstances suggest otherwise. In both of these cases, the normal lie represents a crucial mechanism for preserving necessary social routines.

In the same way, normal lies also are important in maintaining civil social environments. Thus, when a truthful child announces someone's obesity, foul smell, or physical handicap while on a shopping trip at the mall, parents are quick to instruct him or her in the polite albeit deceptive practices of less-than-honest tact. Similarly, the daily contact between neighbors inherent in most city and suburban layouts leads us to tell a rather bothersome neighbor that she or he is "really no trouble at all." In both of these cases, honesty would surely prove a socially destructive policy—the normal lie allows individuals to preserve the interaction environment.

What processes allow us to normalize an otherwise deviant behavior such as lying? Sociologists Gresham Sykes and David Matza (1957) identify five specific techniques of neutralization that prove useful in this regard. **Techniques of neutralization** are methods of rationalizing deviant behavior. In essence, these techniques allow actors to suspend the control typically exerted by social norms. Freed from norms in this way, social actors can engage in deviance. Using the techniques of neutralization—denial of responsibility, denial of injury, denial of victim, condemning the condemner, and appealing to higher loyalties—individuals effectively explain away the deviant aspects of a behavior such as lying. Individuals convince themselves that their actions, even if norm violating, were justified given the circumstance. Once an individual has learned to use these techniques, she or he can apply them to any deviant arena, thereby facilitating an array of deviant behaviors: stealing, fraud, vandalism, personal violence, and so on.

Employing Sykes and Matza's techniques, then, one might *deny responsibility* for a lie, attributing the action to something beyond one's control: "My boss forced me to say he wasn't in." One might *deny injury* of the lie, arguing that the behavior caused no real harm: "Yes, I lied about my age. What's the harm?" One might *deny the victim* of the lie by arguing that the person harmed by the lie deserves such a fate: "I told her that her presentation was perfect. I can't wait for it to bomb; she deserves it." *Condemning one's condemner* allows an individual to neutralize a lie by shifting the focus to how often one's accuser lies: "Yes, I lied about where I was tonight, but how often have you lied to me about that very thing?" Finally, *appealing to higher loyalties* neutralizes lying by connecting it to some greater good: "I didn't tell my wife I was unfaithful because I didn't want to jeopardize our family."

Just as individuals learn to neutralize certain lies, they also learn appropriate reactions to normal lies. With time and experience, individuals learn that challenging normal lies can be counterproductive. Such challenges can disrupt the social scripts that make collective existence possible. **Social scripts** document the shared expectations that govern those interacting within a particular setting or context.

If the social audience wishes to maintain smooth social exchange, then each member must learn to tolerate certain lies. By doing so, individuals downplay deviations from the social script. Like actors on a stage, individuals ignore momentary lapses and faux pas so that the "performance" can continue (Goffman 1959, 1974).

The new U.S. military policy of "Don't ask, don't tell," for example, is built on such logic. Military officials look the other way in order to avoid the potential disruption embodied in a truthful response to the question of homosexuality. Similarly, the spouse who fails to question a partner's change in routine or habit may do so in an effort to shield the marriage from the threat posed by potential truths.

A variety of social settings require that we take someone at their word or accept things at face value. We learn to listen with half an ear, to take things "with a grain of salt," or to recognize that people don't always "say what they mean or mean what they say." All such options are strategies of interaction maintenance—strategies that demand tolerance for the normal lie.

This excursion on lying raises important points about deviance in general. Despite norms forbidding it, deviance happens. Studies show that nearly every member of the U.S. population engages in some deviant behaviors during their lifetime (Adler and Lamber 1993). Indeed, Emile Durkheim (1938), a central figure in sociology, suggested that deviance would occur even in a society of saints.

Theorist Edwin Lemert contended that certain types of deviance are universal. Everyone, at one time or another, engages in such acts. Lemert referred to these universal occurrences of deviance as primary deviance. **Primary deviance** refers to isolated violations of norms. Such acts are not viewed as deviant by those committing them and often result in no social sanctions. Deviance remains primary in nature as long as such acts "are rationalized or otherwise dealt with as functions of a socially acceptable role" (Lemert 1951: 75–76). (Note that normal lying fits easily within this category.)

Herein lies the importance of techniques of neutralization and social scripts of tolerance. The techniques and scripts can keep us and our behaviors within the confines of primary deviance. They can keep us from moving to a more significant type of deviance, which Lemert refers to as secondary deviance. **Secondary deviance** occurs when a labeled individual comes to view herself or himself according to that which she or he is called.

Although all of us engage in primary deviance, relatively few of us become ensnared by secondary deviance. The techniques of neutralization allow the social actor to rationalize periodic infractions of the rules. Social scripts of tolerance allow the social audience to accept such infractions as well. As such, social audiences refrain from publicly labeling the "neutralized" actor as deviant. By anchoring an individual in primary deviance, the techniques of neutralization ease the return to a conforming status.

When it comes to norms on lying, or any other social behavior, conformity may be, as conventional wisdom suggests, the best policy. However, when we understand the complexity involved in the workings of norm violations, we cannot help but note that deviating from the "best policy" may not be all that deviant after all.

LEARNING MORE ABOUT IT

"The Lie" by Georg Simmel is a classic sociological essay on the topic. See *The Sociology of Georg Simmel*, edited by K. Wolff (New York: Free Press, 1950, pp. 312–316). Paul Ekman's *Telling Lies* (New York: W. W. Norton, 1992) is a highly readable and comprehensive examination of experimental research on lying. For a comprehensive sociological review of lying see J. Barnes's *A Pack of Lies: Toward A Sociology of Lying* (New York: Cambridge University Press, 1994).

For a detailed consideration of normal lying in an occupational setting, consult Janet Ruane, Karen Cerulo, and Judith Gerson's 1994 article, "Professional Deceit: Normal Lying in an Occupational Setting" (*Sociological Focus* 27 (2): 91–109). For an engaging review of how a variation on the normal lie operates in the world of students, see Stan Bernstein's 1972 article "Getting It Done: Notes on Student Fritters." (*Urban Life and Culture 1*: 2).

Gresham Sykes and David Matza's 1957 article "Techniques of Neutralization: A Theory of Delinquency" (*American Sociological Review 22*: 664–670) offers readers some insight into the dynamics that feed the legitimation process.

EXERCISES

1. Consider the normal lie as it exists in the world of advertising. Collect a sample of ads targeting different audiences: adults versus children, men versus women, yuppies versus the elderly. Is there any pattern in the ads' reliance on normal lying as a marketing technique? What would be the ramifications of unmasking the normal lie in advertising?

2. Consider the function of normal lying in the successful completion of the student role. Are there ways in which dishonesty has been institutionalized in the student role? What do your own experiences and the experiences of your friends suggest are the important sources of such deception?

Social Institutions:
Marriage and Family

■

CONVENTIONAL WISDOM TELLS US . . .

The Nuclear Family Is the Backbone of American Society

■

MOM, DAD, AND THE KIDS—IS THIS THE UNIT ON WHICH AMERICAN SOCIAL LIFE IS BUILT? THIS ESSAY DOCUMENTS THE HISTORY OF FAMILY IN AMERICA, SHOWING THAT THE NUCLEAR FAMILY IS A RELATIVELY RECENT PHENOMENON AND ONE THAT SOON MAY BE REPLACED BY OTHER FORMS OF FAMILY. IN ADDITION, THE STABILITY OF THE NUCLEAR FAMILY IS EXPLORED IN LIGHT OF IDYLLIC STEREOTYPES.

■

A tour of Broadway, listening to a top-40 radio station, or hearing a speech by a major political figure—all show us to be a nation hooked on nostalgia. We yearn for the "good old days," a time when life was simpler, the nation was prosperous, and nuclear families prayed and stayed together.

A return to the family—the plea rests at the heart of 1990s rhetoric. Today's popular culture touts the world of the Andersons ("Father Knows Best"), the Cleavers ("Leave It to Beaver"), and the Cunninghams ("Happy Days") as an American ideal. Working dads, stay-at-home moms, and care-free yet respectful kids—conventional wisdom promotes such units as the cornerstone of this nation.

Many believe that only a return to our nuclear "roots" can provide a cure for our ills. Only the rebirth of nuclear family dominance can restore the backbone of our floundering society. Are conventional sentiments correct? Will a return to this nation's nuclear roots bring stability to American society?

A macro-level analysis of family in America suggests this nation's family "roots" are not necessarily located in the nuclear unit. (A **macro-level analysis** focuses on broad, large-scale social patterns as they exist across contexts or through time.) Rather, the shape and form of the "typical" American family has changed quite frequently throughout our nation's history. Historically speaking, the nuclear family is a fairly recent as well as a relatively rare phenomenon. (At present, only about 26% of American families fit the nuclear model.) The **nuclear family** refers to a self-contained, self-satisfying unit composed of father, mother, and children. Knowing this, it is difficult to identify the nuclear family as either *the* traditional family format or the rock upon which our nation was built. Further, social history reveals that the nuclear family's effects on American society has often proved less positive than nostalgic images suggest.

Historically, American families have displayed a variety of forms. In pre-industrial times, the word *family* conjured up an image quite different from the nuclear ideal. Preindustrial families were truly interdependent economic units. All members of the household—parents, children, and quite often boarders or lodgers—made some contribution to the family's economic livelihood. Work tasks overlapped gender and age groups. However, parental contributions were ended frequently by early mortality. In the pre-industrial era, average life expectancy was only 45 years (Rubin 1996). One-third to one-half of colonial children had lost at least one parent by the time they reached 21 years of age (Greven 1970).

During the early stages of industrialization, the face of the family changed. Many families of the era began to approximate the "dad-mom-and-the-kids" model. Yet early industrialization also was a time when the number of extended families in the United States reached its historical high. An **extended family** is a unit comprising father, mother, their children, and other blood relatives such as grandparents or aunts and uncles. Although the extended family has never been a dominant form in U.S. society, 20% of this period's families contained grandparents, aunts, uncles, or cousins (Hareven 1978).

The stay-at-home mom—a mom who focused exclusively on social activities and household management—first appeared in America's middle-class Victorian families. This new role for Victorian women, however, came on the backs of working-class mothers and children. Many women and children of the working class were hired as domestics for middle-class families. In the early days of industrialization, such women and children also were frequently employed as factory workers. Only as industrialization advanced were working-class women relegated to the home sphere (Reskin and Padavic 1994). By the late 1800s, a typical family included a mother who worked exclusively at home. Children, however, continued to work outside the home for wages. Indeed, at the turn of the century, children comprised nearly a fourth of all textile workers in the South (Wertheimer 1977). In the Northeast, children were regularly employed in industry or the mines (Bodnar 1987; Schneiderman 1967). Approximately 20% of American children were relegated to orphanages because parents could not afford to raise them (Katz 1986).

The modern nuclear family that Americans so admire did not fully come into its own until the 1950s. A careful review of families emerging from this period suggests a unit that both confirms and contradicts conventional wisdom's idyllic models.

Historian Stephanie Coontz (1992) notes that the nuclear unit of the 1950s emerged as a product of the times. The family model of the era developed in response to a distinct set of socioeconomic factors. The post-World War II decade saw great industrial expansion in the United States. The nation enjoyed a tremendous increase in real wages. Further, Americans experienced an all-time high in their personal savings, a condition that resulted largely from U.S. war efforts. The nuclear family became a salient symbol of our country's newfound prosperity.

Consumerism was a significant hallmark of 1950s' nuclear families. Spending devoted to products that enhanced family life brought significant increases in our nation's GNP (gross national product). Indeed, the buying power of the 1950s family was phenomenal. During the postwar era, for example, home ownership increased dramatically. Federal subsidies enabled families to buy homes with minimal down payments, and low interest (2–3%) guaranteed 30-year mortgages. It is estimated that half the suburban homes of the 1950s were financed in this way (Coontz 1992).

Consumerism added a new dimension to the American family. Cars, cheap gas, and new highways made mobility a part of family life. The purchase of televisions converted the home into a true entertainment center. Indeed, 86% of the U.S. population owned TVs by the decade's end, bringing about a 50% decrease in movie theater attendance (Jones 1980). Other new and improved appliances made the home an efficient and comfortable place to live. The growth of the credit card industry strengthened the nuclear family's consumer patterns and encouraged a "buy now and pay later" mentality (Dizard and Gadlin 1990; Ritzer 1995). And pay later we did. Some would argue that the debt-laden 1990s are the legacy of the spend-and-grow mentality established in the 1950s.

The buying power of the 1950s nuclear family suggested a unit with the potential to fulfill all needs. At first glance, this development may seem a positive aspect of the era, but some argue that it marked the beginning of a harmful trend in our society—the decline of community commitment. Such critics contend that by emphasizing the "private" values of the individual and the family, the nuclear unit intensified individualism and weakened civic altruism (Bellah, Madssen, Sullivan, Swidler, and Tipton 1985; Collier 1991; Sennett 1977). Thus, the seeds of our later decades of self-indulgence and excess may well have been planted in the nuclear family era of the 1950s. As historian Coontz observes, "The private family . . . was a halfway house on the road to modern 'me-first' individualism" (1992:98).

Consumerism, however, is only a part of the nuclear family's legacy. There were profound changes in domestic behavior patterns as well. In contrast to the ideal lives enjoyed by the Andersons, the Cleavers, or the Cunninghams, home life of the 1950s showed some problematic developments.

For example, couples married at younger ages than earlier generations had. The formation of a nuclear family was an integral part of "making it" in the United States. As a result, many people moved rapidly toward that goal. But the trend toward early marriage was not without cost. National polls showed that 20% of the period's married couples rated their marriages as unhappy—interestingly, a figure higher than any displayed in current polls. In the heyday of the nuclear family, millions of couples resolved their marital differences by living apart (Komarovsky 1962; May 1988; Mintz and Kellogg 1988).

The 1950s also saw couples starting families at younger ages than their predecessors. In addition, families were larger and grew more quickly than families of previous decades. More than ever before or since, married couples faced enormous pressure to have children. Indeed, *Life* magazine declared children to be a built-in recession cure (Jones 1980). But the emphasis on childbearing had some unintended consequences. The period saw a substantial increase in fertility rates, largely due to teenage pregnancies. (Kids were having kids—sound familiar?) Half of all 1950s brides were teenagers who had children within 15 months of getting married (Ahlburg and DeVita 1992). The number of out-of-wedlock babies placed for adoption increased by 80% between 1944 and 1955, and the proportion of pregnant brides doubled during this era (Coontz 1992).

City living was largely abandoned by families in the 1950s. The new young families of the era put down roots in the suburbs, which seemed ideal for breaking with old traditions. The suburbs were well suited to the newly emerging idea of the family as a self-contained unit, a unit that would supplant the community as the center of emotional investment and satisfaction. Fully 83% of the population growth in the fifties occurred in the suburbs. Indeed, *Fortune* magazine noted that more people arrived in the suburbs each year than had ever arrived at Ellis Island (Jones 1980).

Changing family lifestyles brought changes to the workplace as well. By 1952, two million more women were in the work force than had been there during World War II. This time, however, female entry into the workplace was not fueled by patriotic duty. Rather, many women were entering the work force to cover the rising costs and debts associated with the nuclear family's consumer mentality (Rubin 1996). Others went to work to help young husbands complete educational and career goals.

The working women of the 1950s faced a workplace less receptive to them than it had been to the "Rosie the Riveters" of the World War II era. The industries that had welcomed women during the war years now preferred to keep American women at home or in dead-end jobs. Popular magazines of the day ran articles examining the social menace and private dysfunction of working women.

The pressures and rejections faced by women in the workplace had important links to the amazing increase in production and use of newly developed tranquilizers: 462,000 pounds of tranquilizers were consumed in 1958 and 1.15 million pounds of tranquilizers were consumed in 1959! Consumers were overwhelmingly female (Coontz 1992).

In considering the realities of the nuclear family, it becomes clear that neither it nor any other family form can be a remedy for social ills. Debates on the virtue of the "good old days" or attempts to identify the perfect family form thus seem an exercise in futility. Each historical period, with its own combination of economic, political, and social forces, redefines perfection.

These thoughts may help us to better appreciate the risk entailed in trying to build current social policy around institutions whose times may have come and gone. Perhaps the best course of action today is to resist nostalgic "retrofitting" and instead assist the family in making adaptive changes to our current social circumstances. Such changes may well be the new "traditions" that future generations will yearn to restore.

LEARNING MORE ABOUT IT

Stephanie Coontz offers a detailed historical review of the American family from colonial times to the present in *The Way We Never Were: American Families and the Nostalgia Trap* (New York: Basic Books, 1992). In particular, the author systematically debunks many of our most cherished family myths.

For a detailed and thoroughly entertaining account of the 1950s' generation and beyond, readers should consult Landon Jones's *Great Expectations* (New York: Ballantine Books, 1980).

Expressing America: A Critique of the Global Credit Card Society by George Ritzer (Thousand Oaks, CA: Pine Forge, 1995) presents a sociologically informed analysis of the growth of consumerism and the credit industry.

EXERCISES

1. Use your sociological imagination to identify some key factors that prompt our present nostalgia for the past. For example, think in terms of historical and social developments that may help to explain why the past looks so good to us now.

2. We noted in this essay that nuclear families were a product of specific historic and socioeconomic conditions. Consider a family type common to the 1990s, the "blended family." Blended families are units that consist of previously married spouses and their children from former marriages. What are the current historic and socioeconomic conditions that explain the blended family phenomenon? What social policy changes might enhance the success of this family form?

CONVENTIONAL WISDOM TELLS US . . .

Marriage Is a Failing Institution

■

HIGH DIVORCE RATES, COUPLES LIVING
TOGETHER, THE NEED FOR "SPACE," FEAR OF
COMMITMENT—HAVE SUCH TRENDS DOOMED THE
INSTITUTION OF MARRIAGE? HERE, WE DISCUSS
RESEARCH SUGGESTING THAT THE PRACTICE OF
MARRIAGE IS ALIVE AND WELL DESPITE
CONVENTIONAL WISDOM TO THE CONTRARY. WE
ALSO NOTE THE HISTORICAL "POPULARITY" OF
DIVORCE IN AMERICA AND SPECULATE ON WHY
SUCH A TREND MARKS OUR CULTURE.

■

Politicians say it and social commentators lament it: Many of our current social and economic problems stem from deteriorating family values. The conventional wisdom on the matter suggests that high divorce rates are jeopardizing the future of marriage and the family. Many fear that "till death us do part" has become a promise of the past. Are such fears well-grounded? Is marriage really a failing institution?

Most research on the matter suggests little cause for such alarm. Indeed, a variety of indicators document that marriage remains one of society's most viable social institutions. **Marriage** refers to a socially approved economic and sexual union. A **social institution** consists of behavior patterns, social roles, and norms, all of which combine to form a system that ultimately fulfills an important need or function for a society.

In the United States, a higher proportion of the population marries than in *any* other modern industrial society (U.S. Bureau of the Census 1994a). Approximately 90% of all American men and women eventually marry (although the percentage may be declining for women (Bloom and Bennett 1990). Indeed, fewer people remain single today than did at the turn of the century.

In the United States, the marriage institution enjoys much "positive press." Americans identify a good marriage as the key to overall happiness, and the majority of married adults in the United States indicate that they are happy with their marriages. Further, surveys show that married couples are more likely than single individuals to report feeling happy with their lives (Strong and DeVault 1989; NORC 1994).

This happiness quotient is an important resource for married couples because current marital partnerships have the potential to be long-lasting. Overall increases in life expectancy and decreases in death rates mean that couples marrying in the 1990s are more likely to celebrate their 40th wedding anniversary than were their counterparts of the early 1900s (Skolnick 1991).

Marriage in the United States occurs with great frequency and generates high overall satisfaction for those who enter the union. What, then, explains our growing fears regarding the institution's failure? Typically, divorce is cited as the primary threat to the health of the marriage institution. And, indeed, the United States has the highest divorce rate in the world (U. S. Bureau of the Census 1994a). Still our propensity toward divorce is not a recent or modern phenomenon.

Divorce is a rather old practice in America. The United States has ranked number one on the divorce scale since the late 1800s. The first American divorce was recorded in 1639 and occurred in Puritan Massachusetts (Riley

1991). The Puritans viewed unsuccessful marriages as obstacles to the harmony deemed important to their society. Consequently, divorce was regarded as a necessary tool for the *safeguard* of marriage, family, and community (Riley 1991; Salmon 1986; Weisberg 1975).

By the Revolutionary War, divorce was a firmly established practice in the colonies, one defended via the revolutionary values and rhetoric of our newly formed nation. Thomas Jefferson, for example, in preparing notes for a divorce case in Virginia, defended the right to a divorce, using the principles of "independence" and "happiness" (Riley 1991: 31). In 1832, divorce entered the White House. Andrew Jackson was the first to be elected to the presidency despite a much publicized marriage to a divorced woman (Owsley 1977).

By the mid-1800s, divorce was characterized as a right of those whose freedom was compromised by an unsuccessful marriage. In the years following the Civil War, the U.S. divorce rate increased faster than the rates of both general population growth and married population growth (Riley 1991: 79). By World War I, this nation witnessed one divorce for every nine marriages (Glick and Sung-Ling 1986). For a short time after World War II, there was one divorce for every three marriages of women over 30! In 1960, the U.S. divorce rate began to increase annually, until the rate doubled and peaked in 1982. Today, we average nearly one divorce for every two marriages. When viewed within its historical context, it is clear that divorce is an American tradition.

In considering high divorce rates in the United States, we must take care not to interpret these figures as an indictment of the marriage institution. Despite bad experiences in first-time marriages, better than 70% of divorced individuals eventually remarry. About half of these remarriages occur within three years of one's divorce (Cherlin 1992). (Note that second remarriages constitute approximately half of all recent marriages.) High remarriage rates indicate that divorce is clearly a rejection of a specific partner and not a rejection of marriage itself. Indeed, these remarriage patterns have prompted some observers of the family to recognize a new variation on our standard practice of monogamy—namely, serial monogamy. **Monogamy** refers to an exclusive union: one man married to one woman at one time. **Serial monogamy** refers to the practice of successive, multiple marriages— that is, over the course of a lifetime, a person enters into successive monogamous unions.

The prevalence of serial monogamy in the United States suggests that the old adage "Once burned, twice shy" does not seem to apply to the divorced. Indeed, the inclination to remarry—even after one has been "burned"—may provide the greatest testimony to the importance of marriage as a social institution.

Is there a positive side to divorce? Some research suggests that the high divorce rate does provide a latent function in U.S. society. A **latent function** is an unintended benefit or consequence of a social practice or pattern. Studies show that as divorce rates in the U.S. increase, so too do rates of marital satisfaction. Considering high divorce rates in conjunction with increasing marital satisfaction suggests that, in the long run, divorce may make marriage a healthier institution (Veroff, Douvan, and Kulka 1981). By dissolving unhappy unions, divorce frees individuals to create new and happy unions. Within happy marriages, fear of divorce also may encourage continued dedication to maintaining a successful union.

But despite the positive impact divorce can have on the marriage institution, the practice carries several manifest dysfunctions as well. A **manifest dysfunction** refers to an obvious negative consequence of a social practice or pattern. For example, divorce has highly negative effects on the emotional well-being of ex-spouses. Research documents that ex-spouses face an increased incidence of depression, loneliness, and alcohol use. Financial hardship also plagues victims of divorce. Such hardship targets divorced women in particular, as studies show significant decreases in the standard of living for divorced women and their children (Sorenson 1990; Whitehead 1993).

The children of a divorce often pay an undeniably high price. Such children display greater emotional conflict than children in intact families (Wallerstein and Blakeslee 1990). Further, the children of divorce are likely to "lose" one of their parents. Despite a growing trend toward joint parental custody of children, nonresidential parents often have little or no contact with their children. Most children of divorce live with their mothers, and most fathers visit such children rarely or not at all (Furstenberg 1988; Wallerstein and Blakeslee 1990). When stepparents enter the scene, children of divorce frequently must cope with the unwanted replacement of their biological parents (Cherlin and Furstenberg 1994; Nordheimer 1990). All of these factors led researchers Judith Wallerstein and Sandra Blakeslee (1990) to a sobering conclusion: About half the children of divorce experience long-lasting negative effects that seriously alter their quality of life.

Although divorce clearly poses serious problems for a society, the practice appears firmly rooted in the United States. Ironically, some suggest that the prevalence of divorce in our nation may stem from the heightened health and longevity of Americans. Historian Lawrence Stone (1989) argues that divorce is the functional substitute for death. In earlier periods of our history, marriages—good and bad alike—were typically terminated by death.

The high mortality rates that characterized colonial America, for example, guaranteed that most marriages lasted less than 12 years (Fox and Quit 1980). But as life spans grew longer and longer, marriages faced new tests. In the current day, promises of "till death us do part" now constitute oaths that can traverse decades. Surely, such a profound demographic shift has had an effect on our divorce rates (Wells 1982).

In addition to increased life expectancy, some contend that the ready availability of divorce in the United States helps to explain the prevalence of the practice. By 1970, every state in the union permitted divorce. In that same year, no-fault divorce was introduced in California, and many states quickly followed suit.

Yet, although easy access may contribute to the high rate of divorce in the United States, history reveals that the "absence" of a divorce option does little to save bad marriages. For example, in states that were slow to recognize divorce as a legal option (typically, the Southern states), marriages were far from indissoluble. In lieu of legal divorce, other adaptations were readily devised: annulments, desertion, migratory divorces (divorces sought after relocations to other states), premarital contracts, and separation agreements. Indeed, South Carolina's refusal to recognize divorce resulted in a curious development in the state's inheritance laws: mistresses (another popular adaptation to troubled marriages) were legally precluded from inheriting *any more than* 25% of a husband's estate (Riley 1991).

But longer life spans or ease of access do not tell the whole story regarding divorce in America. Our high divorce rates must be examined in light of some core American values. Consider, for example, American values relating to romantic love. Americans have long identified romantic love as the most important dimension of marriage. Indeed, it is the power and passion of love that convinces us to separate from our families of orientation and form new unions with others. A **family of orientation** is the family into which one is born.

The principle of a love-based marriage guarantees excitement and euphoria for the individuals involved. But linking marriage to romantic love simultaneously introduces a high risk to the institution as a whole. Love is a fickle enterprise. When the sparks of passion die, love can be fleeting. Love's fickle nature is exacerbated by the fact that people frequently fall in love with possibilities rather than realities—that is, they fall for what they *want* their future spouses to be rather than what they are (Berscheid and Hatfield 1983).

In short, love can and often does fade. And faded love can leave a marriage with no raison d'être, making it a union ripe for divorce. Indeed, some of the earliest U.S. divorce petitions—petitions filed in the 1600s and

1700s—referenced lost affections and love as a justification for divorce (Riley 1991). Knowing this, love may not be the strongest foundation for the marriage institution. Indeed, many other cultures of the world do not base marriages on love; some regard a loved-based marriage as a foolish endeavor (Jankowiak and Fischer 1992). Instead, marriages are arranged for social or economic reasons. There is some indication that these alternate factors result in more stable unions with higher survival rates than those motivated by love (Levine 1993).

Romantic love is only one American value that may be linked to the nation's high divorce rates. The pursuit of personal freedom, self-actualization, and self-gratification—all values on which the establishment and expansion of our country were based—are also quite compatible with our well-exercised "right" to divorce. Consider that the westward expansion of this country was fueled, in part, by settlers who carried the spirit of rugged individualism. Many who migrated to the West did so without the support or company of recalcitrant spouses. Under such conditions, liberal divorce laws in Western states and territories proved to be a valuable mechanism for resolving such migratory conflicts.

Liberal divorce policies also proved a boon to self-actualizing business entrepreneurs. For example, when social pressure from antidivorce factions saw Nevada increase its divorce residency requirement from six months to a year, Nevada businesspeople vigorously protested the change. Such a change posed a threat to the valuable revenues typically generated by the "divorce trade." Thus, in the interest of capturing more and more of the dollars spent in pursuing a divorce, Nevada eventually dropped its residency requirement to six weeks (Riley 1991).

If core American values contribute to high divorce rates, then a reversal of divorce trends in the United States may demand major cultural changes—changes that would be difficult to execute. For example, increasing marital stability may require that love give way to less romantic criteria in making marriage decisions. Yet, that such a shift would be made seems highly unlikely. A cursory review of television programming, movie plots, literature, or music clearly demonstrates that Americans are "in love" with the notion of love. Further, surveys from the 1960s through the 1980s document an increase in Americans' commitment to love as the basis for marriage (Simpson, Campbell, and Berscheid 1986).

Similarly, individualism's dire effects on many a happy marriage suggest that decreasing divorce rates may require an exchange of individualism for concerns of community. Again, however, such a change is unlikely. Individualism is arguably the "defining" American value. Proposed solutions to other social problems such as welfare, poverty, and homelessness recommend a recommitment to individual accomplishment and responsibility. The me-generation of the 1980s and the economic threats of the 1990s have put concerns for "number 1" at the forefront of American attentions (Collier 1991; Etzioni 1993).

In contrast, concerns of community occupy the "back burner" of the American agenda. For example, a 1991 national poll found that two-thirds of Americans *never* give any time to community activities (Patterson and Kim 1991). Similarly, national leaders, such as Speaker of the House Newt Gingrich, continue to fight community-minded programs such as the National Youth Corp on the grounds that volunteerism should be a "personal decision" rather than an institutionalized practice.

As community lost its place on the American agenda, some speculate that family filled the void. In many ways, family has become the substitute for community. In contrast to the America of the 1930s and 1940s, where "God, Home and Country" were the rule, the America of recent decades finds religion and civic concerns overpowered by issues of family. Current surveys show that Americans define their families as their single highest priority. Further, Americans note that they count on the family to be the primary source of their emotional well-being (Wattenberg 1985).

Ironically, Americans' heavy investments in family may make this unit increasingly vulnerable to the practice of divorce. When family experiences fail to yield the expected emotional benefits, American cultural traditions and laws make it possible to "cut our losses" and invest anew. Oddly enough, our restricted family focus may render the family more, rather than less, vulnerable to disruption (Giddens 1992).

Is marriage a failing institution? Hardly. But along with the health of marriage in America comes the health of divorce. Arguably, divorce is itself an established institution, one which facilitates the pursuit of some core American values. Without some changes to these values, we can well expect both high marriage rates and high divorce rates to be a rather permanent feature of our society.

LEARNING MORE ABOUT IT

Much of the historical data on divorce in this chapter were obtained from Glenda Riley's book, *Divorce: An American Tradition* (New York: Oxford University Press, 1991).

Stephen Parker's *Informal Marriage: Cohabitation and the Law* (New York: St. Martin's Press, 1990) examines "marriages" without that slip of paper. The work also offers a historical review of the institutionalization of marriage.

James Lincoln Collier offers a rather thorough and highly readable review of the moral transformation of American society in his book, *The Rise of Selfishness in America* (New York: Oxford University Press, 1991). In a similar vein, Amatai Etzioni offers a somewhat controversial petition for increased community in *The Spirit of Community: Rights, Responsibilities, and the Community* (New York: Crown, 1993).

EXERCISES

1. Trying to understand divorce in America provides a good opportunity for exercising our sociological imagination. Divorce, as it currently stands in our society, is not just a "private trouble"—a personal failing of the individual. Rather, it is a "public issue"—a phenomenon tied to a myriad of broader social, cultural, and historical events. Confusing public issues with private troubles results in misinformed social policy. Public issues cannot be remedied with individual-oriented solutions appropriate to private troubles. Instead, public issues require that we pay attention to changes in social forces that are larger than and transcend individuals. Recognizing divorce as a public issue, identify three appropriate targets for our reform efforts.

2. Go to your local or university library and collect recent statistics on national divorce rates as broken down by the following groups: African Americans, Asian Americans, Hispanics, and Whites of Western European origin. Attempt to explain any differences you find using information on the cultural values held within each group.

3. Love is the basis on which current American marriages are built. Think of at least two other possible foundations for the institution of marriage. In each case, what are the likely ramifications of changing the "rules" of choosing a mate?

Social Institutions:
The Economy

■

Welfare Is Ruining This Country

■

A FREQUENTLY EXPRESSED OPINION WHEN TALK TURNS TO WELFARE REFORM IS THAT TOO MANY PEOPLE ARE ON THE DOLE, AND TOO MANY RECIPIENTS HAVE OTHER OPTIONS. IN THIS ESSAY, WE REVIEW SOME OF THE LEAST UNDERSTOOD DIMENSIONS OF WELFARE AND EXPLORE EXACTLY WHERE WELFARE MONEYS ARE GOING.

■

Charges against the United States welfare system abound in conventional wisdom. Welfare recipients are thought to be lazy people. They are accused of lacking the motivation to earn an honest living, preferring instead to take handouts from the government. Further, the welfare system itself is believed to be riddled with fraud. It often is discussed as a program plagued by able-bodied con artists, people with no financial need, who nonetheless manage to collect welfare checks.

Conventional wisdom also tells us that welfare fails to help those on the dole. Rather, it creates further dependency among its recipients. As such, many argue that welfare expenditures are ruining this nation. Welfare represents too great a burden for a government facing unsettled financial times.

Is the conventional wisdom regarding welfare accurate? Is welfare simply a tax on the economy, one destroying American initiative? A fair assessment of the system requires us to evaluate the many charges against it.

Are welfare recipients simply lazy? No doubt some are. After all, laziness is a trait found in all social groups. However, it would be wrong to assume that the *typical* welfare recipient is a social loafer. A mother with dependent children is a more accurate portrait of the average welfare recipient. [Note that since the early 1990s, 21% of all U.S. children live in poverty (U.S. Bureau of the Census 1994a).]

So, you might ask: Why doesn't that mother try work instead of welfare? The disturbing truth is that many of the jobs currently available in our country—especially service sector jobs earmarked for women—simply pay too little to keep a family above the poverty line (Edin 1994; Reskin and Padavic 1994). The **poverty line** is the federal government's designation of the annual income a family requires to meet its basic needs. Currently, the poverty line is set at $15,000. This figure is periodically adjusted to reflect inflation as well as family size and region of the country.

Furthermore, accepting a minimum wage job actually can prove a "costly" proposition for the poor. Employment can deprive former welfare recipients of other essential benefits, such as food stamps and health care (Edin 1994). Low-paying jobs also fail to provide a solution to a major obstacle facing poor female heads of households: child care (Popkin 1990).

Hard work, then, does not necessarily save one from the need for government assistance. Census data indicate that over 5% of those working full-time nonetheless remain in the clutches of poverty (U.S. Bureau of Census 1993d). Indeed a family of four with both parents working full-time at minimum wage jobs will just barely keep their collective heads above the poverty line (Schwartz and Volgy 1992). Change the picture to a single-parent family—where only one parent's salary pays the bills—and the likelihood of warding off poverty is greatly reduced. With the development of unforeseen hardships such as illness, layoffs, home or car repairs, and so on, a hardworking, lower-income family could be plunged into official poverty. A hardworking family could find itself in need of welfare.

Do those who enter the welfare ranks engage in welfare abuse and fraud? Surely some do. But a close examination of welfare expenditures shows that such practices are the exception to the rule. For example, childbearing is generally cited as one of the most frequent vehicles of welfare abuse. Welfare recipients are said to bear additional children in order to sustain and/or increase the benefits they receive. Yet official statistics show that three-quarters of all welfare families have two or fewer children. Indeed, the typical family unit within the welfare system consists of a mother with one child (Funiciello 1990).

The image of the "overgrown" welfare household appears more grounded in fiction than in fact. Empirical evidence indicates that welfare payments do not prompt women to have more children. Thus, efforts to limit or decrease such payments may serve only to worsen the growing problem of juvenile poverty (Devine and Wright 1993; Jencks and Edin 1995; Levitan 1985; Wilson 1987).

Do those who enter the welfare system become hopelessly dependent on it? A large body of research says no. Those who turn to the government for financial help tend not to seek that assistance for very long. Despite the rather prevalent belief that welfare is a chronic dependency condition (that is, a long-lasting condition assumed to destroy one's will to work), census figures show that most people are on welfare for relatively short time periods. The average welfare stay is 2 years or less (Bedard 1991; Sherraden 1988).

It is also important to note that most welfare stays are not the result of being born to poverty. Rather, most poor families (half of which are headed by females) enter poverty as the result of life events such as unemployment, illness, or divorce (Sidel 1986). Only a very small percentage of American families remain permanently poor and therefore permanently tied to welfare programs.

Suppose we were all to agree that most welfare recipients are hardworking, honest individuals who simply need some temporary help. Isn't it still the case that the welfare system represents too great a financial burden for our country? To answer this question accurately, we must carefully distinguish among the terms *poverty, public assistance programs* (welfare programs), and *social insurance programs* of the welfare state.

The Bureau of the Census estimates that roughly 40 million Americans—about 15% of our population—live in poverty. **Poverty** refers to an economic state where one's annual income is below that judged necessary to support a predetermined minimal standard of living. Indeed, there are more poor now than at any other time since President Johnson launched his "war on poverty" (U.S. Bureau of the Census 1994b).

Only a portion of those living in poverty enter the welfare system via public assistance programs. **Public assistance programs** are those directed exclusively at the eligible poor—that is, recipients must meet income requirements. In the United States, less than half of the eligible poor receive any kind of cash assistance and only about half receive food stamps (U.S. Bureau of Census 1990b; 1993a). In the late 1980s, total federal payments under the Aid to Families with Dependent Children (AFDC) program were just under $9 billion. Although this figure may seem large to the average wage earner, it represents less than 1% of the annual federal budget (Funiciello 1990; Rubin 1996). In contrast, 27% of the federal budget is devoted to national defense.

As these figures show, America's financial burdens lie not with antipoverty, public assistance programs like AFDC, but elsewhere. More realistically, America's financial woes are located in social insurance programs like Social Security and Medicare. **Social insurance programs** are those that require payroll contributions from future beneficiaries. Neither eligibility for nor benefits from these programs are linked to financial need.

In the early 1990s, the annual costs of Social Security and Medicare reached $264 and $114 billion, respectively. Thus, in reality, social insurance programs—not antipoverty programs—are our largest "welfare" expenditures. Indeed, these social insurance programs constitute the largest part of what we have come to define as America's "welfare state"—a state that transcends poverty per se and instead offers protection based on our more general rights of citizenship (Bowles and Gintis 1982).

When we turn to facts and figures, we can quickly discredit the conventional wisdom on welfare. Yet, we must also concede that year after year conventional wisdom on this subject overpowers facts and figures. Why?

Some of our misconceptions regarding welfare no doubt are fueled by the profound changes occurring in the economic and occupational structure of our society. Americans today face a growing gap between the rich and poor (Center on Budget and Policy Priorities 1992). From 1977 to 1989, the incomes of the wealthiest 1% of Americans nearly doubled, whereas the remainder of the population saw either no improvement or a decline in their incomes (Mandel 1992). Further, census data indicate that the great middle class has decreased in size over the past decade, with those at the lower fringe of the middle class facing the greatest threats (Knutson 1992).

In the face of present economic circumstances, intergenerational upward mobility is no longer a birthright for most Americans. **Intergenerational upward mobility** refers to social status gains by children vis-à-vis their parents. In the 1950s, the average male worker could expect a 50% increase in income over the course of his working lifetime. This expectation is no longer a safe bet for the average worker. Rather, present-day workers find themselves competing in a global economy. As a result of this turn of events, many American jobs have been lost to other countries and wages for low-skill jobs have suffered a marked decline. Consequently, today's workers can look forward to only modest income increases—increases that may be followed by stagnation and backslides (Hout 1988). This disappointing picture is true even for those families headed by college graduates (Children's Defense Fund 1992).

Shifts in the occupational and economic structure of our society have shaken the very core of American values. Americans invest heavily in the idea that they can and will work their way up the socioeconomic ladder; these shifts threaten that belief. The growing inability to achieve the "American Dream" has left many people frustrated and searching for someone to blame. In this regard, the poor—and welfare recipients in particular—are easy scapegoats. The logic of the welfare system is completely inconsistent with fundamental American values: individual effort, equal opportunity, success, and upward mobility. Rather than promoting hard work and achievement, welfare programs institutionalize qualities that are directly opposite. In this way, welfare recipients come to constitute an out-group in our society (Feagin 1975; Lewis 1978). **Out-groups** are considered undesirable and are thought to hold values and beliefs foreign to one's own. An out-group is identified as such by an in-group, which holds itself in high esteem and demands loyalty from its members.

Individuals who can avoid poverty, regardless of their exact income, can count themselves as members of the hardworking in-group. Indeed, it is the negative image of the welfare out-group that keeps many poor and near-poor from accessing various forms of public assistance: "I may be poor, but I'm not on welfare."

The power of American values explains why we cling to conventional wisdom regarding welfare. This power also can help us better understand why few Americans denigrate society's wealthy sector, even when that wealth is gained at the expense of the working and middle class. Note that in 1993, the average salary of top corporate executives was 157 times higher than the average factory worker, 113 times higher than teachers, and 66 times higher than engineers (*Business Week* 1993). When we value individual effort and opportunity, tolerance of wealth must be expected. The wealthiest have already arrived where many of us would like to go. They are proof to us that individual efforts can pay off; they are proof that the American Dream, to which we are so committed, lives on.

To sustain the power of American values, we must lay the blame for poverty on the poor themselves. There is, of course, a certain irony and destructiveness to this process. Personalizing poverty deflects our attention from the social causes of poverty, such as changing occupational structure and lack of education. Such a stance lessens the likelihood that we will successfully reduce poverty. Indeed, without major social changes, social reproduction theory suggests that the American Dream will continue to elude the poor. **Social reproduction theory** maintains that existing social, cultural, and economic arrangements work to "reproduce" in future generations the social class divisions of the present generation.

One proponent of social reproduction theory, Pierre Bourdieu (1977a, 1977b), maintains that the aspirations of lower-class children are adversely affected by their class position. The lower-class child is immersed in a social world hostile to the American Dream. The objective realities of the lower-class environment deflate hopes of success; the restricted opportunity structure inherent in a lower-class location leads to reduced life aspirations.

Social reproduction is not the only obstacle to poverty reduction. Structural functionalists remind us that the elimination of poverty is highly unlikely as long as the poor among us serve valuable social functions. **Structural functionalism** is a theoretical approach that stresses social order. Proponents contend that society is a collection of interdependent parts that function together to produce consensus and stability. **Social functions** refer to the intended and unintended social consequences of various behaviors and practices.

Personalizing poverty sustains a lower class. The lower class, in turn, fulfills many needs for those in other social locations. For example, the poor provide society with a cheap labor pool. They also create countless job opportunities for others: for those wishing to help them—social workers, policy makers, and so on—as well as for those wishing to control them—police and corrections officers. The poor even provide financial opportunities for those wishing to take advantage of them—loan sharks, for example, and corporations seeking tax breaks via the food discard market (Funiciello 1990; Gans 1971; Jacobs 1988). And sustaining the poverty out-group enables the social mainstream to better define and reaffirm some of its most fundamental values and beliefs.

In light of these functions, we must reexamine the notion that welfare is ruining this country. Welfare may breed dependency, but dependency for whom? Given the social functions of the poor, welfare may breed a social dependency of the masses on the few, as the poor ultimately serve as vehicles by which mainstream values are assured.

LEARNING MORE ABOUT IT

To learn more about the gender and racial base of poverty, see Diana M. Pearce's 1983 article, "The Feminization of Ghetto Poverty" (*Society 21:* 1, pp. 70–74). See also J. Devine and J. D. Wright's *The Greatest of Evils* (New York: Aldine de Gruyter, 1993).

To learn more about the poor as social scapegoats, see Jeffrey Reiman's book *The Rich Get Richer and The Poor Get Prison* (New York: Macmillan. 1990).

The classic work on the functions of poverty is Herbert Gans's "The Uses of Poverty: The Poor Pay for All" [*Social Policy* (Summer 1971): 20–24].

EXERCISES

1. American values are one explanation for the triumph of conventional wisdom over facts. Choose another concept from the material covered thus far in your course and provide an alternate explanation of why welfare gets such a "bum rap."

2. The cut-off level for official poverty is arbitrary. Identify five different consequences of setting the cut-off point higher; identify five consequences of setting the cut-off point lower. Are the consequences you identify primarily functional or dysfunctional for mainstream Americans?

CONVENTIONAL WISDOM TELLS US . . .

Immigrants Are Ruining This Nation

■

WHY DON'T YOU GO BACK WHERE YOU CAME
FROM? THIS ANGRY CRY SEEMS TO BE GETTING
MORE AND MORE FAMILIAR AS THE UNITED
STATES FACES THE HIGHEST LEVELS OF
IMMIGRATION IN ITS HISTORY. IS IMMIGRATION
RUINING THIS NATION? THIS ESSAY REVIEWS
THE HISTORICAL IMPACT AND FUTURE TRENDS
OF IMMIGRATION IN THE UNITED STATES.

■

"Why don't you go back where you came from?" It is a familiar taunt that most of us have heard. Here in the United States, it is a question often born of ethnic and racial prejudice. And, increasingly, feelings of prejudice target members of immigrant groups. **Prejudice** refers to the prejudgment of individuals on the basis of their group membership. **Immigrant groups** contain individuals who have left their homelands in pursuit of a new life in a new country.

Immigration has always been a fact of American life. The earliest European settlers were immigrants to the 3–8 million Native Americans who already occupied the continent. At the first census, in 1790, approximately one in five Americans was an"immigrant" slave brought from Africa (U.S. Bureau of the Census 1993c). And since the mid-19th century, approximately 60 million immigrants have arrived in the United States. Undeniably, most Americans are truly indebted to their immigrant ancestors—all but 0.8% of us are descendents of immigrants (Schuman and Olufs 1995).

Since 1990, more than one million *documented* immigrants have entered the United States each year. Indeed, the Census Bureau estimates that immigration rather than increases in the birth rate will account for over 90% of the U.S. population growth that occurs between now and the year 2050. In light of such figures, the conventional wisdom on immigration suggests that the phenomenon has gotten out of hand. More and more, public sentiments urge severe limitations on the acceptance of new immigrants to our shores (Church 1993).

Given America's immigration history, the current conventional wisdom on the subject is ironic. We find ourselves casting doubt on the value of immigrants in a nation long considered the "land of immigrants." As evidenced by annual parades and festivals, a great many hyphenated-Americans take pride in their diverse ancestral roots. At the same time, our daily newspapers and television newscasts document anti-immigrant sentiments that currently run high and frequently run violent. Commentaries filled with fear, distrust, and hate are becoming a staple of talk-radio broadcasts. Even some presidential primary candidates have attempted to win election by "wooing" the anti-immigrant vote.

Is the current conventional wisdom on immigration justified? Do these sentiments reflect a new anti-immigrant trend? Or are these anti-immigrant sentiments more common and long-standing than we realize?

The immigration history of the United States is nothing if not complex. Despite the message delivered by the "Lady in the Harbor," the United States has seldom greeted immigrants with totally open arms. Descendents of the first immigrant settlers, white Anglo-Saxon Protestants from England, were slow to welcome other newcomers. Rather, they expressed concern about "new" and undesirable immigrants, and organized against those arriving from Germany, Ireland, Poland, Italy, and other white ethnic countries (Fallows 1983). In the same decade that the Statue of Liberty first beckoned immigrants to our shores, a group of U.S. residents founded the first all-WASP (White Anglo-Saxon Protestant) country club; these residents also established the *Social Register*, a list identifying the exclusive "founding" families of the United States (Baltzell 1987). In the 1920s, President Hoover freely expressed clear anti-immigrant sentiments when he encouraged New York City's mayor, Fiorello La Guardia, the son of immigrants, to go back where he belonged. And from 1921 to 1968, the government used a quota system to regulate and limit immigration. These examples suggest that, although the United States proudly touts its immigration history, immigration in the United States has always been characterized by a love–hate relationship.

Americans' love–hate stance toward immigration may be the product of certain core cultural values. A **cultural value** is a general sentiment that people share regarding what is good or bad, right or wrong, desirable or undesirable.

We are a nation strongly committed to economic opportunity and advancement. At various times and to various parties, the labor of immigrants has provided one sure route to economic betterment. For example, estimates suggest that nearly half of colonial-era European immigrants came to America as indentured servants who were willing to work off their debts for a chance at a better life in the new land. Similarly, the forced immigration of African slaves provided cheap labor for the South's labor-intensive agricultural development (Daniels 1990). The construction of the transcontinental railroad and the economic development of the West depended on the willing and able labor of Chinese immigrants. And Japanese immigrants were welcomed as cheap, reliable labor for Hawaiian sugar plantations. In short, immigration has benefited many U.S. enterprises, industries, and corporations.

The ties that link immigrants to traditional American cultural values have not only benefited big business. The immigration experience has advanced the lives of countless immigrants as well. Indeed, the crush of immigrants in the mid-19th century was prompted by the immigrants' hopes that they could escape their own poverty via the economic expansion that was taking place in the United States. Such promises of economic betterment continue to attract immigrants to our shores, even amidst current trends toward economic globalization. The promise proves a potent one. Even the lowest-paying jobs in the United States are an improvement over those most new immigrants left behind. Wages for unskilled labor in the United States, for example, are 7 times higher than wages in South Korea, 10 to 15 times higher than wages in Central America, and 35 times higher than wages in China (Backer, Smith, and Weiner 1993, Bonacich, Cheng, Chinchilla, Hamilton, and Ong 1994; Braun 1991; Peterson 1992).

Cultural emphasis on economic advancement and opportunity helps to explain the affinity between the United States and immigrants. But such emphasis also helps to explain our long history of resisting immigrants. American tolerance for immigrants decreases whenever immigrants prove a threat to the economic well-being of "traditional" American workers. Indeed, the strongest support for immigration restrictions has often come from organized labor (Schuman and Olufs 1995).

Recall that Chinese immigrants played a critical role in the construction of the transcontinental railroad. However, the Chinese Exclusion Act of 1882 was passed when Chinese immigrants began to be viewed as a threat to the white labor force. Similarly, Mexicans were welcomed immigrants to the United States during the labor shortages imposed by World War II and again during the farm labor shortages of the 1950s. However, in the 1960s and the 1980s, when traditionally white labor jobs were in jeopardy, attempts were made to stem the flow of Mexican immigrants (Schuman and Olufs 1995).

In the 1990s, economic changes have created a double bind for the traditional American work force. Specifically, many low-wage jobs are leaving America for more profitable locations abroad. Further, more and more foreign workers are entering America and offering direct competition for the low-wage jobs that remain. These economic realities play a role in fueling current anti-immigrant sentiments.

Americans' approach-avoidance toward immigrants is further explained by referring to the basic processes of group dynamics. We refer specifically to conventional patterns by which in-groups and out-groups develop. The people who constitute the group to which one belongs form an **in-group.** An in-group holds itself in high esteem and demands loyalty from its members. In-groups then define others as members of an **out-group.** Out-groups are considered undesirable and are thought to hold values and beliefs foreign to one's own. American society consists of a variety of ethnic groups. These groups frequently are ranked relative to their tenure in the country.

But each wave of immigration to a country establishes new population configurations. In general, the most established immigrant groups cast themselves in the role of the in-group. Such groups define themselves as the "senior" and, thus, most valid representatives of a nation. These in-groups cast those that follow them in the role of out-group. Recent arrivals are stigmatized as foreign elements to an established mold.

Research demonstrates that members of in-groups carry unrealistically positive views of their group. At the same time, in-group members share unrealistically negative views of the out-group (Tajfel 1982). Because newcomers are viewed relative to those with earlier claims, the very process of immigration perpetuates social conflict. Indeed, the mechanics of immigration seem to guarantee a hostile boundary between the old and the new, between established ethnic groups versus recent arrivals.

In light of Americans' historical relationship with immigrants, should we simply dismiss current anti-immigrant sentiments as "business as usual"? Perhaps not.

Figure 17.1 shows that the large majority of early immigrants to the United States were of European descent. Indeed, these European origins frequently are credited with facilitating past immigrants' transition to U.S. culture. The many shared customs and characteristics of various European ethnic groups facilitated the assimilation of each new European immigrant wave. **Assimilation** is the process by which immigrant groups come to adopt the dominant culture of their new homeland as their own.

By the year 2050, most immigrants will hail from Latin American, Asia, Africa, the Middle East, or the Pacific Islands. Even today, the vast majority of immigrants are from Asian (37%) or Latin American (47%) nations (U.S. Immigration and Naturalization Service 1992). These facts, in and of themselves, should hardly be cause for concern. The immigration history of such groups has been relatively successful. Asian Americans, for example, have the highest median family income and the lowest unemployment rates of any minority group in the United States today (Ong 1994). Further, various Asian-American subgroups boast impressive indicators of success. The poverty rate of Japanese Americans is half that of the United States as a whole. Similarly, the proportion of Chinese Americans who graduate from college is twice the national average (U.S. Bureau of Census 1993c). Indeed, Asian Americans have a remarkable record for gaining entrance to our best colleges and universities (Brand 1987).

Hispanic immigrants to the United States can point to similar triumphs. Although it is true that the economic conditions of Hispanic Americans tend

FIGURE 17.1

Population Ancestry (U.S. Bureau of the Census 1994)

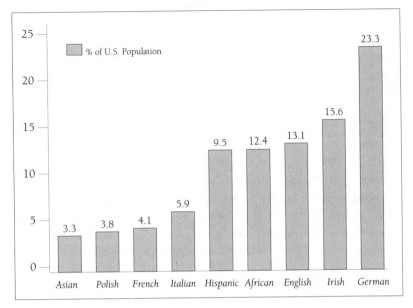

to lag behind national averages (the income of Hispanics is only two-thirds the U.S. average), the number of affluent Hispanic households—those with an income of $50,000 or more—is on the rise. Such households increased by 284% from the early 1970s to the late 1980s (O'Hare 1990). Further, during the latter half of the 1980s, the number of Hispanic professionals increased by 50% (Schwartz 1989). Hispanic households also reaffirm important core American values. The family, for instance, is greatly respected in Hispanic culture, a sentiment reflected in high rates of marriage and low rates of divorce for Hispanic Americans.

In light of the success rates posted by "model" Asian and Hispanic Americans, we must consider that current anti-immigrant sentiments may be based on issues of race. Visible physical differences, as well as a lack of familiar cultural practices, make the assimilation of "new" immigrant groups more difficult than it was for earlier immigrants. New, non-European immigrants may lack the physical and cultural similarities necessary for eventual acceptance as part of society's in-group.

If immigration and population trends develop as predicted, anti-immigrant sentiments fueled by issues of race may get worse before they get better. Demographers tell us that the dominant white population of U.S. society will become the numerical minority by the year 2050. By 2050, African Americans, Hispanics, Asian Americans, and Native Americans are expected to account for half the U.S. population (Pear 1992). If these projections are accurate, future immigration, in a very profound sense, will change the status quo. The practice of assimilation may necessarily give way to multiculturalism. **Multiculturalism** accentuates rather than dilutes ethnic and racial differences. Such an environment might strip in-groups of dominance and power. In contrast to the adversarial stance of the in-group/out-group design, a multicultural structure demands that all groups be viewed as equally valued contributors to the mainstream culture.

Immigration projections suggest that the United States is moving closer to being a microcosm of the world. Our nation will experience an increase in the diversity that already characterizes the younger generations of Americans. Such changes could bring us closer to fully realizing the motto that appears on all U.S. currency: *E Pluribus Unum*—One formed from many. Thus, current and future attitudes toward immigrants in America will hinge on our readiness to deal with fundamental population change.

Certainly, some Americans will resist this development, arguing that it threatens our national identity and changes our national "face." Contemporary movements against bilingual education are evidence of such resistance. Nevertheless, others will view our changing population as a positive economic opportunity. Consider that economists forecast a very different world for coming generations of Americans. More and more of us will be earning our livings in the service sector of an increasingly global, postindustrial economy. Postindustrial economies place a high premium on knowledge and information (Drucker 1993). Thus, those who can work with symbols and ideas as a means to problem solving and revenue enhancement can expect to do best in the new economic arena (Reich 1991).

Framed in this way, new immigration patterns may help supply us with a new source of cultural capital (Archdeacon 1992). **Cultural capital** refers to attributes, knowledge, or ways of thinking that can be converted or used for economic advantage. By their familiarity with cultures now central to the world market, immigrants to the United States may well give our nation a competitive edge in a global playing field. Once again, immigrants to the United States may be the national resource that makes the United States a significant player in a new world economy.

LEARNING MORE ABOUT IT

For opposing views on the economic consequences of immigration in the United States, see a work by Vernon Briggs and Stephen Moore entitled *Still an Open Door?: U.S. Immigration Policy and the American Economy* (Washington, DC: The American University Press, 1994).

Those interested in an in-depth consideration of diversity issues facing today's college students should consult David Schuman and Dick Olufs' *Diversity on Campus* (Boston: Allyn and Bacon, 1995).

For an interesting and now classic discussion of the underside of American values, see Philip Slater's *The Pursuit of Loneliness: American Culture at the Breaking Point* (Boston: Beacon Press, 1970).

George Borgas offers a thorough discussion of the economic impact of immigrants in his book, *Friends or Strangers: The Impact of Immigrants on the U.S. Economy* (New York: Basic Books, 1990).

EXERCISES

1. Visit a library that has back copies of local telephone directories. Examine the entries in the yellow pages for a variety of categories—beauty salons, physicians, restaurants, and so on. What insights about immigration patterns can be gleaned from your data as you move from year to year.

2. Prepare several in-depth interviews with first-generation Americans—that is, people who were born in another country and immigrated to the United States. Find out about the conditions of their immigration, the reception they received in their new community, and, if appropriate, the reception they received at their new workplace or their new school. Try to vary the immigration background of your interview subjects; that is, choose individuals who traveled from different foreign countries. Consider whether one's status as an immigrant functions as a master status (see Essay 5 or 11).

3. Use your own college community to locate children of recent immigrants. Prepare an interview guide that will allow you to explore whether these individuals exist in two social worlds or cultures. (For example, how do language, food, fashion patterns, and so on vary from school to home?)

Social Institutions:
Education

∎

CONVENTIONAL WISDOM TELLS US . . .

Education Is the Great Equalizer

■

CONVENTIONAL WISDOM TELLS US THAT
EDUCATING THE MASSES WILL BRING EQUAL
OPPORTUNITIES TO PEOPLE OF ALL RACES,
ETHNICITIES, AND GENDERS. IN THIS ESSAY, WE
EXPLORE THE TRUTH OF THIS CLAIM AND
REVIEW THE PROGRESS WE HAVE MADE IN
BRINGING A QUALITY EDUCATION TO ALL.

■

The United States has earned a reputation as the land of opportunity, and the opportunity that so many of us desire is the improvement of our socio-economic lot. Intergenerational upward mobility is a key dimension of the American Dream. **Intergenerational upward mobility** refers to social status gains by children vis-à-vis their parents.

Historically, education has been offered as the route by which such mobility can best be realized. Our free common public school system, established just prior to the Civil War, was founded on the principle that everyone, regardless of social background, should be educated. Lester Ward, a prominent sociologist of the late 1800s thought that universal education would eliminate the inequalities associated with social class, race, and gender. Similarly, educational reformer Horace Mann promoted an expanded educational system as the antidote to poverty (Katz 1971).

Such sentiments have survived the test of time. We are a nation fueled by the belief that education will lead to equal opportunity for individual achievement and success. Former "Education President" George Bush aptly captured this cultural value, characterizing education as the "great lifting mechanism of an egalitarian society. It represents our most proven pathway to a better life."

The conventional wisdom on education reflects a structural functionalist view of society. **Structural functionalism** is a theoretical approach that stresses social order. Proponents contend that society is a collection of interdependent parts that function together to produce consensus and stability. This perspective links education to social stability in two ways. First, in taking their place in the education system, students learn the key norms, values, and beliefs of American culture. Second, by affording all students a chance to develop their skills and talents, education can channel the "best and the brightest" to key social positions.

Does the conventional view of education paint an accurate portrait? Is America's education system really the great equalizer?

To be sure, the American education system has grown dramatically over the past century. At the turn of the century, only 10% of U.S. youth earned a high school degree and only 2% earned a college degree (Vinorskis 1992). By World War I, primary education became compulsory in every state; by World War II, the same was true for secondary education.

At present, about 80% of Americans earn a high school degree; the majority of high school graduates go on to spend some time at college, with about 20% of Americans actually earning a college degree. Further, the face of our nation's college population has become more socially diverse over the past one hundred years. At the turn of the century, college students were primarily the sons of white, upper-class professionals. In contrast, today's college population includes the sons and daughters of all social classes and all racial and ethnic groups (U.S. Bureau of the Census 1993b).

In support of conventional wisdom, one must note a strong and positive association between income and education (Kosters 1990). Heads of households with professional graduate degrees earn about five times more than heads of households with less than a ninth-grade education [over $80,000 versus less than $20,000 dollars per year (*Mortenson Report* 1993)]. Further, much evidence suggests that the key to securing a good job rests not on one's knowledge or ability, but rather on the amount of education one achieves (Bowles and Gintis 1976). The benefits of education seem to touch even those who detour from life's conventional path: Earning a high school degree or working on a college degree while in prison is associated with lower rates of recidivism (Holloway and Moke 1986).

The statistics just quoted suggest that education's links to "the good life" are right on target. However, on closer examination one finds several situations that can weaken the strength of that bond. Education's "lifting mechanism" may not be fully functional for all social groups.

Several studies show that the economically disadvantaged fail to reap the benefits of higher education (Mehan 1992). Working-class and minority youths are less likely to attend college than are their upper-class counterparts. This trend holds true despite the intelligence of the student (Sewell and Shah 1968). Recent census data show that the "smart but poor" student is less likely to attend college than the "not-so-smart but rich" student. In fact, only 5% of the poorest fourth of 18–24-year-olds complete college compared with 65% of those in the wealthiest quarter (*Mortenson Report* 1993).

When lower-class students do attend college, they are more likely to attend a two-year rather than a four-year institution. This distinction is important as studies show that community colleges simply don't yield the same long-term dividends for students as four-year institutions. Students entering two-year colleges are far less likely to ultimately obtain their bachelor degrees than students entering four-year colleges (Veles 1985). In addition, studies confirm that one year at a community college results in lower occupational salaries and status dividends than one year at a four-year college (Monk-Turner 1990).

The greatest financial return on a college degree is reserved for graduates of elite or selective private colleges (Coleman and Rainwater 1978;

Useem and Karabel 1986). "Selective" colleges, however, are very selective about their student body. Gatekeeping practices of elite universities ensure that access to such institutions is restricted largely to members of the most privileged social classes. Educational ability proves less important than family background in gaining admission to Ivy League institutions (Karen 1990; Persell and Cookson 1990).

Education's equalizing mechanism often seems to fail ethnic and racial minorities as well. Both high school and college completion rates are lower for African Americans, Hispanic Americans, and Native Americans than they are for Whites (U.S. Census Bureau 1992, 1993b). Despite recent increases in the percentage of African-American and Hispanic-American high school graduates who go on to attend college, these figures continue to lag behind the percentage recorded for Whites. Further, minority students are less likely to pursue graduate education (Carter and Wilson 1993).

Such trends lead many to doubt the effectiveness of classroom instruction for minorities. These doubts are fueled further by the fact that as many as 40% of minority students report functional illiteracy (National Commission on Excellence in Education 1983). **Functional illiteracy** refers to a level of reading and writing skills lower than those possessed by the average eighth-grade student. Note that the negative effects of minority status exist over and above the effects of social class. Consequently, poor minorities are doubly disadvantaged when it comes to education and mobility.

Perhaps the most dramatic failure of education's equalizing powers is witnessed in the area of gender. The educational history of women in the United States bespeaks little in the way of equal opportunity or achievement. In the 1900s, the doors to high schools and subsequently colleges were opened to women. Indeed, in 1907, there were 110 women's colleges in the United States. However, only 32% of these women's colleges met even the most basic standards of a true higher-education program. Rather, most women's colleges were engaged in the task of preparing women for their "place" in society—homemakers. Government aid policies of the era reinforced this traditional tracking. Vocational training such as cooking, sewing, and home economics qualified for federal subsidies; commercial training did not (Stock 1978).

Women who wanted a "real" higher education were limited by restrictive college admission policies. Most elite schools of the East simply refused to accept women. Western institutions had more liberal policies, but such policies generally were driven by financial motives. Western colleges admitted women in an effort to ward off financial disaster. The most blatant example of this practice occurred at the University of Chicago. Faced with bankruptcy in 1873, the university decided to admit women. But when the financial situation of the university improved, the institution's stance toward female admissions changed dramatically. Women immediately were relegated to a separate junior college (Stock 1978).

The post-World War II era further compromised women's access to education. Prior to World War II, the percentage of women attending college increased steadily. However, postwar college admissions gave absolute priority to war veterans. Such policies forced women back into the home, despite the work they had done during the war to keep America producing (Stock 1978). Further, the postwar policy signaled the beginning of a long-term trend. Even today, women do not enjoy educational returns equal to those of men; the financial benefits of education are significantly less for women than for men at every level of educational achievement (see Essay 10).

Instances of class, racial, ethnic, and gender inequality lead many to doubt the conventional wisdom on education. Indeed, conflict theorists question education's ability to equalize. **Conflict theorists** analyze social organization and social interactions by attending to the differential resources controlled by different sectors of a society. Conflict theorists suggest that the U.S. education system actually transmits inequality from one generation to the next (Bidwell and Friedkin 1988; Bowles and Gintis 1976; Kozol 1991; Weis 1988).

The conflict view of education parallels structural functionalism in acknowledging the role of education within the socialization process. **Socialization** refers to the process by which we learn the norms, values, and beliefs of a social group, as well as our place within that social group. But in contrast to structural functionalists, conflict theorists argue that the goals of socialization vary according to the social class of students.

In Essay 11, we noted Jonathan Kozol's observations regarding racial inequalities in U.S. schools. Kozol argued that Whites and Non-Whites often learn different lessons within American schools. Kozol notes similar inequalities in comparisons of various social classes. (Indeed, Kozol argues that much racial inequality in the United States is fueled by factors that link minority racial status to low economic status.)

Through their elementary and high school education, lower- and working-class students are taught attitudes and skills that best prepare them for supervised or labor-intensive occupations; these include respect for authority, passivity, the willingness to obey orders, and so on. In contrast, middle- and upper-class children are taught skills essential to management-level jobs and professional careers—that is, responsibility and dependability. College and postcollege education offers privileged students continued training in the management and professional skills. The underrepresentation of lower- and working-class students at the college level and beyond excludes such students from similar training and, ostensibly, from upward career mobility (Kozol 1991).

Beyond socialization, the funding and delivery of education also can maintain and reinforce class divisions. Consider, for instance, that local property taxes fund a large portion of public school budgets (Pisko and Stern 1985). As a result, less affluent communities are plagued with poorly funded schools. In 1993, for example, the 47 largest urban school districts in the United States spent approximately $900 less per student than did their wealthy suburban counterparts. Such discrepancies translate into larger class sizes, older textbooks, fewer teachers, and less equipment—particularly hi-tech equipment such as computers—in urban schools. Some states have taken the issue to the courts, petitioning that such arrangements be ruled discriminatory and unconstitutional. (More than 25 states are involved in such lawsuits.) To date, however, little progress has been made (Kozol 1991).

Teachers themselves also may play a role in transmitting educational inequality (Brophy 1983). Studies show, for example, that the social characteristics of students often affect teacher expectations of student performance. Low expectations are most likely to be found in the most disadvantaged schools—inner city schools with large enrollments of poor and minority students (Hallinan and Sorensen 1985).

Teachers' social characteristics can also influence their performance expectations. High-status teachers frequently display rather low expectations for their poor and minority students (Alexander, Entwisle, and Thompson 1987). But in this regard there is also some encouraging news. Teachers who hold positive performance expectations appear to motivate positive results in their students. Indeed, high expectations and demands for academic excellence appear to offset the otherwise negative effects associated with class, race, and ethnicity (Hoffer, Greeley, and Coleman 1987).

Finally, conflict theorists cite tracking as an important source of educational inequality. **Tracking** is a practice by which students are divided into groups or classes that reflect their differential intellectual ability. Although tracking is meant to group students in terms of academic ability, in reality it tends to create economic, racial, and ethnic clusters. Further, studies that compare the performance of low-, medium-, and high-ability tracks show that tracking benefits only the high-ability groups (Shavit and Featherman 1988). Thus, critics of tracking argue, the practice does little to equalize opportunity. Rather, tracking creates a self-fulfilling prophecy (Eder 1981). A **self-fulfilling prophecy** is a phenomenon whereby that which we believe to be true, in some sense, becomes true for us. Within the tracking system, students do as well or as poorly as they are expected to do (Alexander and Cook 1982; Goodlad 1984; Strum 1993).

The inequalities found in the U.S. education system are likely to worsen in the near future. American youth must be ready to compete in an increasingly global and information-driven economy. As such, jobs that require some college education are expected to increase in number (Rubin 1996). An education system that restricts access to college and postcollege training guarantees a bleak future for the "undereducated." Students who are absent from these settings also will be chronically absent from upward mobility.

The inequalities found in the U.S. education system also present an unavoidable irony. Education indeed *can* be a great equalizer—but at present, it is not. This tool of upward mobility is most likely to be placed in the hands of those who already are located in advantaged positions. Thus, rather than *creating* opportunity, the current educational system more accurately *sustains* the status quo. Our greatest educational challenge, then, may be to devise an ideology that can resolve such contradictions within the system.

LEARNING MORE ABOUT IT

For an interesting history of the links between education and credentials, see Randall Collins' *The Credential Society: An Historical Sociology of Education.* (New York: Academic Press, 1979).

A now classic critique of the American education system comes from Samuel Bowles and Herbert Gintis in *Schooling in Capitalist America: Educational Reform and the Contradictions of Economic Life* (New York: Basic Books, 1976). A more recent presentation of the argument can be found in Jonathan Kozol's *Savage Inequalities* (New York: Crown, 1991).

EXERCISES

1. Obtain a college catalogue representing each of the following categories: (a) an Ivy League college, (b) a four-year state college, and (c) a local community college. Compare the mission statement contained in each

school's catalogue. Also compare each school's programs of study and the types of courses it offers. Use your data to prepare a discussion regarding the equal opportunity philosophy of U.S. colleges and universities.

2. Access the most recent edition of the *World Almanac*. Obtain information on the following four items: high school graduation rate by state, student–teacher ratio per state, per capita personal income per state, state revenues for the public schools. Identify those states that represent the top five and the bottom five of each data category. Is there any overlap in these top five and bottom five groups? Speculate on your findings.

Conclusion:
Why Do Conventional
Wisdoms Persist?

■

Love knows no reason . . . beauty is only skin deep . . . honesty is the best policy . . . education is the great equalizer. These statements represent just a few of the conventional wisdoms that we so often hear throughout our lives.

In the introduction to this book, we noted that many of these adages contain some elements of truth. Within certain settings or under certain conditions, conventional wisdom can prove accurate. Yet, throughout *Second Thoughts*, we also have noted that social reality is generally much more involved and much more complex than conventional wisdom would have us believe. Traditional adages and popular sayings rarely provide us with a complete picture of the broader social world. Knowing this, one might ask why individuals continue to embrace conventional wisdom. Given the limited usefulness of such assertions and tenets, why do such adages persist?

THE POSITIVE FUNCTIONS OF CONVENTIONAL WISDOM

Conventional wisdom represents a people's attempt at "knowing." Such adages promise some insight into what is actually occurring. In this way, a culture's conventional wisdom comes to serve a variety of positive social functions; conventional wisdom can induce many productive outcomes for those who invoke them. Here, we speak specifically to five positive social functions served by conventional wisdom.

First, by providing an explanation for an unexpected or mysterious occurrence, *conventional wisdom helps social members confront the unknown and dispel the fear the unknown can generate.* When conventional wisdom proclaims that "immigrants are ruining this country," it provides members of a society with a tangible explanation for their increasing inability to "make ends meet." Similarly, when conventional wisdom tells us that "the media breeds violence," it offers a concrete cause for the perennial and always frightening problems of crime, violence, loneliness, and chaos.

By identifying the causes for looming social problems, conventional wisdom not only dispels fear, it also implies a hopeful resolution. As we noted in Essay 6, naming a problem's cause often gives the sense that a solution cannot be far away. Further, identifying the cause of frightening social conditions offers a protective shield to the broader population. For example, consider a frequently heard bit of wisdom of the 1980s and 1990s: "Homeless people are mentally ill." Here, conventional wisdom cites a reason for a phenomenon most Americans find foreign and frightening. Further, identifying mental illness as the instigator of the homeless condition gives most "sane" people a secure guarantee—homelessness could never happen to them. This piece of wisdom, like so many other adages, locates the source of a problem within the individual. Thus, as long as other social members distinguish themselves from the "problemmed" individual, they can protect themselves from the problem itself.

Conventional wisdom also can function to maintain social stability. Consider the common belief, "Every dog has its day." This adage urges people to be patient, to keep striving, or to leave revenge to fate—all dimensions necessary to peaceful coexistence. Similarly, consider the adage, "Education is the great equalizer." This belief provides an incentive for citizen commitment to an institution whose greatest social contribution may be the consignment to the population of national customs, norms, and values. In the same way, conventional wisdom that warns "united we stand, divided we fall" can effectively squelch protest or disagreement. Such a sentiment can enhance cooperation and dedication to a particular group or goal.

In these examples, and others like them, conventional wisdom "steers" a population toward behaviors that maintain smooth social operations. It keeps societies balanced by making constructive effort a matter of "common knowledge."

Under certain conditions, *conventional wisdom can function to legitimate the actions of those who invoke it.* Often, speakers will create or tap popular adages with a specific goal in mind. In such cases, conventional wisdom takes on the guise of political, religious, or social rhetoric. "Wisdom" emerges as strategically selected and stylized speech delivered to influence an individual or group.

As rhetoric, conventional wisdom proves effective in instituting policy or law because it promotes a vision of sound "common sense." For example, we witness politically conservative members of the U.S. Congress forwarding wisdom such as "welfare is ruining this country" or "welfare breeds dependency." They do so because such rhetoric projects a prudent justification for shaving federal contributions to this cause. Similarly, politicians often espouse wisdom that claims that "capital punishment deters murderers" or "affirmative action programs favor unqualified minorities." They offer these claims, despite factual evidence to the contrary, because such rhetoric effectively employs popular assumptions in the service of the speaker's special interests.

At yet another level, *conventional wisdom can strengthen or solidify a social group's identity.* Conventional wisdom often underscores shared values or attributes. In so doing, such beliefs can enhance collective identity. Adages such as "Great minds think alike" or "Like father like son," sayings such as "The apple doesn't fall far from the tree" or "Birds of a feather flock together" bond individuals by accentuating their similarities. Such wisdom unites individuals by underscoring the common ground they share.

In some cases, however, note that conventional wisdom supports solidarity by creating a "them-versus-us" milieu. Such approaches may unite the members of one group by accentuating the group's hatred or fear of others. For example, Whites who feel threatened by the influx of Non-White immigrants to the United States may readily espouse wisdom that advises individuals to "stick with their own kind." As like-minded individuals rally around such wisdom, White group solidarity can be heightened. Similarly, males who find it difficult to accept growing numbers of females in the workplace may rally around the traditional adage, "A woman's place is in the home." Using conventional wisdom to legitimate their fears, the threatened group can comfortably join in opposition.

Finally, it is important to note that *conventional wisdom often is created or tapped as a tool for power maintenance.* When certain religious traditions defined "the love of money as the root of all evil," such wisdom effectively maintained the divide between the "haves" and the "have-nots." Dissuading the masses from the struggle for material goods allows those in power to maintain their control over limited resources. (Note that such reasoning led social philosopher Karl Marx to refer to religion as "the opium of the people." Marx argued that religion promoted a passive acceptance among the poor of an unfair economic structure.) Similarly, adages such as "You've come a long way baby" or "Good things come to those who wait" serve to dampen efforts toward gender, racial, or ethnic equality. If common consensus suggests that minority group goals have been satisfactorily achieved or addressed, then the continued struggle toward true equality becomes difficult to sustain.

CONVENTIONAL WISDOM AS KNOWLEDGE

Whatever its functions, conventional wisdom appears to offer individuals an intelligence boost—a phenomenon social psychologist David Myers (1987) refers to as the "I-knew-it-all-along" effect. No matter what happens, there exists a conventional wisdom to cover or explain social behaviors; there always exists a saying or belief that predicts all outcomes. Herein lies conventional wisdom's most troubling feature: A society's "common knowledge" simultaneously proclaims contradictory "facts." For example, conventional wisdom assures us that "haste makes waste," while at the same time warning us that "he who hesitates is lost." Whereas one adage suggests that "too many cooks spoil the broth," another claims that "many hands make light work."

All in all, conventional wisdoms abound for every possible behavior and outcome. Such claims form a stockpile of knowledge to which socialization affords us access. Once introduced to a culture's conventional wisdom, social actors draw on this stockpile of ancient and contemporary adages to make almost any discovery seem like common sense. Thus, when I discover that separation intensifies my romantic attraction, I confirm the phenomenon by saying "absence makes the heart grow fonder." If, instead, separation dampens the fires of my romance, I confirm my experiences noting that "out of sight is out of mind." Indeed, conventional wisdom allows me to confirm any of my impressions and experiences—whatever they might be—and thereby frames those experiences as if they constitute a general norm or the ultimate truth.

The drawbacks of conventional wisdom are heightened by the fact that once introduced, these wisdoms take on a life of their own. Such adages become a "taken-for-granted" part of our culture; they state what is known, implicitly suggesting that such topics need not be further considered. In this way, conventional wisdom constitutes tenacious knowledge—information that endures even if there's no empirical evidence to support it. The mere passing of time, the longevity of an idea or belief becomes a sufficient indicator of a tenet's veracity. Facts or observations that contradict the adage lose out to the test of time.

The "staying power" of conventional wisdom may be tied to dimensions of wisdom per se. Indeed, equating conventional adages with wisdom may help to accentuate their appeal. Wisdom is a highly valued commodity in our society. It is born of good judgment and experience. Further, it can offer us a sense of inner peace—an ability to live with what we know. Wisdom cannot be taught; courses in wisdom are not part of the college curriculum. Indeed, our formal education experiences often convince us that wisdom is not to be found in books or in research. Rather, wisdom emerges from the ordinary, the common, the everyday. In the final analysis, the wise person is one who has "lived."

In turning to our experiences for wisdom, however, we return to a problem cited earlier and explored at some length in this book's introduction—namely, the limitations of experientially based knowledge. If we base our wisdom solely on personal experiences, we will likely build dubious knowledge. Although our speculations about various social topics typically start with personal experiences, such experiences may not offer us the best empirical evidence for verification.

Our experiences are subjective and therefore vulnerable to distortion and personal bias. They require a "correction" factor, one that can control for distortions emerging from personal prejudices or sloppy thinking. Social scientific inquiry offers one such correction factor. The sociological approach to knowledge follows a set of standardized rules and procedures that can maximize our chances of obtaining valid and reliable knowledge. Although sociology may start with what we already know, good sociology does not end there. Rather, good sociology explores commonsense notions about the social world by collecting and comparing varied reports and observations in the interest of building an all-encompassing picture of reality.

IN CLOSING

Joseph Story, an early Associate Justice of the U.S. Supreme Court, is quoted as saying: "Human wisdom is the aggregate of all human experience, constantly accumulating, selecting and reorganizing its own materials." Story's statement suggests that true wisdom requires a wealth of experience. It is in that spirit that we prepared *Second Thoughts*. In each essay, we proposed a wisdom that requires us to consider a myriad of experiences and facts. We advocated an approach to knowledge that remains open-ended, a stance that treats new information as an opportunity to rethink what we know. In this way, we cast all social actors as perpetual students of their environment—students who regularly question assumptions and who seek to see beyond themselves.

LEARNING MORE ABOUT IT

The flaws inherent in relying on conventional wisdom for knowledge are effectively portrayed in a 1949 classic by sociologist Paul Lazarsfeld entitled "The American Soldier: An Expository Review" (*Public Opinion Quarterly 13* (3): 378–380). A similarly striking demonstration comes from social psychologist Karl Halvor Teigen in his 1986 article "Old Truths or Fresh Insights?: A Study of Students' Evaluations of Proverbs" (*Journal of British Social Psychology 25* (1): 43–50). Both provide interesting and very readable excursions on this topic.

In a related vein, anthropologist Claude Levi-Strauss explores the origins of myth in his book *The Raw and the Cooked: Introduction to a Science of Mythology* (New York: Harper & Row, 1964).

Howard Kahane provides a detailed exploration of both the tools and pitfalls of everyday reasoning and problem solving in *Logic and Contemporary Rhetoric: The Use of Reason in Everyday Life,* 6th ed. (Belmont, CA: Wadsworth, 1992).

Source List for Additional Information and Action

■

The following organization list provides some suggestions for those who wish to further pursue any of the topics addressed in this book. Some of these organizations serve as information sources, others are action-oriented. The list is just a sampling of the many groups connected to the issues discussed in this text. Interested readers can find full descriptions of these organizations, as well as listings for many others like them, by consulting the *Encyclopedia of Associations* [Carol Schwartz and Rebecca Turner, eds. (Detroit, MI: Gale Research Co.)].

COOPERATION

Cooperative Education Association
11710 Beltsville Drive, Suite 520, Beltsville, MD 20705; (301) 572-CEA9

Cooperative Learning Center
University of Minnesota, Minneapolis, MN 55455; (612) 625-5000

Future Problem Solving Program
318 West Ann St., Ann Arbor, MI 48104-1337; (313) 998-7876
(Fosters creative thinking in problem-solving efforts.)

Grace Contrino Abrams Peace Education Foundation
2627 Biscayne Blvd., Miami, FL 33137; (800) 749-8838

International Association for the Study of Cooperation in Education
Box 1582, Santa Cruz, CA 95061-1582; (408) 426-7926

National Commission for Cooperative Education
501 Stearns Center, 360 Huntington Ave., Boston, MA 02115;
(617) 373-3770

CHILDREN

Action for Child Protection
4724C Park Rd., Charlotte, NC 28209; (704) 529-1080

American Bar Association Center on Children and the Law
1800 M St. NW, Washington, DC 20036; (202) 331-2250

American Humane Association—Children's Division
63 Inverness Drive E, Englewood, CO 80112-5117; (800) 227-4645

Association for the Care of Children's Health
7910 Woodmont Ave., Suite 300, Bethesda, MD 20814;
(301) 654-6549

Association for Children for Enforcement of Support
723 Phillips Ave., Suite J, Toledo, OH 43612; (800) 537-7072
(Concerned with child support issues.)

Child Abuse Listening and Mediation
PO Box 90754, Santa Barbara, CA; 93190-0754, (805) 965-2376

Child Trend
4301 Conneticut Ave. NW, Suite 100, Washington, DC 20008;
(202) 362-5580
(Collects statistics and research regarding U.S. children and families.)

Child Welfare League of America
440 1st St. NW, Suite 310, Washington, DC 20001; (202) 638-2952

Children, Inc.
PO Box 5381, 1000 Westover Rd., Richmond, VA 23220; (800) 538-5381
(International organization spanning 22 countries.)

Children's Defense Fund
25 E St. NW, Washington, DC 20001; (800) CDF-1200
(Long-range advocacy for children and teenagers.)

Children's Express Foundation
1400 New York Ave. NW, Suite 510, Washington, DC 20005;
(202) 737-7377
(Produces publications in which children ages 8–13 can express their views on social life.)

Children's Foundation
725 15th St. NW, Suite 505, Washington, DC 20005; (202) 347-3300
(Concerned with social and economic issues facing children.)

Children's Watch
89 Hancock St., Cambridge, MA 02139; (617) 492-4890
(Multinational guardian for children's rights worldwide.)

International Child Health Foundation
Century Building No. 325, 10630 Little Patuxat Pkwy., Columbia, MD
20814; (301) 596-4514

National Association of Child Advocates
1625 K St. NW, Suite 510, Washington, DC 20006; (202) 347-3300

National Safe Kids Campaign
111 Michigan Ave. NW, Washington, DC 20010-2970; (202) 884-4993

LOVE

Love Notes
Box 54321, Albuquerque, NM 87153; (505) 837-2160
(Promotes love, friendship, and positive relationships.)

Scientific Marriage Foundation
Hopkins Syndicate, 802 S. Washington, Bloomington, IN 47401;
(812) 331-7753
(Helps individuals locate mates via science and psychology.)

Society of Limerents
c/o Dorothy Tennov, RR 2, Box 251, Millsboro, DE 19966; (302) 934-7067
(Avenue for expression and research of individual love experiences.)

STRESS

American Institute of Stress
124 Park Ave., Yonkers, NY 10703; (800) 24RELAX

International Stress Management Association
c/o Dr. F. J. McGuigan, U.S. International University, Institute of Stress
Management, 10455 Pomerado Rd., San Diego, CA 92131;
(619) 693-4698

AGE

Aging in America
1500 Pelham Parkway South, Bronx, NY 10461; (718) 824-4004

American Senior Citizens Association
PO Box 41, Fayetteville, NC 28302; (919) 323-3541

Center for Understanding Aging
200 Executive Blvd., Suite 201, PO Box 246, Southington, CT 06489;
(203) 621-2079

Generations United
c/o Child Welfare League of America, 440 1st St. NW, Suite 310,
Washington, DC 20001; (202) 638-2952

Gray Panthers
2025 Pennsylvania Ave. NW, Suite 821, Washington, DC 20006;
(202) 347-8800

National Council of Senior Citizens
1331 F St. NW, Washington, DC 20004-1171; (202) 347-8800

NAMES

African-American History Association
PO Box 115268, Atlanta, GA 30310; (404) 344-7405

American Name Society
c/o Professor Wayne H. Finke, Baruch College, Department of Modern
Languages and Comparative Literature, 17 Lexington Ave., Box 350,
New York, NY 10010; (212) 387-1570

Ancestry Research Club
PO Box 476, Salt Lake City, UT 84110; (800) 531-1790

Immigrant Genealogical Society
1310B Magnolia Rd., PO Box 7369, Burbank, CA 91510-7369;
(818) 848-3122

North Central Name Society
c/o Laurence Seits, Waubonsee Community College, Sugar Grove, IL
60554; (708) 466-4811

Also note that there are over 150 organizations devoted to specific family
surnames (for example, the Adams' family organization, the Stewart
family organization, and so on).

BEAUTY

American Fitness Association
6285 E. Spring St., No. 404, Long Beach, CA 90808; (310) 402-3952

American Society for Aesthetic Plastic Surgery
3922 Atlantic Ave., Long Beach, CA 90807; (310) 595-4275

National Foundation for Facial Reconstruction
317 E. 34th St., Suite 901, New York, NY 10016; (212) 263-6656
(Sponsors surgical and rehabilitation programs.)

Uglies Unlimited
3912 St. Michael's Court, Sugarland, TX 77479; (713) 980-9830
(Serves as the "guardian of ugly human beings.")

BODY WEIGHT

Anorexia Nervosa and Related Eating Disorders
PO Box 5102, Eugene, OR 97405; (503) 344-1144

Council on Size and Weight Discrimination
PO Box 305, Mount Marion, NY 12456; (914) 679-1209

Eating Disorders Organization
445 East Granville Rd., Worthington, OH 43085-3195; (614) 436-1112

Largess
PO Box 9404, New Haven, CT 06534-0404; (203) 787-1624
(Provides information on size discrimination.)

Little People of America
7238 Piedmont Dr., Dallas, TX 75227-9324; (800) 24DWARF

National Association to Advance Fat Acceptance
PO Box 188620, Sacramento, CA 95818; (800) 442-1214

The Obesity Foundation
5600 So. Quebec, Suite 109A, Englewood, CO 80111; (303) 850-0328

Tall Clubs International
PO Box 13, Stafford, TX 77497-0013; (800) 521-2512

OCCUPATIONS

American Labor Education Center
2000 P St. NW, Suite 300, Washington, DC 20036; (202) 828-5710
(Provides training materials for various occupations.)

Equal Employment Advisory Council
1045 15th St. NW, Suite 1220, Washington, DC 20005; (202) 789-8650

Equal Rights Advocates
1663 Mission St., Suite 550, San Francisco, CA 94103; (415) 621-0672

National Association of the Professions
292 Madison Ave., 4th floor, New York, NY 10017; (800) 221-2168

Work In America Institute
700 White Plains Rd., Scarsdale, NY 10583; (914) 472-9600
(Researches more effective uses of human resources.)

POVERTY

Box Project
PO Box 435, Plainville, CT 06062; (203) 747-8182
(Matches "helping families" with "needy families" in the Mississippi Delta
area. Helping families provide goods and support.)

Center for Community Change
1000 Wisconsin Ave. NW, Washington, DC 20007; (202) 342-0519

National Alliance to End Homelessness
1518 K St. NW, Suite 206, Washington, DC 20005; (202) 638-1526

National Coalition for the Homeless
1612 K St. NW, Suite 1004, Washington, DC 20006; (202) 775-1322

National Research Center on Homelessness and Mental Illness
262 Delaware Ave., Delmar, NY 12054; (800) 444-7415

Public Voice for Food and Health Policy
1001 Connecticut Ave. NW, Suite 522, Washington, DC 20036;
(202) 659-5930

GENDER

Catalyst
250 Park Ave. S, New York, NY 10003; (212) 777-8900
(Works with business to effect change for women.)

National Association for Women in Careers
675 No. Court, Suite 200, Palatine, IL 60067; (708) 358-4965

National Chamber of Commerce for Women
10 Waterside Plaza, Suite 6H, New York, NY 10010; (212) 685-3454

National Women's Health Network
1325 G St. NW, Washington, DC 20005; (202) 347-1140

National Women's History Project
7738 Bell Rd., Windsor, CA 95492-8518; (707) 838-6000

National Women's Mailing List
PO Box 68, Jenner, CA 95450; (707) 632-5763
(This is an information exchange network.)

Societas Docta
2207 Glynnwood Dr., Savannah, GA 31404; (912) 354-4634
(Encourages minority Ph.D. candidates.)

Tradeswomen, Inc.
PO Box 40664 B, San Francisco, CA 94140; (415) 821-7334
(Serves women in nontraditional blue-collar occupations.)

Women's Health Action and Mobilization
PO Box 733, New York, NY 10009; (212) 560-7177

The Women's Institute
PO Box 6005, Silver Spring, MD 20916; (301) 871-6106
(Develops presentations on problems and issues of concern to women.)

RACE

Coalition for Harmony of Races in the U.S. (CHORUS)
PO Box 59848, Rockville, MD 20859; (301) 926 2590

Fund for an Open Society (OPEN)
311 S. Juniper St., Ste. 400, Philadelphia, PA 19107; (215) 735-6915
(Provides financial help with mortgages and loans designed to integrate neighborhoods.)

National Association for the Advancement of Colored People (NAACP)
4805 Mt. Hope Dr., Baltimore, MD 21215; (410) 358-8900

National Catholic Conference for Interracial Justice (NCCIJ)
3033 4th St. NE, Washington, DC 20017-1102; (202) 529-6480

Women for Racial and Economic Equality (WREE)
198 Broadway, Rm. 606, New York, NY 10038; (212) 385-1103

MURDER

Accuracy In Media
4455 Conneticut Ave. NW, Suite 330, Washington, DC 20008;
(202) 364-4401

American Crime Fighters
5466 Lake Ave., Sanford, FL 32773; (407) 322-7011

American Justice Institute
300 Capital Mall, Suite 1170, Sacramento, CA 95814; (916) 487-9334

National Alliance for Safe Schools
PO Box 30177, Bethesda, MD 20824; (301) 907-7888

National Coalition on TV Violence
33290 W 14 Mile Rd., Suite 498, West Bloomfield, MI 48322;
(810) 489-3177

National Crime Prevention Council
1700 K St. NW, 2nd floor, Washington, DC 20006; (202) 466-6272

Strategies for Media Literacy
1095 Market St., Suite 617, San Francisco, CA 94103; (415) 621-2911
(Devoted to helping the public "read" and "read through" the violent
messages conveyed in various media presentations.)

Violence Policy Center
1300 N St. NW, Washington, DC 20005; (202) 783-4071

HONESTY

Center for Academic Ethics
c/o Dr. Arthur Brown, Wayne State University, 311 Education Bldg.,
Detroit, MI 48202; (313) 577-8290

Hastings Center
255 Elm Rd., Briar Cliff Manor, NY 10510; (914) 762-8500
(Concerned with medical ethics.)

Society for Business Ethics
Rosemont College, Department of Philosophy, Rosemont, PA 19010;
(215) 687-6819

MARRIAGE, DIVORCE, AND FAMILY

AMEND
777 Grant St., Suite 600, Denver CO 80203; (303) 832-6363
(Therapy for abusers, advice for victims.)

American Family Communiversity
1820 West Hubbard St., Suite 204, Chicago, IL 60622; (312) 563-9733
(This group studies and attempts to upgrade policy affecting marriage.)

Association for Couples in Marriage Enrichment
PO Box 10596, Winston-Salem, NC 27108; (800) 634-8325
(Promotes community service designed to foster successful marriages.)

Children's Rights Council
220 I St. NE, Washington, DC 20002; (202) 547-6227
(Provides information aimed at minimizing hostility during child
custody cases.)

Committee for Single Adoptive Parents
PO Box 15084, Chevy Chase, MD 20825; (202) 966-6367

Family Research Laboratory
University of New Hampshire, Durham, NH 03824; (603) 862-1234

Institute for the Study of Matrimonial Laws
c/o Sidney Siller, 11 Park Pl., Suite 1116, New York, NY 10007;
(212) 766-4030

National Coalition Against Domestic Violence
PO Box 18749, Denver CO 80218; (303) 839-1852

National Council on Child Abuse and Family Violence
1155 Conneticut Ave. NW, Suite 400, Washington, DC 20036;
(800) 222-2000

Parents Anonymous
675 West Foothill Blvd., Suite 220, Claremount, CA 91711;
(909) 621-6184
(Helps parents learn effective, nonviolent child-rearing strategies.)

Single Mothers by Choice
PO Box 1642, Gracie Square Station, New York, NY 10028;
(212) 988-0993

Single Parents' Resource Center
141 West 28th St., Suite 302, New York, NY 10001; (212) 947-0221

Stepfamily Foundation
333 West End Ave., New York, NY 10023; (800) sky-step

United Fathers of America
595 The City Dr., Suite 202, Orange, CA 92668; (714) 385-1002

Women Helping Women
c/o Ruth Kvalheim, 525 No. Van Buren St., Stoughton, WI 53589;
(608) 873-3747

WELFARE

ARISE
718 State St., Springfield, MA 01109; (413) 734-4948
(Aims to empower low-income individuals via education on social/
economic rights, health care, housing, and voting.)

Catholic Charities USA
1731 King St., Suite 200, Alexandria, VA 22314; (703) 549-1390

CEGA Services
PO Box 81826, Lincoln, NE 68501; (402) 464-0602
Library Hotline: (800) 228-2213
(Information agency addressing economic issues.)

Coalition for Economic Survival
1296 N. Fairfax Ave., Los Angeles, CA 90046; (213) 656-4410
(Addresses economic concerns of senior citizens and low-income families.)

Operation PUSH
930 E. 50th St., Chicago, IL 60615; (312) 373-3366
(International organization directed toward educational and economic equity and parity.)

Social Legislation Information Services
440 1st St. NW, Suite 310, Washington, DC 20001; (202) 638-2952

IMMIGRATION

American Civic Association
131 Front St., Binghamton, NY 13905; (607) 723-9419
(Naturalized citizens helping the foreign born.)

Ancestry Research Club
PO Box 476, Salt Lake City, UT 84110; (800) 531-1790

Association of Multi-Ethnic Americans
PO Box 191726, San Francisco, CA 94119-1726; (510) 523-2632

Church World Service Immigration and Refugee Program
475 Riverside Dr., Rm. 656, New York, NY 10115; (212) 870-3153
(Coordinates the resettlement of refugees.)

Ethnic Anonymous
c/o F. J. Nubee, 1631 Belmont Ave., #107, Seattle, WA 98122;
(206) 325-8091
(Self-help group designed to confront and heal the problems of prejudice.)

Immigration and Refugee Service of America
1717 Massachusetts Ave. NW, Suite 701, Washington, DC 20036;
(202) 797-2105
(Promotes cultural pluralism.)

National Immigration Project of the National Lawyer's Guild
14 Beacon St., Suite 506, Boston, MA 02108; (617) 227-9727
(Works for more progressive immigration laws.)

Refugee Policy Group
1424 16th St. NW, Suite 401, Washington, DC 20036; (202) 797-2105

EDUCATION

A Better Chance
419 Boylston St., Boston, MA 02116; (617) 421-0950
(Identifies, recruits, and helps place minority students in leading
secondary and public schools.)

Cities in Schools
401 Wythe St., Suite 200, Alexandria, VA 22314; (703) 519-8999
(Promotes school attendance and performance among underprivileged
children.)

Common Destiny Alliance
c/o Willis D. Hawley, College of Education, University of Maryland,
3119 Benjamin Building, College Park, MD 20742-1121;
(301) 405-2334

Contact Center
PO Box 81826, Lincoln, NE 68501; (800) 228-8813
(Literacy center.)

Creative Education Foundation
1050 Union Rd., Buffalo, NY 14224; (716) 675-3181

Moby Dick Academy
Box 589, Ocean Park, WA 98640; (206) 665-4577
(Alternative education institution.)

National Coalition of Advocates for Students
100 Boylston St., Suite 737, Boston, MA 02116; (617) 357-8507

National Dropout Prevention Network
Clemson University, 205 Martin St., Box 345111, Clemson, SC
29634-5111; (800) 443-6392

National Women Students' Coalition
c/o USSA, 815 15th St. NW, Suite 838, Washington, DC 20005;
(202) 347-8772

Plan of Action for Challenging Times
635 Divisadero St., San Francisco, CA 94117; (415) 922-2550
(Helps motivate minority students who face poor economic
circumstances.)

REFERENCES

Adler, S. J., and Lamber, W. 1993. "Common Criminals: Just About Everyone Violates Some Laws, Even Model Citizens." *Wall Street Journal* (March 12): A6.

Ahlburg, D., and DeVita, C. 1992. "New Realities of the American Family." *Population Bulletin* 47: 2. (Washington, DC: Population Reference Bureau).

Alexander, K., and Cook, M. 1982. "Curricula and Coursework: A Surprise Ending to a Familiar Story." *American Sociological Review* 47: 626–640.

Alexander, K., Entwisle, D., and Thompson, M. 1987. "School Performance, Status Relations, and the Structure of Sentiment: Bringing the Teachers Back In." *American Sociological Review* 52(5): 665–682.

Alford, R. D. 1988. *Naming and Identity: A Cross Cultural Study of Personal Naming Practices.* New Haven, CT: HRAF Press.

Allan, G. 1989. *Friendship: Developing A Sociological Perspective.* Boulder, CO: Westview Press.

Allen, C. 1994. "First They Changed My Name" *Ms.* 4(4): 25–27.

Altheimer, E. 1994. *Weight Loss and the Distortion of Body Image.* Henry Rutgers Scholars Thesis, Rutgers University.

Amabile, T. M. 1982. "When Self-Descriptions Contradict Behavior." *Social Cognition* 1: 311–335.

Amasile, T. M., and Kabat, L. G. 1982. "When Self-Descriptions Contradict Behavior." *Social Cognition* 1: 311–335.

American Association of Retired Persons (AARP). 1989. A Profile of Older Americans. Washington, DC: AARP Fulfillment.

American Society for Aesthetic Plastic Surgery, Inc. 1995. "1994 National Plastic Surgery Statistics." Arlington Heights, IL: Communications Office.

Anderson, T. 1985. "Unique and Common First Names of Males and Females." *Psychological Reports* 57: 204–206.

Aneshensel, C. 1992. "Social Stress: Theory and Research. *Annual Review of Sociology* 18: 15–38.

Archdeacon, T. 1992. "Reflections on Immigration to Europe in Light of U.S. Immigration History." *International Migration Review* 26 (Summer): 524–548.

Archer, D., and Gartner, R. 1987. *Violence and Crime in Cross-National Perspective.* New Haven: Yale University Press.

Aronson, E., 1980. *The Social Animal.* San Francisco: Freeman.

Aronson, E., and Cope, V. 1968. "My Enemy's Enemy Is My Friend." *Journal of Personality and Social Psychology* 8: 8–12.

Aronson, E., Stephan, C., Sikes, J., Blaney, N., and Snapp, M. 1978. *The Jigsaw Classroom.* Beverly Hills, CA: Sage.

Aronson, E., and Thibodeau, R. 1992. "The Jigsaw Classroom: A Cooperative Strategy for Reducing Prejudice." In J. Lynch, C. Modgil, and S. Modgil (Eds.), *Cultural Diversity in the Schools*. London: Falmer Press.

Atchley, R. 1994. *Social Forces and Aging: An Introduction to Social Gerontology* (7th ed.). Belmont, CA: Wadsworth.

Atkin, C. 1982. "Changing Male and Female Roles." In M. Schwartz (Ed.), *TV and Teens: Experts Look at the Issues*. Reading, MA: Addison-Wesley.

Axelrod, R. 1984. *The Evolution of Cooperation*. New York: Basic Books.

Babbie, E. 1994. *What Is Society: Reflections On Freedom, Order, and Change*. Thousand Oaks, CA: Pine Forge Press.

Backer, S., Smith, G., and Weiner, E. 1993. "The Mexican Worker." *Business Week* (April): 84–92.

Baltzell, E. D. 1987. *The Protestant Establishment: Aristocracy and Caste in America*. New Haven, CT: Yale University Press.

Barnes, J. A. 1994. *A Pack of Lies: Toward a Sociology of Lying*. New York: Cambridge University Press.

Basow, S. 1992. *Gender: Stereotypes and Roles* (3rd ed.). Monterey, CA: Brooks/Cole.

Bastian, L., and Taylor, B. 1991. *School Crime: A National Crime Victimization Survey Report*. Washington, DC: Bureau of Justice Statistics (September).

Bean, C. 1992. *Women Murdered by the Men They Love*. New York: Hawthorne.

Beck, M. 1990. "Trading Places." *Newsweek* 16 (July): 48–54.

Becker, H. 1963. *The Outsiders*. Glencoe, IL: Free Press.

Bedard, M. 1991. "Captive Clientele of the Welfare Supersystem: Breaking the Cage Wide Open." *Humanity and Society* 15: 23–48.

Bellah, R., Madssen, R., Sullivan, W., Swidler, A., and Tipton, S. 1985. *Habits of the Heart: Individualism and Commitment in American Life*. Berkeley: University of California Press.

Bem, S. L. 1993. *The Lenses of Gender: Transforming the Debate on Sexual Inequality*. New Haven: Yale University Press.

Bengston, V., Rosenthal, C., and Burton, L. 1990. "Families and Aging: Diversity and Heterogeneity." In R. Binstock and L. Geroge (Eds.), *Handbook of Aging and the Social Sciences* (3rd ed.). New York: Academic.

Berger, P. 1963. *Invitation To Sociology*. New York: Anchor Books.

Berger, P., and Luckmann, T. 1967. *The Social Construction of Reality*. New York: Anchor.

Berke, R. L. 1994. "Crime Is Becoming the Nation's Top Fear." *New York Times* (January 23), Section 1: 1, 16.

Bernstein, S. 1972. "Getting It Done: Notes on Student Fritters." *Urban Life and Culture* 1 (October): 2.

Berscheid, E. 1981. "An Overview of the Psychological Effects of Physical Attractiveness and Some Comments upon the Psychological Effects of Knowledge of the Effects of Physical Attractiveness." In W. Lucker, K. Ribbens, and J.A. McNamera (Eds.), *Logical Aspects of Facial Form*. Ann Arbor: University of Michigan Press.

_____. 1982. "America's Obsession with Beautiful People." *U. S. New and World Report* (January 11): 59–61.

Berscheid, E., and Hatfield, E. 1983. *Interpersonal Attraction* (2nd ed.). Reading, MA: Addison-Wesley.

Besnard, P., and Desplanques, G. 1993. *La Cote des Prénoms en 1994*. Paris: Balland.

Bidwell, C., and Friedkin, N. 1988. "The Sociology of Education." In N. Smelser (Ed.), *Handbook of Sociology* (pp. 449–471). Newbury Park, CA: Sage.

Bishop, J. E. 1986. "'All For One . . . One For All?' Don't Bet On It." *Wall Street Journal* (December 4): 31.

Blackstone, W. 1979. *Commentaries on the Laws of England*. Chicago: University of Chicago Press. (Original work published 1765–1769.)

Blake, R. R., and Moulton, J. S. 1979. "Intergroup Problem Solving in Organizations: From Theory to Practice." In W. G. Austin and S. Worschel (Eds.), *The Social Psychology of Intergroup Relations*. Monterey, CA.: Brooks/Cole.

Blau, J. 1992. *The Visible Poor: Homelessness in the U.S.* New York: Oxford Press.

Bleiszner, R., and Adams, R. C. 1992. *Adult Friendships*. Newbury Park, CA: Sage.

Bloom, D. E., and Bennett, N. G. 1985. *Marriage Patterns in the United States*. Cambridge, MA: National Bureau of Economic Research.

_____. 1986. "Childless Couples." *American Demographics* 8: 23–25.

_____. 1990. "Modeling American Marriage Patterns." *Journal of American Statistical Associations* 85(412): 1009–1017.

Blumstein, P., and Schwartz, P. 1985. *American Couples: Money, Work, Sex*. New York: Wm. Morrow.

Bodnar, J. 1987. "Socialization and Adaptation: Immigrant Families in Scranton." In H. Graff (Ed.), *Growing Up in America: Historical Experiences*. Detroit: Wayne State Press.

Bonacich, E., Cheng, L., Chinchilla, N., Hamilton, N., and Ong, P. (Eds.). 1994. *Global Production: The Apparel Industry in the Pacific Rim*. Philadelphia: Temple University Press.

Borgas, G. 1990. *Friends or Strangers: The Impact of Immigrants on the U.S. Economy*. New York: Basic Books.

Bourdieu, P. 1977a. "Cultural Reproduction and Social Reproduction." In J. Karabel and A. H. Halsey (Eds.), *Power and Ideology in Education*. New York: Oxford University Press.

_____. 1977b. *Outline of a Theory of Practice*. Cambridge: Cambridge University Press.

_____. 1984. *Distinction: A Social Critique of the Judgment of Taste*. Cambridge: Harvard University Press.

Bowles, S., and Gintis, H. 1976. *Schooling in Capitalist America: Educational Reform and the Contradiction of Economic Life*. New York: Basic Books.

_____. 1982. "The Crisis of Liberal Democratic Capitalism: The Case of the U.S." *Politics and Society* 11: 51–59.

Brand, D. 1987. "The New Whiz Kids." *Time* (August 31): 42–51.

Braun, D. D. 1991. *The Rich Get Richer.* Chicago: Nelson Hall.

Braveman, P. Egerter, S., Bennett, T., Showstack, J. 1990. "Differences in Hospital Resource Allocation Among Sick Newborns According to Insurance Coverage." *Journal of the American Medical Association 266:* 3300–3308.

Brenner, J. G., and Spayd, L. 1993. "A Pattern of Bias in Mortagage Loans." *Washington Post* (July 8).

Briggs, V., and Moore, S. 1994. *Still an Open Door?: U.S. Immigration Policy and the American Economy.* Washington, DC. The American University Press.

Brillon, Y. 1987. *Victimization and Fear of Crime Among the Elderly.* Toronto: Butterworth.

Brophy, J. 1983. "Research on the Self-Fulfilling Prophecy and Teacher Expectations." *Journal of Educational Psychology 75:* 631–661.

Brown, J. F. 1994. "35 Black Men Quizzed in Union, S. C." *Afro-American* (November 12): A:1:3.

Bryan, J. H., and Walbek, N. H. 1970. "Preaching and Practicing Generosity." *Child Development 41:* 329–353.

Burt, M. 1992. *On the Edge: The Growth of Homelessness in the 1980s.* New York: Russell Sage Foundation.

Business Week. 1993. "The Widening Gap Between CEO Pay and What Others Make." (April 26): 56–57.

Buss, D. M., and Barnes, M. 1986. "Preferences in Human Mate Selection." *Journal of Personality and Social Psychology 50:* 559–570.

Busse, T. V., and Seraydarian, L. 1978. "The Relationship Between First Name Desirability and School Readiness, IQ, and School Achievement." *Psychology in the Schools 16:* 297–302.

Carter, B. 1991. "Children's T.V., Where Boys Are King." *New York Times* (May 1): A, 1:2.

Carter, D., and Wilson, R. 1993. *Minorities in Higher Education.* Washington, DC: American Council on Education.

Casale, A. M., and Lerman, P. 1986. *USA Today: Tracking Tomorrow's Trends.* Kansas City, MO: Andrews, McNeil, & Parker.

Cash, T. F,. and L. H. Janda. 1984. "The Eye of the Beholder." *Psychology Today* (December): 46–52.

Cash, T. F., and Pruzinsky, T. 1990. "The Psychology of Physical Appearance: Aesthetics, Attributes, and Images." In T. F. Cash and Pruzinsky, T. *Body Images: Development, Deviance, and Change.* New York: Guilford Press.

Center on Budget and Policy Priorities. 1992. "Where Have All the Dollars Gone?" Washington, DC: CBPP (August).

Cerulo, K. 1995. *Identity Designs: The Sights and Sounds of a Nation.* ASA Rose Book Series. New Brunswick, NJ: Rutgers University Press.

Cherlin, A. 1992. *Marriage, Divorce, Remarriage.* Cambridge, MA: Harvard University Press.

Cherlin, A., and Furstenberg, F., Jr. 1994. "Stepfamilies in the U.S.: A wReconsideration." *Annual Review of Sociology 20:* 359–381.

Chesler, P., and Goodman, E. J. 1976. *Women, Money, and Power.* New York: Morrow.

Chideya, F. 1995. *Don't Believe the Hype: Fighting Cultural Misinformation About African-Americans.* New York: Plume.

Children's Defense Fund. 1991. *Child Poverty in America.* Washington, DC: Author.

———. 1992. *Vanishing Dreams: The Economic Plight of America's Young Families.* Washington, DC: Author.

Chira, S. 1992. "Bias Against Girls Is Found Rife in Schools, with Lasting Damage." *New York Times* (February 12) A1.

Church, G. 1993. "Send Back Your Tired, Your Poor . . ." *Time* (June 21): 26–27.

Clarke, E. H. 1873. *Sex in Education: or A Fair Chance for Girls.* Boston: J. R. Osgood.

Clifford, M. M., and Walster, E. H. 1973. "The Effects of Physical Attractiveness on Teacher Expectation." *Sociology of Education* 46: 245–258.

Cockerham, W. 1991. *This Aging Society.* Englewood Cliffs, NJ:Prentice-Hall.

———. 1995. *Medical Sociology* (6th ed.). Englewood Cliffs, NJ: Prentice-Hall.

Colburn, D. 1992. "A Vicious Cycle of Risk." *Washington Post Health Magazine* (July 28): WH 10:1.

Cole, T. 1992. *The Journey of Life: Aging in America.* New York: Cambridge University Press.

Coleman, R., and Rainwater, L. 1978. *Social Standing in America: New Dimensions of Class.* New York: Basic Books.

Collier, J. L. 1991. *The Rise of Selfishness in America.* New York: Oxford University Press.

Collins, P. H. 1990. *Black Feminist Thought.* New York: Routledge.

Collins, R. 1979. *The Credential Society: An Historical Sociology of Education.* New York: Academic Press.

Combs, A. 1992. *Cooperation: Beyond the Age of Competition.* Philadelphia: Gordon and Breach.

Condry, J. C., and Condry, S. 1976. "Sex Differences: A Study of the Eye of the Beholder." *Child Development* 47: 812–819.

Conner, G., and Smith, D. 1991. "Home Mortgage Disclosure Act: Expanded Data on Residential Lending." *Federal Reserve Bulletin* (November).

Cooley, C. H. 1902. *Human Nature and Social Order.* New York: Scribner.

———. 1909. *Social Organization.* New York: Charles Scribner.

Coontz, S. 1992. "Introduction" and "The Way We Wish We Were." In *The Way We Never Were: American Families and the Nostalgia Trap.* New York: Basic Books.

Coopersmith, S. 1967. *Antecedents of Self-Esteem.* San Francisco: Freeman.

Coser, L. 1956. *The Function of Social Conflict.* Glencoe, IL: Free Press.

———. 1963. *Sociology Through Literature: An Introductory Reader.* Englewood Cliffs, NJ: Prentice Hall.

Courts, F. 1939. "Muscular Tension and Memorization." *Journal of Experimental Psychology* 25: 235–256.

Cowan, R. 1991. "More Work for Mother: The Post-War Years." In Laura Kramer (Ed.), *The Sociology of Gender.* New York: St. Martin's Press.

Cowe, R. 1990. "New Ice Cream Plans to Lick Rivals." *Guardian II* (April 2): 3.

Crocker, P. 1985. "The Meaning of Equality for Battered Women Who Kill Men in Self-Defense." *Harvard Women's Law Journal 8*: 121–153.

Crowley, G. 1991. "Children in Peril." *Newsweek Special Issue* (Summer): 21.

Crystal, G. 1991. "How Much CEOs Really Make." *Fortune* (June 17): 72–80.

Cupito, M. C. 1986. "Children Do Help Elderly." *Columbus Ohio Dispatch* (October 23): column 1.

Dahrendorf, R. 1959. *Class and Class Conflict in Industrial Society.* Stanford, CA: Stanford University Press.

Daly, M., and Wilson, M. 1988. *Homicide.* New York: Aldine de Gruyter.

Daniels, R. 1990. *A History of Immigration and Ethnicity in American Life.* New York: Harper Perennial.

Davis, F. J. 1991. *Who Is Black: One Nations' Definition.* University Park, PA: Penn State University Press.

Davis, K., and Moore, W. 1945. "Some Principles of Stratification." *American Sociological Review 27*(1): 5–19.

Dedman, B. 1989. "Blacks Turned Down for Home Loans from S&L's Twice as Often as Whites." *Atlanta Constitution* (January 22) A,1:4.

Degher, D., and Hughes, G. 1992. "The Identity Change Process: A Field Study of Obesity." *Deviant Behavior 2*: 385–401.

Denton, N., and Massey, D. 1989. "Racial Identity Among Caribbean Hispanics: The Effect of Double Minority Status on Residential Segregation." *American Sociological Review 54*: 790–808.

Dentzer, S. 1991. "The Graying of Japan." *U.S. News and World Report* (September 30): 790–808.

Deustch, M., and Krauss, R. M. 1960. "The Effect of Threat on Interpersonal Bargaining." *Journal of Abnormal and Social Psychology 1*: 629–636.

Devine, J., and Wright, J. D. 1993. *The Greatest of Evils.* New York: Aldine de Gruyter.

Dion, K. K. 1979. "Physical Attractiveness and Interpersonal Attraction." In M. Cook and G. Wilson (Eds.), *Love and Attraction.* New York: Pergamon Press.

Dion, K. K., and Berscheid, E. 1974. "Physical Attractiveness and Peer Perception Among Children." *Sociometry 37*: 1–12.

Dion, K. K., Berscheid, E., and Walster, E. 1972. "What Is Beautiful Is Good." *Journal of Personality and Social Psychology 24*: 285–290.

Dion, K. L. 1979. "Intergroup Conflict and Intragroup Cohesiveness." In W. G. Austin and S. Worschel (Eds.), *The Social Psychology of Intergroup Relations.* Monterey, CA.: Brooks/Cole.

Dizard, J. E., and Gadlin, H. 1990. *The Minimal Family.* Amherst: University of Massachusetts Press.

Donato, K. 1990. "Keepers of the Corporate Image: Women in Public Relations." In B. Reskin and P. Roos (Eds.), *Job Queues, Gender Queues. Explaining Women's Inroads into Male Occupations.* Philadelphia: Temple University Press.

Drucker, P. 1993. "The Rise of the Knowledge Society." *Wilson Quarterly* (Spring): 52–71.

DuBois, W. E. B. 1982. *The Souls of Black Folks.* New York: Penguin. (Original work published 1903.)

Dunne, J. G. 1986. "The War That Won't Go Away." *New York Review of Books* (September 25): 25–29.

Durkheim, E. 1966. *The Rules of Sociological Method* (8th ed.). S. A. Solovay and J. H. Mueller, trans. New York: Free Press. (Original work published 1938.)

Dutton, D. 1989. "Social Class, Health, and Illness." In P. Brown (Ed.), *Perspectives in Medical Sociology.* Belmont, CA: Wadsworth.

Eaton, W. W. 1978. "Life Events, Social Support, and Psychiatric Symptoms: A Re-Analysis of the New Haven Data." *Journal of Health and Social Behavior* 19(2): 230–234.

Eder, D. 1981. "Ability Grouping as a Self-Fulfilling Prophecy: A Micro-Analysis of Teacher Student Interaction." *Sociology of Education* 54:(3) 151–162.

Edin, K. 1994. "The Myth of Dependency and Self-Sufficiency: Women, Welfare, and Low-Wage Work." Working Paper No. 67. Center for Urban Policy and Research. New Brunswick: Rutgers University.

Effran, M. G., and Patterson, E. W. J. 1974. "Voters Vote Beautiful: The Effect of Physical Appearance on a National Election." *Canadian Journal of Behavioral Science* 6: 352–356.

Ekman, P. 1992. *Telling Lies.* New York: W. W. Norton.

Elles, L. 1993. *Social Stratification and Socioeconomic Inequality.* Westport, CT: Praeger.

Ellis, A., and Beechley, R. M. 1954. "Emotional Disturbance in Children with Peculiar Given Names." *Journal of Genetic Psychology* 85: 337–339.

Ellis, H. C. 1972. "Motor Skills in Learning." In *Fundamentals of Human Learning and Cognition.* Dubuque, IA: Wm. C. Brown.

Epstein, C. Fuchs. 1988. *Deceptive Distinctions: Sex, Gender, and the Social Order.* New Haven, CT: Yale University Press.

Epstein, E., and Guttman, R. 1984. "Mate Selection in Man: Evidence, Theory, and Outcome." *Social Biology* 31: 243–278.

Equal Employment Opportunity Commission. 1993. "EEOC Reports Job Bias Charges On Record Pace Through 3rd Quarter." Press release, August 9.

Etzioni, A. 1984. *Capital Corruption.* New York: Harcourt Brace Jovanovich.

———. 1993. *The Spirit of Community: Rights, Responsibilities, and the Community.* New York: Crown.

Evans, C. K. 1992. *Unusual and Most Popular Baby Names.* Lincolnwood, IL: Publications Intl.

Exter, T. 1992. "Home Alone in 2000." *American Demographics.* 14(9) (September): 67.

Fallows, J. 1983. "Immigration: How It Is Affecting Us." *The Atlantic Monthly* 252.

Family Research Council. 1992. *Free to Be Family.* Washington, DC.

Feagin, J. R. 1975. *Subordinating the Poor.* Englewood Cliffs, NJ: Prentice-Hall.

Feingold, A. 1988. "Cognitive Gender Differences Are Disappearing." *American Psychologist* 43: 95–103.

Feldman, S. 1971. "The Presentation of Shortness in Everyday Life." Paper presented at the annual meetings of the American Sociological Association.

Felson, R. B., and Reed, M. 1986. "Reference Groups and Self-Appraisals of Academic Ability and Performance." *Social Psychology Quarterly 49:* 103–109.

———. 1987. "The Effect of Parents on the Self-Appraisals of Children." *Social Psychology Quarterly 49:* 302–308.

Ferraro, K. 1989. "Policing Woman Battering." *Social Problems 26:* 61–74.

Festinger, L., Schachter, S., and Back, K. 1950. *Social Pressures in Informal Groups: A Study of Human Factors in Housing.* New York: Harper and Brothers.

Fingerhut, L. A., and Kleinman, J. C. 1990. "International and Interstate Comparisons of Homicide Among Young Males." *Journal of the American Medical Association 263* (June 17): 3292–3295.

Finkelstein, J. 1991. *The Fashioned Self.* Philadelphia: Temple University Press.

Fischer, C. 1982. *To Dwell Among Friends: Personal Networks in Town and City.* Chicago: University of Chicago Press.

Fischer, D. H. 1977. *Growing Old in America.* New York: Oxford University Press.

Flanagan, T. J., and McLeod, M. (Eds.). 1983. *Sourcebook of Criminal Justice Statistics—1982.* Department of Justice, Bureau of Justice Statistics. Washington, DC: U.S. Government Printing Office.

Foucault, M. 1971. *The Order of Things: An Archeology of Human Sciences.* New York: Pantheon.

Fox, V., and Quit, M. 1980. *Loving, Parenting, and Dying: The Family Cycle in England and America, Past and Present.* New York: Psychohistory Press.

Freudenheim, B. 1988. "Who Lives Here, Go-Getter or Grouch?" *New York Times* (March 31): 15–16.

Funiciello, T. 1990. "The Poverty of Industry" *Ms.* (Nov/Dec): 32–40.

Furstenburg, F., Jr. 1979. "Pre-marital Pregnancy and Marital Instability." In G. Levinger and O. C. Moles (Eds.), *Divorce and Separation.* New York: Basic Books.

———. 1988. "Good Dads-Bad Dads: Two Faces of Fatherhood." In Cherlin, A. (Ed.), *The Changing American Family and Public Policy.* Washington, DC: Urban Institute Press.

Furstenburg, F. F., Jr., and Talvitie, K. G. 1980. "Children's Names and Parental Claims: Bonds Between Unmarried Fathers and Their Children." *Journal of Family Issues 1:* 31–57.

Gans, H. 1971. "The Uses of Poverty: The Poor Pay for All." *Social Policy* (Summer): 20–24.

Gelles, R., and Cornell, C. 1990. *Intimate Violence in Families* (2nd ed.). Newbury Park, CA: Sage.

Gelles, R., and Straus, M. 1988. *Intimate Violence.* New York: Simon and Schuster.

Gelles, R. J., and Loseke, D. R. (Eds.). 1993. *Current Controversies on Family Violence.* Newbury Park, CA: Sage.

General Social Science Surveys 1972–1993: Cumulative Codebook. 1993. Chicago: National Opinion Research Center.

George, S. 1977. *How the Other Half Dies: The Real Reasons for World Hunger.* Totowa, NJ: Rowman and Allanheld.

Gerbner, G., and Gross, L. 1972. "Living with Television: The Violence Profile." *Journal of Communication 26:* 173–199.

Gerbner, G., Gross, L., Jackson-Beek, M., Jeffries-Fox, S., and Signorielli, N. 1978. "Cultural Indicators: Violence Profile No. 9." *Journal of Communication 28:* 176–206.

Gergen, K. 1971. *The Concept of Self.* New York: Holt, Rinehart, and Winston.

Gettleman, T. E., and Thompson, J. K. 1993. "Actual Differences and Stereotypical Perceptions in Body Image and Eating Disturbance: A Comparison of Male and Female Heterosexual and Homosexual Sample." *Sex Roles 29* (7/8): 545–562.

Gibbs, N. 1988. "Grays on the Go." *Time* (February 22): 66–75.

Giddens, A. 1992. *The Transformation of Intimacy, Sexuality, Love and Eroticism in Modern Societies.* Stanford, CA: Stanford University Press.

Gil, D. 1986. "Sociocultural Aspects of Domestic Violence." In M. Lystad (Ed.), *Violence in the Home: Interdisciplinary Perspectives* (pp. 124–149). New York: Brunner/Mazel.

Gilbert, D., and Kahl, J. A. 1993. *The American Class Structure: A New Synthesis* (4th ed.). Belmont, CA: Wadsworth.

Glenn, N. D., and Supancic, M. 1984. "The Social and Demographic Correlates of Divorce and Separation in the United States." *Journal of Marriage and the Family 46:* 563–575.

Glick, P., and Sung-Ling, L. 1986. "Recent Changes in Divorce and Remarriage." *Journal of Marriage and Family 48:* 737–747.

Goffman, E. 1959. *The Presentation of Self in Everyday Life.* New York: Anchor.

———. 1963. *Stigma: Notes on the Management of Spoiled Identity.* Englewood Cliffs, NJ: Prentice-Hall.

———. 1974. *Frame Analysis.* Cambridge: Harvard University Press.

Goleman, D. 1985. *Vital Lies, Simple Truths.* New York: Simon and Schuster.

Goodlad, J. 1984. *A Place Called School: Prospects for the Future.* New York: McGraw-Hill.

Gouldner, H., and Strong, M. S. 1987. *Speaking of Friendship: Middle-Class Women and Their Friends.* New York: Greenwood Press.

Greven, P. J. 1970. *Four Generations: Population, Land, and Family in Colonial Andover.* Ithaca, NY: Cornell University Press.

Grover, K. J., Russell, C. S., and Schumm, W. 1985. "Mate Selection Processes and Marital Satisfaction." *Family Relations 34:* 383–386.

Hacker, A. 1992. *Two Nations: Black and White, Separate, Hostile, Unequal.* New York: Scribner.

Hall, W. 1986. "Social Class and Survival on the S. S. Titanic." *Social Science and Medicine 22:* 687–690.

Hallinan, M., and Sorenson, A. 1985. "Ability Grouping and Student Friendships." *American Educational Research Journal 22:* 485–499.

Hamilton, N. L., Broman, C., and Hoffman, W. 1990. "Hard Times and Vulnerable People: Initial Effects of Plant Closings on Auto Workers' Mental Health." *Journal of Health and Social Behavior 31:* 123–140.

Hareven, T. 1978. "The Dynamics of Kin in an Industrial Community." In John Demos and Sarane Boocock (Eds.), *Turning Points: Historical and Sociological Essays on the Family.* Chicago: University of Chicago Press.

Harris, L. 1981. *Aging in the Eighties: America in Transition.* Washington, DC: National Council on Aging.

Harris, M. J., and Rosenthal, R. 1985. "Mediation of Interpersonal Expectancy Effects: 31 Meta-analyses." *Psychological Bulletin 97:* 363–386.

Harris, T. G. 1978. Introduction to E. H. Walster and G. W. Walster, *A New Look At Love.* Reading, MA: Addison-Wesley.

Harrison, P. 1984. *Inside the Third World: The Anatomy of Poverty* (2nd ed.). New York: Penguin.

Hartman, H. 1976. "Capitalism, Patriarchy, and Job Segregation by Sex." *Signs 1* (3): 137–170.

Hatfield, E., and Sprechter, S. 1986. *Mirror, Mirror: The Importance of Looks in Everyday Life.* Albany, NY: SUNY Press.

Haug, M., and Folmar, S. 1986. "Longevity, Gender and Life Quality." *Journal of Health and Social Behavior 27.*

Haug, W. F. 1986. *Critique of Commodity Aesthetics.* Minneapolis: University of Minnesota Press.

Heider, F. 1980. *The Psychology of Interpersonal Relations.* New York: Wiley.

Heiland, H. G., Shelley, L. I., and Katoh, H. 1991. *Crime and Control in Comparative Perspectives.* Hawthorne, NY: Aldine de Gruyter.

Hochschild, A.R. 1989. *The Second Shift: Working Parents and the Revolution at Home.* New York: Viking.

Hoffer, T., Greeley, A., and Coleman, J. 1987. "Catholic High School Effects on Achievement Growth." In E. Haertel, T. James, and H. Levin, (Eds.), *Comparing Public and Private Schools* (pp. 67–88). Vol 2: *Student Achievement.* New York: Falmer.

Hoffman, S., and Duncan, G. 1988. "What *Are* the Economic Consequences of Divorce?" *Demography 25.*

Hollingshead, A. B. 1950. "Cultural Factors in the Selection of Marriage Mates." *American Sociological Review 15:* 619–627.

Holloway, J., and Moke, P. 1986. "Post Secondary Correctional Education: An Evaluation of Parolee Performance." Unpublished report, Wilmington College, Wilmington, Ohio.

House, J. 1988. "Social Relationships and Health." *Science 241:* 540–545.

House, J. S., Strecher, V., Metzner, H. L., Robbins, C. A. 1986. "Occupational Stress and Health Among Men and Women in the Tecumseh Community Health Study." *Journal of Health and Social Behavior 31*(2): 123–140.

Hout, M. 1982. "The Association Between Husbands' and Wives' Occupations in Two-Earner Families." *American Journal of Sociology 88* (September): 397–409.

_____. 1988. "More Universalism, Less Structural Mobility: The American Occupational Structure in the 1980s." *American Journal of Sociology 93* (May): 1358–1400.

Howell, M. 1986. "Women, the Family Economy, and Market Production." In B. Hanawalt (Ed.), *Women and Work in Pre-Industrial Europe*. Bloomington: Indiana University Press.

Hughes, E. C. 1945. "Dilemmas and Contradictions of Status" *American Journal of Sociology 50*(5): 353–359.

Hutchinson, J., and Smith, A. 1994. *Nationalism*. New York: Oxford University Press.

Hyde, J. S. Fennema, E., and Lamon, S. J. 1990. "Gender Differences in Mathematics Performance." *Psychological Bulletin 107:* 139–155.

Hyde, J. S., and Linn, M. C. 1988. "Gender Differences in Verbal Ability." *Psychological Bulletin 104:* 53–69.

Iams, J. 1990. "Soviets Line Up For Makeup." *Advertising Age 61*(3) (January 15): 12.

Insko, C. A., and Wilson, M. 1977. "Interpersonal Attraction as a Function of Social Interaction." *Journal of Personality and Social Psychology 35:* 903–911.

Isaacs, H. 1975. *Idols of the Tribe*. Cambridge: Harvard University Press.

Jackson, L. A. 1992. *Physical Appearance and Gender: A Sociobiological and Sociocultural Perspective*. Albany: State University of New York Press.

Jacobs, P. 1988. "Keeping the Poor, Poor." In J. H. Skolnick and E. Currie (Eds.), *Crisis in American Institutions*. Glenview, IL: Scott, Foresman.

Jacobson, D. 1989. "Context and the Sociological Study of Stress." *Journal of Health and Social Behavior 30*(3): 257–260.

Jankowiak, W., and Fischer, E. 1992. "A Crosscultural Perspective on Romantic Love." *Journal of Ethnology 31:* 149–156.

Jedlicka, D., and Kephart, W. M. 1991. *The Family, Society, and the Individual*. New York: Harper and Row.

Jeffries, V., and Ransford, E. 1980. *Social Stratification: A Multiple Hierarchy Approach*. Boston: Allyn and Bacon.

Jencks, C., and Edin, K. 1995. "Do Poor Women Have the Right to Bear Children?" *American Prospect* (Winter), no. 20: 43–52.

Johnson, D. W., and Johnson, R. T. 1989. *Cooperation and Competition: Theory and Research*. Edina, MN: Interaction Books.

Johnson, J. L., McAndrew, F. T., and Harris, P. B. 1991. "Sociobiology and the Naming of Adopted and Natural Children." *Etiology and Sociobiology 12:* 365–375.

Jones, L. 1980. *Great Expectations*. New York: Ballantine Books.

Jones, W., Hansson, R. O., and Phillips A. L. 1978. "Physical Attractiveness and Judgements of Psychopathology." *Journal of Social Psychology 105:* 79–84.

Jordan, M. 1993. "In Cities Like Atlanta, Whites Are Passing on Public Schools." *Washington Post* (May 24): A:1:1.

Kahane, H. 1992. *The Use of Reason in Everyday Life* (6th ed.). Belmont, CA: Wadsworth.

Kalisch, P. A., and Kalisch, B. J. 1984. "Sex-Role Stereotyping of Nurses and Physicians on Prime-Time Television: A Dichotomy of Occupational Portrayals." *Sex Roles 10*: 533–553.

Karen, D. 1990. "Toward a Political Organizational Model of Gatekeeping: The Case of Elite Colleges." *Sociology of Education 63*: 227–240.

Kart, G. 1990. *The Realities of Aging* (3rd ed.). Boston: Allyn and Bacon.

Katz, M. (Ed.). 1971. *School Reform Past and Present*. Boston: Little Brown.

——————. 1986. *In the Shadow of the Poorhouse: A Social History of Welfare in America*. New York: Basic Books.

Kaw, E. 1994. "Opening Faces: The Politics of Cosmetic Surgery and Asian American Women." In N. Sault (Ed.), *Many Mirrors: Body Image and Social Relations* (pp. 241–265). New Brunswick: Rutgers University Press.

Kelley, H. H., and Stahelski, A. J. 1970. "Errors in Perception of Intentions in a Mixed-Motive Game." *Journal of Experimental Social Psychology 6*: 379–400.

Kephart, W. M., and Jedlicka, D. 1991. *The Family, Society, and the Individual*. New York: Harper & Row.

Kessler, R., Price, R., and Wortman, C. 1994. "Lifetime and 12-Month Prevalence of DSM-III-R Psychiatric Disorders in the United States." *Archives of General Psychiatry 51*: 8–19.

Kessler, R. C., and McLeod, J. D. 1985. "Social Support and Mental Health in Community Sample." In S. Cohen and L. Syme (Eds.), *Social Support and Health*. Orlando: Academic Press.

Kessler, R. C., Price, R. H., and Wortman, C. B. 1985. "Social Factors in Psychopathology: Stress, Social Support, and Coping Processes." *Annual Review of Psychology 36*: 531–572.

Kessler-Harris, A. 1982. *Out to Work: A History of Wage-Earning Women in the United States*. New York: Oxford University Press.

Kids Count Data Book. 1991. Washington, DC: Center For Social Policy.

Kilker, E. 1993. "Black and White in America: The Culture and Politics of Racial Classification." *International Journal of Politics, Culture, and Society 7*: 229–258.

Kitson, G. C., Babri, K. B., and Roach, M. J. 1985. "Who Divorces and Why?" *Journal of Family Issues 6*: 285–293.

Knutson, L. L. 1992. "Census: Poverty Has Eroded Middle-Class." *Santa Barbara News-Press* (May 31): A–7.

Kobasa, S. O., Maddi, S. R., and Kahn, S. 1982. "Hardiness and Health." *Journal of Personality and Social Psychology 42*: 168–177.

Kohn, Alfie. 1986. *No Contest: The Case Against Competition*. Boston: Houghton Mifflin.

Komarovsky, M. 1962. *Blue-Collar Marriage*. New Haven: Vintage.

Kornhauser, W. 1959. *The Politics of Mass Society*. New York: Free Press.

Kosters, M. 1990. "Be Cool, Stay in School." *The American Enterprise* (March/April): 60–67.

Kozol, J. 1991. *Savage Inequalities*. New York: Crown.

Kraut, K., and Luna, M. 1992. *Work and Wages: Facts on Women and People of Color in the Workforce.* Washington, DC: National Committee on Pay Equity.

Ladd, E. C. 1987. "Class Differences: An Issue for 1988?" *Public Opinion 10* (May/June): 21–29.

Lake, A. 1975. "Are We Born into Our Sex Roles or Programmed into Them?" *Woman's Day* (January): 25–35.

Langlois, J. H., and Stephan, C. W. 1981. "Beauty and the Beast: The Role of Physical Attractiveness in the Development of Peer Relations and Social Behavior." In S. S. Brehm, S. M. Kassin, and F. X. Gibbons (Eds.), *Developmental Social Psychology.* New York: Oxford University Press.

Lansky, B., and Sinrod, B. 1990. *The Baby Name Personality Survey.* Deephaven, MN: Meadowbrook Press.

Lanzetta, J. T. 1955. "Group Behavior Under Stress." *Human Relations 8:* 29–53.

Lapidus, J., Green, S. K., and Baruh, E. 1985. "Factors Related to Roommate Compatibility in the Residence Hall—A Review." *Journal of College Student Personnel 26:* 420–434.

Laslett, B., and Warren, C. B. 1975. "Losing Weight: The Organizational Promotion of Behavior Change." *Social Problems 23*(1): 69–80.

Latané, B., and Glass, D. C. 1968. "Social and Nonsocial Attraction in Rats." *Journal of Personality and Social Psychology 9:* 142–146.

Laumann, E. O., Gagnon, J. H., Michael, R. T., and Michaels, S. 1994. *The Social Organization of Sexuality.* Chicago: University of Chicago Press.

Lazarsfeld, P. 1949. "The American Soldier: An Expository Review." *Public Opinion Quarterly 13*(3): 376–404.

Lee, T. 1990. "Here Comes the Pink Slip." *American Demographics* (March): 46–49.

Lemert, E. 1951. *Social Pathology: A Systematic Approach to the Theory of Sociopathic Behavior.* New York: McGraw-Hill.

Lennon, M. C. 1989. "The Structural Contexts of Stress." *Journal of Health and Social Behavior 30*(3): 261–268.

Leone, R. 1994. "What's Trust Got to Do with It?" *The American Prospect 17:* 78–83.

Levine, M. P. 1987. *Student Eating Disorders: Anorexia Nervosa and Bulimia.* Washington, DC: National Educational Association.

LeVine, R. A., and White, M. 1992. "The Social Transformation of Childhood." In A. S. Skolnick and J. H. Skolnick (Eds.), *Family in Transition.* New York: Harper Collins.

Levi-Strauss, C. 1964. *The Raw and the Cooked: Introduction to a Science of Mythology.* New York: Harper & Row.

Levine, R. V. 1993. "Is Love A Luxury?" *American Demographics 15*(2): 27–28.

Levitan, S. 1985. *Programs on Aid of the Poor.* Baltimore: Johns Hopkins University Press.

Lewak, R. W., Wakefield, J. A., Jr., and Briggs, P. F. 1985. "Intelligence and Personality in Mate Choice and Marital Satisfaction." *Personality and Individual Differences 6:* 471–477.

Lewis, M. 1978. *The Culture of Inequality.* New York: New American Library.

Lieberson, S., and Bell, E. 1992. "Children's First Names: An Empirical Study of Social Taste." *American Journal of Sociology* 98: 511–554.

Lieberson, S., and Mikelson, K. 1995. "Distinctive African-American Names: An Experimental, Historical, and Linguistic Analysis of Innovation." *American Sociological Review* 60(6): 928–946.

Lin, N. 1982. "Social Resources and Instrumental Action." In P. Marsden and N. Lin (Eds.), *Social Structure and Network Analysis* (pp. 131–145). Beverly Hills, CA: Sage.

Livingston, J. 1996. *Crime and Criminology* (2nd. ed.). Upper Saddle River, NJ: Prentice-Hall.

Locher, P., Unger, R., Sociedade, P., and Wahl, J. 1993. "At First Glance: Accessibility of the Physical Attractiveness Stereotype." *Sex Roles* 28:(11/12): 729–743.

Lord, W. 1981. *A Night To Remember.* New York: Penguin.

Los Angeles Times. 1990. "One Man, 2 Paintings: 160.6 Million" (May 19) F: 1–2.

Lystad, M. (Ed.). 1986. *Violence in the Home: Interdisciplinary Perspectives.* New York: Brunner/Mazel.

Maguire, K., and Pastore, A. L. 1994. *Sourcebook of Criminal Justice Statistics.* Washington, DC: U.S. Government Printing Office.

Makeup sales rise. 1990. *Wall Street Journal* (September 6): 7:6

Mandel, M. 1992. "Who'll Get the Lion's Share of Wealth in the 90's? The Lion." *Business Week* (June): 86–88.

Manning, P. 1974. "Police Lying." *Urban Life* 3: 283–306.

———. 1984. "Lying, Secrecy, and Social Control." In J. Douglas Newton (Ed.), *The Sociology of Deviance* (pp. 268–279). Newton, MA: Allyn and Bacon.

Mare, R. D. 1991. "Five Decades of Educational Assortive Mating." *American Sociological Review* 56(1): 15–32.

Marks, G., Miller, N., and G. Maruyama. 1981. "Effects of Targets' Physical Attractiveness on Assumptions of Similarity." *Journal of Personality and Social Psychology* 41: 198–206.

Martin, T. C., and Bumpass, L. L. 1989. "Recent Trends in Marital Disruption." *Demography* 26: 41.

Marvelle, K., and Green, S. 1980. "Physical Attractiveness and Sex Bias in Hiring Decisions for Two Types of Jobs." *Journal of the National Association of Women Deans, Administrators, and Counselors* 44(1): 3–6.

Massey, D., and Denton, N. 1993. *American Apartheid.* Boston: Harvard University Press.

Mathisen, J. A. 1989. "A Further Look At 'Common Sense' in Introductory Sociology." *Teaching Sociology* 17(3): 307–315.

May, E. 1988. *Homeward Bound: American Families in the Cold War Era.* New York: Basic Books.

Maze, M., and Mayall, D. 1991. *The Enhanced Guide for Occupational Exploration* Indianapolis: JIST Works, Inc.

McConahay, J. B. 1981. "Reducing Racial Prejudice in Desegregated Schools." In W. D. Hawley (Ed.), *Effective School Desegregation.* Beverly Hills, CA: Sage.

McFalls, J. 1990. "The Risks of Reproductive Impairment in the Later Years of Childbearing." *Annual Review of Sociology 16:* 491–519.

McLean, E. A. 1994. "USA Snapshots: Where the Diet Bucks Go." *USA Today* (August 2): B:1:1.

Mead, G. H. 1934. *Mind, Self, and Society.* Chicago: University of Chicago Press.

Mehan, H. 1992. "Understanding Inequality in Schools: The Contribution of Interpretive Studies." *Sociology of Education* 65(1): 1–20.

Mehrabian, A. 1990. *The Name Game: The Decision That Lasts a Lifetime.* Bethesda, MD.: National Press Books.

Meier, R. F. 1989. *Crime and Society.* Boston: Allyn and Bacon.

Menaghan, E. G., and Merves, E. S. 1984. "Coping with Occupational Problems: The Limits of Individual Efforts." *Journal of Health and Social Behavior* 25(4): 406–423.

Mensch, B. 1986. "Age Differences Between Spouses in First Marriages." *Social Biology 33:* 229–240.

Merton, R. 1938. "Social Structure and Anomie." *American Sociological Review 3:* 672–682.

Merton, R. K. 1957. *Social Theory and Social Structure.* Glencoe, IL: Free Press.

Millman, M. 1980. *Such A Pretty Face: Being Fat in America.* New York: W. W. Norton.

Mills, C. W. 1959. *The Sociological Imagination.* London: Oxford University Press.

Minas, J. S., Scodel, A., Marlowe, D., and Rawson, H. 1960. "Some Descriptive Aspects of Two-Person, Zero-Sum Games." *Journal of Conflict Resolution 4:* 193–197.

Mintz, S., and Kellogg, S. 1988. *Domestic Revolutions: A Social History of American Family Life.* New York: Free Press.

Mirowsky, J., and Ross, C. 1989. *The Social Causes of Psychological Distress.* Hawthorne, NY: Aldine.

Mishkind, M. E., Rodin, J., Silberstein, L. R., and Striegel-Moore, R. H. 1986. "The Embodiment of Masculinity." *American Behavioral Scientist* 29: 545–562.

Molnar, S. 1991. *Human Variation: Races, Types and Ethnic Groups* (3rd ed.). Englewood Cliffs, NJ: Prentice-Hall.

Monge, P. T., and Kirste, K. K. 1980. "Measuring Proximity in Human Organizations." *Social Psychology Quarterly 43:* 110–115.

Monk-Turner, E. 1990. "The Occupational Achievements of Community and Four Year College Entrants." *American Sociological Review 55:* 719–725.

Mortenson Report. 1993. "Postsecondary Education Opportunity." *11* (February): 10.

Mortimer, J. T., and Simmons, R. G. 1978. "Adult Socialization." *Annual Review of Sociology 4:* 421–454.

Mosley, W., and Cowley, P. 1991. "The Challenge of World Health." *Population Bulletin 46(4).* Washington, DC: Population Reference Bureau.

Murstein, B. I. 1976. *Who Will Marry Whom?* New York: Springer.

Mutchler, J., and Burr, J. 1991. "A Longitudinal Analysis of Household and Nonhousehold Living Arrangements in Later Life." *Demography 28:* 375–390.

Myers, D. 1987. *Social Psychology.* New York: McGraw Hill.

Myers, P. N., Jr., and Biocca, F. A. 1992. "The Elastic Body Image: The Effect of Television Advertising and Programming on Body Image Distortions in Young Women." *Journal of Communication* 42(3): 108–134.

National Center for Health Statistics. 1990. *Vital Statistics of the U.S.* Washington, DC: U.S. Government Printing Office.

———. 1992. *Health, United States, 1991.* Hyattsville, MD: Public Health Service.

National Commission on Excellence in Education. 1983. *A Nation At Risk.* Washington, DC: U.S. Government Printing Office.

Newberger, E., and Bourne, R. (Eds.). 1985. *Unhappy Families.* Littleton, MA: PSG Publishing.

NORC. 1994. *General Social Surveys, 1972–1994: Cummulative Codebook.* Storrs, CT: Roper Center.

Nordheimer, J. 1990. "Stepfathers: The Shoes Rarely Fit." *New York Times* (October 18): 6.

O'Hare, W. 1990. "The Rise of Hispanic Affluence," *American Demographics* 12(8) (August): 40–43.

Ong, P. 1994. *The State of Asia Pacific America: Economic Diversity Issues, and Policies.* Los Angeles: University of California Asian-American Studies Center and LEAP: Asian Pacific American Public Policy Institute.

Ornstein, N., and Schmitt, M. 1990. "The New World of Interest Politics." *American Enterprise* 1 (January–February): 46–51.

Owsley, H. 1977. "The Marriage of Rachel Donelson." *Tennessee Historical Quarterly* 36 (Winter): 479–492.

Pagnini, D. L., and Morgan, S. P. 1990. "Intermarriage and Social Distance Among U.S. Immigrants at the Turn of the Century." *American Journal of Sociology* 96(3): 405–432.

Parker, R. N. 1989. "Poverty, Subculture of Violence, and Types of Homicide." *Social Forces* 67: 983–1005.

Parker, S. 1990. *Informal Marriage: Cohabitation and the Law.* New York: St. Martin's Press.

Parsons, T. 1964. *The Social System.* Glencoe, Ill.: Free Press.

Patterson, J., and Kim, P. 1991. *The Day America Told the Truth: What People Really Believe About Everything That Really Matters.* New York: Prentice-Hall.

Pear, R. 1992. "New Look at the U.S. in 2050: Bigger, Older and Less White." *New York Times* (July 8).

Pearce, D. 1983. "The Feminization of Ghetto Poverty." *Society* 21(1): 70–74.

Pearlin, L. 1989. "The Sociological Study of Stress." *Journal of Health and Social Behavior* 30(3): 242–256.

Pearlin, L., Menaghan, E. G., Lieberman, M. A., and Mullan, J. T. 1981. "The Stress Process." *Journal of Health and Social Behavior* 22(4): 337–356.

Pearson, D. E. 1993. "Post Mass Culture." *Society* 30(5): 17–22.

People for the American Way and Peter D. Hart Research Associates. 1992. *Democracy's Next Generation II: A Study of American Youth on Race.* Washington, DC: People for the American Way.

Persell, C., and Cookson, P. 1990. "Chartering and Bartering: Elite Education and Social Class." In P. Kingston and L. Lewis (Eds.), *The High Status Track*. Albany, NY: SUNY Press.

Pescosolido, B., and Georgianna, S. 1989. "Durkheim, Suicide, and Religion: Toward a Network Theory of Suicide." *American Sociological Review 54*(1): 33–48.

Peters Atlas of the World. 1990. New York: Harper and Row.

Peterson, K. 1992. "The Manquiladora Revolution in Guatemala." Occasional Paper Series 2. New Haven: Yale Law School, Orville H. Schell Jr. Center for International Human Rights.

Pfohl, S. 1977. "The Discovery of Child Abuse." *Social Problems 24*(3): 310–323.

Pisko, V. W., and Stern, J. (eds). 1985. *The Condition of Education: Statistical Report*. National Center for Education Statistics. Washington, DC: U.S. Government Printing Office.

Pleck, J. 1985. *Working Wives/Working Husbands*. Beverly Hills, CA: Sage.

Polakow, V. 1993. *Lives on the Edge*. Chicago: University of Chicago Press.

Popkin, S. 1990. "Welfare: Views from the Bottom" *Social Problems 17*(1) (February): 64–79.

Porter, S. 1991. "Death Rate for Infants a Tragedy." *The Olympian* (April 15).

The President's Commission on Law Enforcement and Administration of Justice. 1968. The Challenge of Crime in a Free Society. Washington, DC: U.S. Government Printing Office.

Price, S. J., and P. C. McKenry. 1988. *Divorce*. Beverly Hills, CA: Sage.

Public Opinion. 1986. "Opinion Roundup." *Public Opinion 8*(1):1 25–34.

Rapoport, A. 1960. *Fights, Games, and Debates*. Ann Arbor: University of Michigan Press.

Rawlins, W. 1992. *Friendship Matters: Communication, Dialectics, and the Life Course*. New York: Aldine de Gruyter.

Reddy, M. (Ed.). 1993. *American Salaries and Wages Survey* (2nd. ed.). Detroit: Gale Research, Inc.

Reich, R. 1991. *The Work of Nations*. New York: Knopf.

Reiman, J. 1990. *The Rich Get Richer and the Poor Get Prison*. New York: Macmillan.

Reis, H. T., Nezlek, J., and Wheeler, L. 1980. "Physical Attractiveness in Social Interaction." *Journal of Personality and Social Psychology 38*: 604–617.

Rensberger, B. 1981. "Racial Odyssey." *Science Digest* (Jan/Feb).

Renzetti, C. M., and Curran, D. J. 1989. *Women, Men and Society: The Sociology of Gender*. Boston: Allyn and Bacon.

Reskin, B., and Padavic, I. 1994. *Women, Men and Work*. Newbury Park, CA: Pine Forge Press.

Richardson, L. W. 1988. *The Dynamics of Sex and Gender: A Sociological Perspective*. New York: Harper and Row.

Riley, D. 1988. *Am I That Name?* Minneapolis: University of Minnesota Press.

Riley, G. 1991. *Divorce: An American Tradition*. New York: Oxford University Press.

Ritzer, G. 1995. *Expressing America: A Critique of the Global Credit Card Society.* Twin Oaks, CA: Pine Forge Press.

Rivo, M. L., Kofie, V., Schwartz, E., Levy, M. E., and Tuckson, R. 1989. "Comparisons of Black and White Smoking—Attributable Mortality Morbidity and Economic Costs in the District of Columbia." *Journal of the National Medical Association 81*(11): 1125–1130.

Rix, S. (Ed.). 1989. *The American Women 1988–1989: A Status Report.* Women's Research and Education Institute. New York: Norton.

Roberts, D. F. 1975. "The Dynamics of Racial Intermixture in the American Negro: Some Anthropological Considerations." *American Journal of Human Genetics 7:* 361–367.

Rosenhan, D. L. 1973. "On Being Sane in Insane Places." *Science 179:* 250–258.

Rosenthal, R., and Jacobson, L. 1968. *Pygmalion in the Classroom.* New York: Holdt, Rinehart, and Winston.

Rosewater, A. 1989. "Child and Family Trends." In F. Macchiarola and A. Gartner (Eds.), *Caring for America's Children* (pp. 4–19). New York: Academy of Political Sciences.

Ross, C. E., and Huber, J. 1985. "Hardship and Depression." *Journal of Health and Social Behavior 26*(4): 312–327.

Ross, H., and Taylor, H. 1989. "Do Boys Prefer Daddy or His Physical Style of Play?" *Sex Roles 20* (January): 23–33.

Ross, L. 1977. "The Intuitive Psychologist and His Shortcomings: Distortions in the Attribution Process." In L. Berkowitz (Ed.), *Advances in Experimental Social Psychology* (Vol. 10). New York: Academic Press.

Ruane, J. 1993. "Tolerance Revisited: The Case of Spousal Force." *Sociological Focus 26*(4): 333–343.

Ruane, R., Cerulo, K., and Gerson, J. 1994. "Professional Deceit: Normal Lying in an Occupational Setting." *Sociological Focus 27*(2): 91–109.

Rubin, B. 1996. *Shifts in the Social Contract: Understanding Change in American Society.* Twin Oaks, CA: Pine Forge Press.

Rubin, J. Z., Provenzano, F. J., and Luria, Z. 1974. "The Eye of the Beholder: Parents' Views on Sex of Newborns." *American Journal of Orthopsychiatry 44:* 512–519.

Rubin, L. B. 1985. *Just Friends: The Role of Friendship in Our Lives.* New York: Harper and Row.

Rubin, N., Shmilovitz, C., and Weiss, M. 1993. "From Fat to Thin: Informal Rites Affirming Identity Change." *Symbolic Interaction 16*(1): 1–17.

Sacks, H. 1975. "Everyone Has to Lie." In Mary Sanches and Ben Blount (Eds.), *Sociocultural Dimensions of Language Use* (pp. 57–79). New York: Academic Press.

Sadker, M., and Sadker, D. 1985. "Sexism in the Schoolroom of the '80s." *Psychology Today 19:*54–57.

Salmon, M. 1986. *Women and the Law of Property in Early America.* Chapel Hill: University of North Carolina Press.

Schachter, S. 1959. *The Psychology of Affiliation*. Stanford: Stanford University Press.

Schlesinger, P., Dobash, R. E., Dobash, R. P., and Weaver, C. K. 1992. *Women Viewing Violence*. London: BFI.

Schneiderman, R. 1967. *All for One*. New York: P. S. Eriksson.

Schultz, J. W., and Pruitt, D. G. 1978. "The Effect of Mutual Concern on Joint Welfare." *Journal of Experimental Social Psychology* 14: 480–492.

Schuman, D., and Olufs, R. 1995. "Multiculturalism II: The Wider World." In *Diversity on Campus*. Boston: Allyn and Bacon.

Schur, E. 1984. *Labeling Women Deviant*. Philadelphia: Temple University Press.

Schwartz, J. 1989. "Rising Status." *American Demographics* 11(1) (January): 10.

Schwartz, J., and Volgy, T. 1992. *The Forgotten Americans: Thirty Million Working Poor in the Land of Opportunity*. New York: Norton.

Seligmann, J. 1994. "The Death of a Spouse." *Newsweek* (May 9): 57.

Sennett, R. 1977. *The Fall of Public Man*. New York: Knopf.

Sennett, R., and Cobb, J. 1972. *The Hidden Injuries of Class*. New York: Vintage.

Sewell, W., and Shah, V. 1968. "Parents' Education and Children's Education Aspirations and Achievements." *American Sociological Review* 33(2): 191–209.

Shanas, E., and Maddox, G. 1976. "Aging, Health, and the Organization of Health Resources." In R. Binstock and E. Shanas (Eds.), *Handbook of Aging and the Social Sciences*. New York: Van Nostrand Reinhold.

Sharpe, R. 1994. "The Waiting Game." *Wall Street Journal* (March 29): A1, A8.

Shavit, Y., and Featherman, D. 1988. "Schooling, Tracking, and Teenage Intelligence." *Sociology of Education* 61.

Sherif, M. 1966. *In Common Predicament: Social Psychology of Intergroup Conflict and Cooperation*. Boston: Houghton Mifflin.

Sherif, M., Harvey, O. J., White, B. J., Hood, W. R., and Sherif, C. W. 1961. *Intergroup Conflict and Cooperation: The Robbers' Cave Experiment*. Norman, OK: The University Book Exchange.

Sherraden, M. 1988. "Rethinking Social Welfare: Toward Assets." *Social Policy* (Winter): 37–43.

Shipman, P. 1994. *The Evolution of Racism: Human Differences and the Use and Abuse of Science*. New York: Simon and Schuster.

Sidel, R. 1986. *Women and Children Last*. New York: Penguin.

———. 1991. *On Her Own: Growing Up in the Shadows of the American Dream*. New York: Viking Press.

Siegel, J., and Taeuber, C. 1986. "Demographic Perspectives on the Long-Lived Society." *Daedalus* 115.

Sigall, H., and Aronson, E. 1969. "Liking of an Evaluator as a Function of Her Physical Attractiveness and the Nature of the Evaluations." *Journal of Experimental Social Psychology* 5: 93–100.

Signorielli, N., and Morgan, N. 1988. *Cultivation Analysis* Newbury Park, CA: Sage.

Silberner, J. 1990. "Health: Another Gender Gap" *U.S. News & World Report* (September 24): 54–55.

Simmel, G. 1950. "The Lie." In K. Wolff (Ed.), *The Sociology of Georg Simmel* (pp. 312–316). New York: Free Press.

_____. 1950. "The Stranger." In K. Wolff (Ed.), *The Sociology of Georg Simmel* (pp. 402–408). New York: Free Press.

Simmons, J. L. 1966. "Public Stereotypes of Deviants" *Social Problems 13:* 223–232.

Simon, B. L. 1987. *Never Married Women.* Philadelphia: Temple University Press.

Simon, D. R., and Eitzen, D. S. 1990. *Elite Deviance* (3rd. ed.). Boston: Allyn and Bacon.

Simpson, J., Campbell, B., and Berscheid, E. 1986. "The Association Between Romantic Love and Marriage: Kephart (1967) Twice Revisited." *Personality and Social Psychology Bulletin 12:* 363–372.

Skolnick, A. 1991. *Embattled Paradise: The American Family in an Age of Uncertainty.* New York: Basic Books.

Slater, P. 1970. *The Pursuit of Loneliness: American Culture at the Breaking Point.* Boston: Beacon Press.

Slavin, R. E., and Madden, N. A. 1979. "School Practices That Improve Race Relations." *American Educational Research Journal 16:* 169–180.

Smith, A. 1991. *National Identity.* Reno: University of Nevada Press.

Smith, T. W. 1990. *Ethnic Images.* Chicago: National Opinion Research Center (December).

Soldo, B., and Agree, E. 1988. "America's Elderly." *Population Bulletin 43:*1–51.

Sorenson, A. 1990. "Estimating the Economic Consequences of Separation and Divorce: A Cautionary Tale from the U.S." In L. Weitzman and M. Maclean (Eds.), *Economic Consequences of Divorce: The International Perspective.* Oxford, England: Clarendon.

Spencer, G. 1989. *Projections of the Population of the United States, by Age, Sex, and Race: 1988–2080.* Washington, DC: U.S. Government Printing Office.

The State of America's Children. 1991. Washington, DC: The Children's Defense Fund.

Stinchcombe, A. 1963. "Some Empirical Consequences of the Davis-Moore Theory of Stratification." *American Sociological Review 28*(5): 805–808.

Stock, P. 1978. *Better Than Rubies: A History of Women's Education.* New York: G. P. Putnam's Sons.

Stone, L. 1989. "The Road to Polygamy." *New York Review of Books* (March):13.

Straus, M., and Gelles, R. 1986. "Societal Change and Changes in Family Violence from 1975 to 1985 as Revealed by Two National Surveys." *Journal of Marriage and the Family 48:* 465–479.

_____. 1988. "Violence in American Families: How Much Is There and Why Does It Occur?" In E. Nunnaly and C. Chilman (Eds.), *Troubled Relationships* (pp. 141–162). Newbury Park: Sage.

_____. 1990. *Physical Violence in American Families: Risk Factors and Adaptations to Violence in 8,145 Families.* New Brunswick, NJ: Transaction.

Straus, M., Gelles, R., and Steinmetz, S. 1980. *Behind Closed Doors: Violence in American Families.* New York: Doubleday.

Strong, B., and DeVault, C. 1989. *The Marriage and Family Experience.* St. Paul, MN: West.

Strum, C. 1993. "School Tracking: Efficiency or Elitism?" *New York Times* (April 1): B5.

Sumner, W. G. 1963. "Sociology." In *Social Darwinism: Selected Essays of William Graham Sumner* (pp. 9–29). Englewood Cliffs, NJ: Prentice-Hall.

Swidler, A. 1986. "Culture As Action." *American Sociological Review* 51: 273–286.

Sykes, G., and Matza, D. 1957. "Techniques of Neutralization: A Theory of Delinquency." *American Sociological Review* 22: 664–670.

Syme, S. L., and Berkman, L. F. 1987. "Social Class, Susceptibility and Sickness." In H. D. Schwartz (Ed.), *Dominant Issues in Medical Sociology* (2nd ed.). New York: Random House.

Tajfel, H. 1982. "Social Psychology of Intergroup Relations." *Annual Review of Psychology 33:* 1–39. Palo Alto, CA: Annual Reviews.

Teigen, K. H. 1986. "Old Truths or Fresh Insights? A Study of Students' Evaluations of Proverbs." *Journal of British Social Psychology* 25(1): 43–50.

Thoits, P. 1983. "Dimensions of Life Events That Influence Psychological Distress: An Evaluation and Synthesis of the Literature." In H. Kaplan (Ed.), *Psychosocial Stress: Trends in Theory and Research* (pp. 33–103). New York: Academic Press.

———. 1984. "Explaining Distributions of Psychological Vulnerability: Lack of Social Support in the Face of Life Stress." *Social Forces* 63(2): 453–481.

Thomas, B., and Reskin, B. 1990. "A Woman's Place Is Selling Homes: Occupational Change and the Feminization of Real Estate Sales." In B. Reskin and P. Roos (Eds.), *Job Queues, Gender Queues. Explaining Women's Inroads into Male Occupations.* Philadelphia: Temple University Press.

Thorne, B. 1995. "Girls and Boys Together . . . But Mostly Apart: Gender Arrangements in Elementary School." In D. M. Newman (Ed.), *Sociology: Exploring the Architecture of Everyday Life* (pp. 93–102). Thousand Oaks, CA: Pine Forge.

Thornes, B., and Collard, J. 1979. *Who Divorces?* London: Routledge and Kegan Paul.

Toda, M., Shinotsuka, H., McClintock, C. G., and Stech, F. L. 1978. "Development of Competitive Behavior As a Function of Culture, Age, and Social Comparison." *Journal of Personality and Social Psychology* 36: 825–839.

Tumin, M. 1967. *Social Stratification: The Forms and Functions of Inequality.* Englewood Cliffs, NJ: Prentice-Hall.

Turner, M. A., Fix, M., and Struyk, R. J. 1991. "Hiring Discrimination Against Young Black Men." *The Urban Institute Policy and Research Report* (Summer): 4–5.

United Nations Development Programme. 1993. *Human Development Report 1990.* New York: Oxford University Press.

U.S. Bureau of the Census. 1990a. "Marital Status and Living Arrangements: 1989 and 1990." *Current Population Reports,* Series P-20, no. 445.

———. 1990b. "Money Income and Poverty Status in the U.S.: 1989." Washington, DC: Government Printing Office.

_____. 1992. *The Hispanic Population of the United States.* Washington, DC: U.S. Government Printing Office.

_____. 1993a. "Poverty in the United States: 1992." *Current Population Reports,* Series P-60, no. 185. Washington, DC: U.S. Government Printing Office.

_____. 1993b. *Statistical Abstracts: 1993* (112th ed.). Washington, DC: U.S. Government Printing Office.

_____. 1993c. "Money Income of Households, Families and Persons in the United States: 1992." *Current Population Reports,* Series P-60, no. 184. Washington, DC: U.S. Government Printing Office.

_____. 1993d. "Earnings of Year-Round, Full-Time Workers." Washington, DC: U.S. Government Printing Office (January 22).

_____. 1994a. *Statistical Abstract of the United States.* Washington, DC: U.S. Government Printing Office.

_____. 1994b. "1993 Annual Income and Poverty Reports." Washington, DC: U.S. Government Printing Office (October 6).

U.S. Bureau of Justice Statistics. 1991. *Sourcebook of Criminal Justice Statistics, 1990.* T. Flanagan and K. McGuire (Eds.). Washington, DC: U.S. Government Printing Office.

U.S. Department of Agriculture. 1993. Agricultural Research Service, Family Economics Research Group. "Expenditures on a Child by Families, 1992." Hyattsville, MD: The Groups.

U.S. Department of Education. 1993. *Adult Literacy in America.* Washington, DC: National Center for Education Studies.

U.S. Federal Bureau of Investigation. 1993. *Uniform Crime Reports.* Washington, DC: U.S. Government Printing Office.

_____. 1994. *Uniform Crime Reports.* Washington, DC: U.S. Government Printing Office.

U.S. Immigration and Naturalization Service. 1992. *Immigrants to the U.S., 1820–1991.* Washington, DC: U.S. Government Printing Office.

U.S. National Center for Health Statistics. 1989. *Current Estimates from the National Health Survey, 1988.* Washington, DC: U.S. Government Printing Office.

Useem, M., and Karabel, J. 1986. "Pathways to Top Corporate Management." *American Sociological Review 51.*

Van Hasselt, B. B., Morrison, R. L., Bellack, A. S., and Straus, M. (Eds.). 1987. *Handbook of Family Violence.* New York: Plenum.

Veles, W. 1985. "Finishing College: The Effects of College Type." *Sociology of Education 58:* 191–200.

Verbrugge, L. 1985. "Gender and Health: An Update on Hypotheses and Evidence." *Journal of Health and Social Behavior 26:* 156–182.

Vernacci, R. L. 1992. "Study Finds Poor Access To Physicians." *Associated Press Report* (February 28).

Veroff, J., Douvan, E., and Kulka, R. 1981. *The Inner American: A Self-Portrait from 1957 to 1976.* New York: Basic Books.

Vinorskis, M. 1992. "Schooling and Poor Children in 19th Century America." *American Behavioral Scientist 35*(3): 313–331.

Vito, G. F., and Holmes, R. M. 1994. *Criminology: Theory, Research, and Policy.* Belmont, CA: Wadsworth.

Waldman, S. 1992. "Deadbeat Dads." *Newsweek* (May 4): 46–52.

Walker, K. 1995. "Always There For Me: Friendship Patterns and Expectations Among Middle and Working Class Men and Women." *Sociological Forum* 10(2): 273–296.

Wall Street Journal. 1993. "Civil Rights: The Next Generation." (August 31): A10.

Wallerstein, J., and Blakeslee, S. 1990. *Second Chances: Men, Women and Children a Decade after Divorce.* New York: Ticknor and Fields.

Walster, E., Aronson, V., Abrahams, D., and Rottman, L. 1966. "Importance of Physical Attractiveness in Dating Behavior." *Journal of Personality and Social Psychology* 4: 508–516.

Ward, D., Carter, T., and Perrin, R. 1994. *Social Deviance: Being, Behaving, and Branding.* Needham Heights, MA: Allyn and Bacon.

Washington Post. 1992. (February 6): A4.

Watson, W. H., and Maxwell, R. J. (Eds.). 1977. *Human Aging and Dying: A Study in Sociocultural Gerontology.* New York: St. Martin's Press.

Wattenberg, B. 1985. *The Good News Is the Bad News Is Wrong.* New York: Simon and Schuster.

Weber, M. 1968. *Economy and Society.* New York: Bedminster. (Original work published 1922.)

Weis, L. (Ed.). 1988. *Class, Race, and Gender in American Education.* Albany, NY: Suny Press.

Weisberg, K. 1975. "'Under Great Temptations Here': Women and Divorce in Puritan Massachusetts" *Feminist Studies* 2(2/3): 183–193.

Wells, R. 1982. *Revolutions in Americans' Lives: A Demographic Perspective on the History of Americans, Their Families and Their Society.* Westport, CT: Greenwood Press.

Wertheimer, B. 1977. *We Were There: The Story of Working Women in America.* New York: Pantheon.

West, C. 1993. *Race Matters.* Boston: Beacon Press.

Wheaton, B. 1982. "A Comparison of the Moderating Effects of Personal Coping Resources on the Impact of the Exposure to Stress in Two Groups." *Journal of Community Psychology* 10: 293–311.

————. 1983. "Stress, Personal Coping, Resources, and Psychiatric Symptoms: An Investigation of Interactive Models." *Journal of Health and Social Behavior* 24(3): 208–229.

————. 1990. "Life Transitions, Role Histories, and Mental Health." *American Sociological Review* 55(2): 209–223.

White, G. 1980. "Physical Attractiveness and Courtship Progress." *Journal of Personality and Social Psychology* 39: 660–668.

White, L., and Edwards, J. 1990. "Emptying the Nest and Parental Well-Being: An Analysis of National Panel Data." *American Sociological Review* 55: 235–242.

Whitehead, B. 1993. "Dan Quayle Was Right." *The Atlantic Monthly* (April): 47–84.

Wichman, H. 1970. "Effects of Isolation and Communication on Cooperation in a Two-Person Game." *Journal of Personality and Social Psychology 16*: 114–120.

Wilder, D. A., and Shapiro, P. N. 1984. "Role of Outgroup Cues in Determining Social Identity." *Journal of Personality and Social Psychology 47*: 342–348.

Will, J. A., Self, P. A., and Dalton, N. 1976. "Maternal Behavior and Perceived Sex of Infant." *American Journal of Orthopsychiatry 49*: 135–139.

Williams, K. R. 1984. "Economic Sources of Homicide: Re-estimating the Effects of Poverty and Inequality." *American Sociological Review 49*: 283–289.

Willis, F. N., Willis, L. A., and Grier, J. A. 1982. "Given Names, Social Class, and Professional Achievement." *Psychological Reports 54*: 543–549.

Wilson, W. J. 1980. *The Declining Significance of Race: Blacks and Changing American Institutions* (2nd ed.). Chicago: University of Chicago Press.

_____. 1987. *The Truly Disadvantaged: The Inner City, the Underclass, and Public Policy.* Chicago: University of Chicago Press.

Witkin-Lanoil, G. 1984. *The Female Stress Syndrome: How to Recognize and Live with It.* New York: Newmarket Press.

Worchel, S., and Norvell, N. 1980. "Effect of Perceived Environmental Conditions During Cooperation on Intergroup Attraction." *Journal of Personality and Social Psychology 38*: 764–772.

World Almanac. 1995. R. Farmighetti (Ed.). Mahwah, NJ: Funk and Wagnall.

World Bank. 1994. *World Development Report 1994.* New York: Oxford University Press.

Wright, J. W. (Ed.). 1995. *Universal Almanac.* Kansas City: Andrews and McMeel.

Wrightsman, L. S., Jr. 1960. "Effects of Waiting with Others on Changes in Levels of Felt Anxiety." *Journal of Abnormal and Social Psychology 13*: 17–22.

Wrightsman, L., O'Connor, J., and Baker, N. (Eds.). 1972. *Cooperation and Competition.* Belmont, CA: Brooks/Cole.

Young, R. K., Kennedy, A. H., Newhouse, A., Browne, P., and Thiessen, D. 1993. "The Effects of Names on Perception of Intelligence, Popularity, and Competence." *Journal of Applied Social Psychology 23*(21): 1770–1788.

Zajonc, R. B. 1970. ""Brainwash: Familiarity Breeds Comfort." *Psychology Today* (February): 32–35, 60–62.

Zeitlin, M., Lutterman, K. G., and Russell, J. W. 1977. "Death in Vietnam: Class, Poverty, and the Risks of War." In M. Zeitlin (Ed.), *American Society Incorporated* (2nd ed.) (pp. 143–155). Chicago: Rand McNally.

Zelizer, V. 1985. *Pricing the Priceless Child.* New York: Basic Books.

_____. 1994. *The Social Meaning of Money.* New York: Basic Books.

GLOSSARY/INDEX